A
A

Enter Sydney Omarr's world of accurate day-by-day predictions for every aspect of your life. With expert readings and forecasts, you can chart a course to romance, adventure, good health, or career opportunities while gaining valuable insight into yourself and others. Offering a daily outlook for 18 full months, this fascinating guide shows you:

- The important dates in your life
- What to expect from an astrological reading
- The initials of people who will be influential in your life
- How the stars can help you stay healthy and fit
- Your lucky lottery numbers
  And more!

Let this expert's sound advice guide you through a year of heavenly possibilities—for today and for every day of 2000!

SYDNEY OMARR'S DAY-BY-DAY ASTROLOGICAL GUIDE FOR

ARIES—March 21–April 19
TAURUS—April 20–May 20
GEMINI—May 21–June 20
CANCER—June 21–July 22
LEO—July 23–August 22
VIRGO—August 23–September 22
LIBRA—September 23–October 22
SCORPIO—October 23–November 21
SAGITTARIUS—November 22–December 21
CAPRICORN—December 22–January 19
AQUARIUS—January 20–February 18
PISCES—February 19–March 20

IN 2000

WIN A PERSONALIZED HOROSCOPE FROM SYDNEY OMARR!

Enter the Sydney Omarr Horoscope Sweepstakes!

No Purchase necessary.
Details below.

Name _____

Address _____

City _____ State _____ Zip _____

Mail to:

SYDNEY OMARR HOROSCOPE SWEEPSTAKES
P.O. BOX 9248
Medford, NY 11763

Offer expires August 31, 1999

SYDNEY OMARR'S

DAY-BY-DAY ASTROLOGICAL GUIDE
FOR THE NEW MILLENNIUM

PISCES

February 19–March 20

2000

A SIGNET BOOK

SIGNET
Published by New American Library, a division of
Penguin Putnam Inc., 375 Hudson Street,
New York, New York 10014, U.S.A.
Penguin Books Ltd, 27 Wrights Lane,
London W8 5TZ, England
Penguin Books Australia Ltd, Ringwood,
Victoria, Australia
Penguin Books Canada Ltd, 10 Alcorn Avenue,
Toronto, Ontario, Canada M4V 3B2
Penguin Books (N.Z.) Ltd, 182–190 Wairau Road,
Auckland 10, New Zealand

Penguin Books Ltd, Registered Offices:
Harmondsworth, Middlesex, England

First published by Signet, an imprint of New American Library,
a division of Penguin Putnam Inc.

First Printing, July 1999
10 9 8 7 6 5 4 3 2 1

CONTENTS

INTRODUCTION:

The Year 2000—Business as Usual?

The year 2000 will be ushered in with celebration like never before. However, the very next day could mark one of the biggest snafus in history!

Unless millions of computer users and businesses worldwide have prepared in advance, the change in the initial digits from 19 to 20 of the date 2000 could shut down the technology that regulates every aspect of our lives. Now referred to as the "Y2K bug," this critical flaw that keeps computers locked in the 20th century has nearly every organization that depends on computers racing to beat the clock to avoid a major shutdown. Billions of lines of code must be rewritten before the chimes strike midnight. And suspense will mount during the hours before the century officially closes, as we wait to see what will happen.

The Millennium takes on even more significance when we realize that we're initiating a new era by making critical changes in the technology we've come to depend on. Because of the urgent time factor, everyone from government computer experts to teenage hackers must pull together to guarantee a smooth transition before the midnight deadline. In an extraordinary way, the technology is drawing us together as we make a global effort to resolve this problem.

Astrologers forecasted the union of technology and global cooperation with the entrance of the planet Uranus (technology) into the sign of Aquarius (humanitarian consciousness) in 1996. And it is also the harbinger of the next century, one where remarkable technological advances will be available to more people than ever before; however, the inevitable problems that will occur may also happen on a global scale and require us to work more closely together to discover solutions.

So the stroke of midnight will be a test of whether we are prepared for the challenges of the next century. Will there be shutdowns, accidents, faulty calculations, inaccurate data? Will you just be frustrated temporarily by not being able to use your bank card or by the store losing track of the Christmas gift you returned? Working together for a smooth crossing of the threshold of the Millennium might set the stage for cooperation in other areas, paving the way for better international communications and mutual understanding.

Astrologers have been looking at the horoscope for the Millennium for other clues to what lies ahead. We find that the first day of the Millennium is marked by an alignment of two tiny but powerful forces in astrology, the distant planet Pluto and the tiny planetoid Chiron. In astrology, Pluto is associated with transformation by renewal, Chiron with healing our wounds and helping others to heal. They are aligned in the sign of Sagittarius, which speaks of wide-reaching aspirations and long-term goals, and they are placed in the communications area of the horoscope as the clock chimes 12:01 EST. Let's hope that this Millennium will be a time of global healing and transformation, so that we may greet the new century with hope and enthusiasm.

In this year's guide, we show you some ways that you can harmonize your own life and goals to the rapid changes taking place. For fun, you can compare your planets with our extensive celebrity list, get a new leap-year lease on love, or find out how to use the Internet to connect with the wide world of astrology.

Besides learning the basic information, you can go beyond your sun sign to find out what astrology is all about. Using this book, you can look up your other planets and rising sign and find out what they mean.

The sometimes confusing symbols you see on a horoscope are explained in the chapter on the astrological glyphs. And, of course, there is all you need to know about your sun sign.

Let this guide help you use astrology as a valuable tool to create prosperity, happiness, and growth in the Millennium!

CHAPTER 1

Leaping into the Millennium—Predictions

In the U.S. Capitol building, there is a famous frieze of the shooting death of the Indian chief, Tecumseh, who figures prominently in this year's predictions. Every twenty years, there's a fateful lineup of two huge planets, Jupiter and Saturn, which coincides with an old prophecy of gloom and doom known as "Tecumseh's Curse."

Tecumseh, whose name, ironically, means "shooting star," was a brilliant Shawnee chief and orator. Threatened by the rapid territorial expansion of the white man and the concept of land division and property ownership, he attempted to unite the native American tribes to fight off the foreign invaders, but was shot in Canada in 1813 by American forces. Later, William Henry Harrison, who had defeated Indian attacks led by Tecumseh's brother at the famous battle of Tippecanoe, became the first U.S. president to die in office. But some believed that Tecumseh had put a curse on the United States presidency. Seemingly a coincidence, the list of American presidents who did not complete their term in office at twenty-year intervals after Harrison's death gave rise to the legend of "Tecumseh's Curse."

The next conjunction of Jupiter and Saturn after Harrison's term came during Lincoln's term, followed in twenty years by Garfield, then by McKinley, all assassinated by shooting. Both Presidents Harding and Franklin Delano Roosevelt died in office. The seventh president whose term fell under a Jupiter/Saturn conjunction was John F. Kennedy, also assassinated by shooting. And the last was President Reagan, who was shot during his term but survived.

At this writing, the term of current President Bill Clinton lasts until the time of the next conjunction in May 2000. However, he is experiencing a kind of "character assassination" leading to impeachment hearings that threaten his presidency and could result in his leaving office. The president taking office in 2001 will also be under the influence of this conjunction, which happens twice more in that year.

Long before Tecumseh, this conjunction has been regarded as one that brings sweeping and traumatic social and political events, wars, and destruction. The conjunction on May 28, 2000 follows several ominous celestial events and a pileup of seven planets in the sign of Taurus on May 3. So those of you who are born in fixed signs (Taurus, Leo, Scorpio, and Aquarius) can expect to be most influenced.

On a more positive note, it is important to recognize that lineups of planets are not events that happen in isolation. They are part of a natural, cyclical growth process. The stage for the events in the year 2000 has been set in motion by major astrological events in the past. So think of this event in context of what has been building up for some time.

What Types of Experiences Can You Expect?

The Millennium itself produces optimism, forward thinking, and futurism, all encouraged by Jupiter. But then Saturn, the taskmaster of the zodiac, brings reality checks, obstacles, demands for responsibility, duty, organization, structure, and follow-through into the picture. So this year we will all be concerned with the tradeoffs, the prices to be paid for all our growth and expansion. We will be setting limits on negative growth, such as overpopulation, destruction of the environment, and overspending of any kind.

The Saturn/Jupiter conjunction in the fixed earth sign of Taurus suggests that, as in the days of Tecumseh, there will be issues of territory, including land rights and physical boundaries—claiming it, gaining it, expanding it, fighting over it. In 1940–41, when the last Taurus meeting of these two planets happened, World War II was under way. At this moment, in Eastern Europe and in the Middle East, there are rumblings of global involvement in local territorial wars.

In your personal life, big plans run up against obstacles and bureaucratic red tape. You may be at odds with authority figures. In other words, when you try to spread your wings and fly, you may have trouble getting off the ground. Unless you bring practicality and discipline into play, you will run into restrictions that result in frustration.

As you may notice from the glyph chapter in this book, Jupiter's symbol is a variation on Saturn's glyph upside down. This is your clue that the two planets actually complement each other. Saturn, the planet associated with constriction, discipline, rules, obligations, and limitations, is the reverse of Jupiter, which is associated with expansion, optimism, options, opportunities, and luck. Saturn's long-lasting rewards come to you with hard work; Jupiter's rewards come to you with little effort—they're lucky breaks. Without Saturn's limitation, however, Jupiter is like a vehicle with no brakes. Saturn without Jupiter is like a vehicle stalled. In other words, Jupiter's enthusiasm needs Saturn's emphasis on structure and discipline in order to accomplish its goals, and vice versa.

At the same time, these planets can work at cross purposes. Saturn's fears and limitations can dampen Jupiter's hope and enthusiasm. Jupiter's expansion can come to a halt under Saturn's demand for reality checks and authority figures. Saturn can be a real drag on Jupiter.

The key is to find a balance to harmonize both of these complementary principles, bringing dreams down to earth

7

and getting a wider perspective on fears that are the basis of our limitations. When Saturn and Jupiter work together, we can adjust our expectations to reality, give form to our hopes, and overcome our fears. As Franklin D. Roosevelt said, "We have nothing to fear but fear itself." With this conjunction, there should be a dialogue between structure and opportunity, and between ideals and reality, that can be very fruitful in preparing us to meet the challenges of the next century. Together, these planets promise great accomplishments, but there is a tradeoff, a price to be paid by meeting obligations and taking on responsibilities.

Where Might It Affect Your Life?

The people who will be most affected will be those born during the previous conjunction in Taurus (1940–1941), who will have both Saturn and Jupiter returning to their natal positions. This second "Saturn Return" is a time of maturity, of leadership and responsibility, the beginning of assuming the duties of the wise elder of the community.

Here is where the conjunction might most affect your life according to your sun sign and rising sign. First look up your rising sign in the chart on page 134 in this book then read the following descriptions.

If Your Sun or Rising Sign Is Aries—

The principles of expansion vs. contraction will be evident in your second house of possessions, income, and self-esteem. You can make financial progress by combining new ideas with discipline, organization, and structure. Schemes that promise great rewards with no practical basis will not fly. It will also be important to balance your budget, stick to an investment plan, and guard against extravagance.

If Your Sun or Rising Sign Is Taurus—

Since the conjunction, and a major pileup of planets, takes place in your sign in May, you hold the power cards. This means you'll be in an authority position; you may be imposing structures on others or shaking others up. Though you will have many opportunities and a good deal of luck coming your way, you will also be aware that there will be a tradeoff, a price to pay. You'll be highly visible, so be sure that you look and feel your best.

If Your Sun or Rising Sign Is Gemini—

This conjunction falls in your most spiritual and vulnerable place, making this a time to open up and examine past experiences. Many of you may delve deeply into your subconscious. Watch what you put your faith in, for there is a potential for disillusion here. Something you believe in fervently will be tested, but this could take you into a new dimension. More Geminis may be involved with charity, hospitals, prisons, and religious institutions, creating much-needed changes in these places.

If Your Sun or Rising Sign Is Cancer—

The Saturn/Jupiter conjunction will fall in your house of goals, values, and group activities. This is a time when you will test your ideals in relationship to society. You will be forced out of your shell in some way. You will have opportunities to get involved in clubs, unions, or politics, but you may have some conflict between being popular and playing by the rules. You might discover talents you didn't know you had, such as organizing groups or public speaking. It's a year to shine before the public.

If Your Sun or Rising Sign Is Leo—

You will have many new opportunities in your career or public life, but along with the prestige, these bring extra responsibilities and hard work. You may feel that the job of your dreams is at last attainable, only to find that your workload will also be doubled. You'll be especially concerned about your public image, so show yourself at your very best. Keep your energy high by cultivating good habits.

If Your Sun or Rising Sign Is Virgo—

Though you may love your own comfortable home turf, you could find that you are challenged to accept a position in a new and different atmosphere. It is important to open your mind to other cultural or religious points of view. This would be an excellent time to study something new, to apply your mind in a disciplined way. There could be a conflict between new ideas and the traditional ways of thinking, between keeping yourself on the cutting edge versus clinging to the past. Be cautious, but also give way to adventure.

If Your Sun or Rising Sign Is Libra—

The conjunction will fall in the area of life where you share resources with others, and this is where issues of power and control dominate in your financial and most intimate life. This could complicate investments, savings, and the cost of living. It is a very important time to deal with funds from outside sources, inheritance, or with tax matters. You could be pushing to increase your income as this year begins, but not getting the backing or funding you need, or the funds may come with restrictions. Wheeling and dealing will face many challenges, but the results could bring you long-term security.

If Your Sun or Rising Sign Is Scorpio—

You'll get more accomplished if you do it with someone else. The pileup of planets in Taurus in May falls in your partnership sector, where you'll be making some lasting and permanent changes. Go for long-term benefits, perhaps turning over the reins to another for a while. The emphasis is on changing or improving relationships, making and meeting commitments, and on legal issues.

If Your Sun or Rising Sign Is Sagittarius—

Pay special attention to the care and maintenance department of your life. This is not the time to take your health for granted or burn the candle at both ends, so listen to your body and make sure everything is in working order. Consider alternate methods of healing that are pleasurable and uplifting as well as effective. Take courses to improve yourself. The events of May 2000 mean that you will be rethinking your job situation. Routine may weigh you down, but you can enhance your reputation by getting the job done and upgrading your skills if necessary. Don't promise more than you can deliver.

If Your Sun or Rising Sign Is Capricorn—

Since Capricorn is a Saturn-ruled sign, you may be especially favored by this conjunction, benefiting from the up-side of both planets. Your self-expression and creativity can take leaps forward now. It's an excellent time to expose your talents to a larger audience. Though you may have extra opportunities for romance, there may also be restrictions involved. The object of your affections may have other obligations or you may attract lovers who are not free to follow their hearts. Matters involving children—both the joys and responsibilities of their upbringing—will be more important than ever to you.

If Your Sun or Rising Sign Is Aquarius—

Your home and personal life will be emphasized by this conjunction, which could give you conflicting emotions

11

about your domestic scene. Perhaps you'll want to move or sell, yet there will be an equally strong pull that might hold you back from taking the decisive step. The grass may look greener elsewhere, but not prove to be so. You may have some wonderful ideas about practical home products or interior design, and you could be highly successful here. You could also resolve some long-standing family issues if you keep an open mind.

If Your Sun or Rising Sign Is Pisces—

How you communicate with others will be emphasized by this conjunction. The buildup of planets in Taurus, a fixed earth sign, indicates a tendency toward stubbornness, so make an extra effort to be flexible and to listen to other points of view. Friends and relatives could be more demanding, perhaps imposing extra duties and responsibilities for their care. There may be elderly friends or family that require your attention. There may be some changes in your neighborhood that require you to get involved. Take extra care of your car and matters concerning local transportation. Taking up new studies or hobbies now could be especially beneficial. Consider learning a new language or computer skills, or taking a writing course to broaden your horizons. The discipline of Saturn and the good luck of Jupiter might help you write that novel or play you've had on the back burner.

CHAPTER 2

The Leap Year Guide to Love

Though the year 2000 is a leap year, when ladies traditionally make the first romantic moves, today it's no longer unusual for women to chase the object of their desire aggressively, no matter what the year. One of the main reasons women turn to astrology is to help them attract a lover or to figure out what's going wrong in a relationship.

Probably the question astrologers hear most is: What sign is best for me in love? Or: I'm a Taurus and my lover is a Gemini. What are our prospects? You might be wondering if you can trust that first spark of chemistry—should you lower your expectations if you're a Leo with a fatal attraction to a sexy Scorpio? Old-fashioned astrologers would warn ominously, "This relationship is doomed from the start!" It used to be that some sun-sign combinations were treated like champagne and tomato juice—never the twain should meet. Others were considered blessed by the stars with perfect compatibility. Today's astrologers are more realistic, acknowledging that, though some combinations will be more challenging, there are too many long-lasting relationships between so-called incompatible sun signs to brand any combination as totally unworkable. We've gone far beyond stereotyping to respecting and enjoying the differences between people and using astrology to help us get along with them.

Each sun sign does have certain predictable characteristics in love, however, which can help you better understand the dynamics of the relationship. But we must be careful not to oversimplify. Just because someone is a so-called "incompatible" sign is no reason the relationship can't work out. For a true in-depth comparison, an astrologer considers the interrelationships of all the planets and houses (where they fall in your respective horoscopes).

Since romantic bonds between other planets can offset difficulties between sun signs, it's worthwhile to analyze several of the most important ones. You can do this by making a very simple chart that compares the moon, Mars, and Venus, as well as the sun signs of the partners in a relationship. You can find the signs for Mars and Venus in the tables in this book. Unfortunately complete moon tables are too long for a book of this size, so it might be worth your while to consult an astrological ephemeris (a book of planetary tables) in your local library or to have a computer chart cast to find out each other's moon placement.

Simply look up the signs of Mars and Venus in this book (and the moon, if possible) for each person and list them, with the sun sign, next to each other. Then add the element (earth, air, fire, or water) of each sign. The earth signs are Taurus, Virgo, and Capricorn. The air signs are Gemini, Libra, and Aquarius. The fire signs are Aries, Leo, and Sagittarius. And the water signs are Cancer, Scorpio, and Pisces.

Here's an example:

	SUN	MOON	MARS	VENUS
ROMEO	Aries/Fire	Leo/Fire	Scorpio/Water	Taurus/Earth
JULIET	Pisces/Water	Leo/Fire	Aries/Fire	Aquarius/ Air

As a rule of thumb, signs of the *same* element or *complementary* elements (fire with air and earth with water) get along best. So you can see that this particular Romeo and Juliet could have some challenges ahead, with an emotional bond (the moon) creating a strong tie.

The Lunar Link—
The Person You Need

The planet in your chart that governs your emotions is the moon. (Note: The moon is not technically a planet, but is usually referred to as one by astrologers.) So you would naturally take this into consideration when evaluating a potential romantic partnership. If a person's moon is in a good relationship to your sun, moon, Venus, or Mars, preferably in the same sign or element, you should relate well on some emotional level. Your needs will be compatible; you'll understand each other's feelings without much effort. If the moon is in a compatible element, such as earth with water or fire with air, you may have a few adjustments, but you will be able to make them easily. With a water–fire or earth–air combination, you'll have to make a considerable effort to understand where the other is coming from emotionally.

The Venus Attraction—
The One You Want

Venus is what you respond to, so if you and your partner have a good Venus aspect, you should have much in common. You'll enjoy doing things together. The same type of lovemaking will turn you both on, so you'll have no trouble pleasing each other.

Look up both partners' Venus placements in the charts on page 78. Your lover's Venus in the same sign or a sign of the same element as your own Venus, Mars, moon, or sun is best. Second-best is a sign of a compatible element (earth with water, air with fire). Venus in water with air, or earth with fire means that you may have to make a special effort to understand what appeals to each other. And you'll have to give each other plenty of space to enjoy activities that don't particularly appeal to you. By the way, this chart can work not only for lovers, but for any relationship where compatibility of tastes is important to you.

The Mars Connection— This One Lights Your Fire!

Mars positions reveal your sexual energy—how often you like to make love, for instance. It also shows your temper—do you explode or do a slow burn? Here you'll find out if your partner is direct, aggressive, and hot-blooded or more likely to take the cool, mental approach. Mutually supportive partners have their Mars working together in the same or complementary elements. But *any* contacts between Mars and Venus in two charts can strike sexy sparks. Even the difficult aspects— your partner's Mars three or six signs away from your sun, Mars, or Venus—can offer sexual stimulation. Who doesn't get turned on by a challenge from time to time? Sometimes the easy Mars relationships can drift into dullness.

The Solar Bond

The sun is the focus of our personality and therefore the most powerful component involved in astrology. Once again, earth and water or fire and air combinations will have an easier time together. Mixtures earth and water with fire and air can be much more challenging. However, each pair of sun signs has special lessons to teach and learn from each other. There is a negative side to the most ideal couple and a positive side to the most unlikely match—Each has an up and a down side. So if the outlook for you and your beloved (or business associate) seems like an uphill struggle, take heart! Such legendary lovers as Juan and Eva Peron, Ronald and Nancy Reagan, Harry and Bess Truman, Julius Caesar and Cleopatra, Billy and Ruth Graham, and George and

Martha Washington are among the many who have made successful partnerships between supposedly incompatible sun signs.

How to Seduce Every Sign . . .

The Aries Lover

It's not easy to make the first move on an Aries, since this sign always likes to be first. Try challenging your Aries in some way—this sign loves the chase almost as much as the conquest. So don't be too easy or accommodating—let them feel a sense of accomplishment when they've won your heart.

Be sure your interests and appearance are up to the minute. You can wear the latest style off the fashion show runway with an Aries, especially if it's bright red. Aries is a pioneer, an adventurer, always ahead of the pack. Play up your frontier spirit. Present the image of the two of you as an unbeatable team, one that can conquer the world, and you'll keep this courageous sign at your side.

Since they tend to idealize their lovers, Aries is especially disillusioned when their mates flirt. Be sure they always feel like number one in your life.

The Taurus Lover

Taurus is often seduced by surface physical beauty alone. Their five senses are highly susceptible, so find ways to appeal to all of them! Your home should be a restful haven from the outside world. Get a great sound system, some comfortable furniture to sink into, and keep the refrigerator stocked with treats. Most Taureans would rather entertain on their own turf than gad about town, so it helps if you're a good host or hostess.

Taurus like a calm, contented, committed relationship. This is not a sign to trifle with. Don't flirt or tease if you want to please. Don't rock the boat or try to make

17

this sign jealous. Instead, create a steady, secure environment with lots of shared pleasures.

Taurus is an extremely sensual, affectionate, nurturing lover, but can be quite possessive. Taurus likes to "own" you, so don't hold back with them or play power games. If you need more space in the relationship, be sure to set clear boundaries, letting them know exactly where they stand. When ambiguity in a relationship makes Taurus uneasy, they may go searching for someone more solid and substantial. A Taurus romance works best where the limits are clearly spelled out. Taurus needs physical demonstrations of affection—so don't hold back on hugs.

The Gemini Lover

Variety is the spice of life to this flirtatious sign. Guard against jealousy—it is rarely justified. Provide a stimulating sex life—this is a very experimental sign—to keep them interested. Be a bit unpredictable. Don't let lovemaking become a routine. Most of all, sharing lots of laughs together can make Gemini take your relationship very seriously.

Keeping Gemini interested is like walking a tightrope. Though this sign needs stability and a strong home base to accomplish their goals, they also require a great deal of personal freedom. A great role model is Barbara Bush, a Gemini successfully married to another Gemini.

This is a sign that loves to communicate, so sit down and talk things over. Be interested in your partner's doings, but have a life of your own and ideas to contribute. Since this is a gadabout social sign, don't insist on quiet nights at home when your Gemini is in a party mood.

Gemini needs a steady hand, but at the same time plenty of rope. Focus on common goals and abstract ideals. Gemini likes to share, so be a twin soul and do things together. Keep up on their latest interests. Stay in touch mentally and physically, using both your mind and your hands to communicate.

The Cancer Lover

The song "Try a Little Tenderness" must have been written by a Cancer. This is probably the water sign that requires the most TLC. Cancers tend to be very private people who may take some time to open up. They are extremely self-protective and will rarely tell you what is truly bothering them. They operate indirectly, like the movements of the crab. You may have to divine their problem by following subtle clues, then draw them out gently and try to voice any criticism in the most tactful, supportive way possible.

Family ties are especially strong for Cancer. They will rarely break a strong family bond. Create an intimate family atmosphere, with the emphasis on food and family get-togethers. You can get valuable clues to Cancer appeal from their mothers and their early family situation. If their early life was unhappy, it's even more important that they feel they have found a close family with you.

Encouraging their creativity can counter Cancer's moodiness, which is also a sure sign of emotional insecurity. Find ways to distract them from negative moods. Calm them with a good meal for instance, or a trip to the seashore. Cancers are usually quite nostalgic and attached to the past. So be careful not to throw out their old treasures or photos.

The Leo Lover

Appeal to Leo pride by treating this sign royally. Be well groomed and dressed, someone they're proud to show off.

Leo thinks big, and likes to live like a king, so don't you be petty or miserly. Remember special occasions with a beautifully wrapped gift or flowers. Make an extra effort to treat them royally. Keep a sense of fun and playfulness, and loudly applaud Leo's creative efforts. React, respond, be a good audience! If Leo's ignored, this sign will seek a more appreciative audience—fast!

(Cheating Leos are almost always looking for an ego boost.)

Be generous with compliments. You can't possibly overdo here. Always accentuate the positive. Make them feel important by asking for advice and consulting them often. Leo enjoys a charming sociable companion, but be sure to make them the center of attention in your life.

The Virgo Lover

Virgos love to feel needed, so give them a job to do in your life. They are great fixer-uppers. Take their criticism as a form of love and caring, of noticing what you do. Bring them out socially—they're often very shy. Calm their nerves with good food, a healthy environment, trips to the country.

Virgos may seem cool and conservative on the surface, but underneath you'll find a sensual romantic. Think of Raquel Welch, Sophia Loren, Jacqueline Bisset, Garbo—it's amazing how seductive this practical sign can be! They are idealists, however, looking for someone who meets their high standards. If you've measured up, they'll do anything to serve and please you.

Mental stimulation is a turn-on to this Mercury-ruled sign. An intellectual discussion could lead to romantic action, so stay on your toes and keep well informed. This sign often mixes business with pleasure, so it helps if you share the same professional interests—you'll get to see more of your busy mate. With Virgo, the couple who works and plays together, stays together.

The Libra Lover

Do not underestimate Libra's need for beauty and harmony. To keep them happy, avoid scenes. Opt for calm, impersonal discussion of problems (or a well-reasoned debate) over an elegant dinner. Pay attention to the niceties of life. Send little gifts on Valentines Day and don't forget birthdays and anniversaries. Play up the romance to the hilt—with all the lovely gestures and trimmings—but tone down intensity and emotional drama (Aries, Scorpio take note). Surround your Libra with a physically tasteful atmosphere—elegant, well-designed furnishings and calm colors. Be well groomed and tastefully dressed and be sure to emphasize good conversation and good manners.

Bear in mind that Libra truly enjoys life with a mate and needs the harmony of a steady relationship. Outside affairs can throw them off balance. However, members of this sign are natural charmers who love to surround themselves with admirers, and this can cause a very possessive partner to feel insecure. Most of the time, Librans are only testing their charms with harmless flirtations and will rarely follow through, unless they are not getting enough attention or there is an unattractive atmosphere at home.

Mental compatibility is what keeps Libra in tune. Unfortunately this sign, like Taurus, often falls for physical beauty or someone who provides an elegant lifestyle, rather than someone who shares their ideals and activities, the kind of compatibility that will keep you together in the long run.

The Scorpio Lover

Pluto-ruled Scorpio is fascinated by power and control in all its forms. They don't like to compromise—it's "all or nothing." They don't trust or respect anything that comes too easily, so be a bit of a challenge and keep them guessing. Maintain your own personal identity in spite of Scorpio's desire to probe your innermost secrets.

Sex is especially important to this sign, which will demand fidelity from you (though they may not deliver it themselves). Communication on this level is critical. Explore Scorpio's fantasies together. Scorpio is a detective, so watch your own flirtations—don't play with fire. This is a jealous and vengeful sign, so you'll live to regret it. Scorpios rarely flirt for the fun of it themselves. There is usually a strong motive behind their actions.

Scorpios are often deceptively cool and remote on the

outside, but don't be fooled: This sign always has a hidden agenda and feels very intensely about most things. The disguise is necessary because Scorpio does not trust easily; but when they do, they are devoted and loyal and will stick with you through the toughest times. You can lean on this very intense and focused sign. The secret is in first establishing that basic trust through mutual honesty and respect.

Scorpio has a fascination with the dark, mysterious side of life. If unhappy, they are capable of carrying on a secret affair. So try to emphasize positive, constructive solutions with them. Don't fret if they need time alone to sort out problems. They may also prefer time alone with you to socializing with others, so plan romantic getaways together to a private beach or a secluded wilderness spot.

The Sagittarius Lover

Be a mental and spiritual traveling companion. Sagittarius is a footloose adventurer whose ideas know no boundaries, so don't try to fence them in. Sagittarians resent restrictions of any kind. For a long-lasting relationship, be sure you are in harmony with Sagittarius's ideals and spiritual beliefs. They like to feel that their life is constantly being elevated and taken to a higher level. Since down-to-earth matters often get put aside in the Sagittarian's scheme of things, get finances under control (money matters upset more relationships with Sagittarians than any other problem), but try to avoid being the stern disciplinarian in this relationship (find a good accountant).

Sagittarius is not generally a homebody—unless there are several homes. Be ready and willing to take off on the spur of the moment, or they'll go without you! Sports, outdoor activities, and physical fitness are important—stay in shape with some of Sagittarius Jane Fonda's tapes. Dress with flair and style—it helps if you look especially good in sportswear. Sagittarius men like beautiful legs, so play up yours. And this is one of the great animal lovers, so try to get along with the dog, cat, or horse.

The Capricorn Lover

Capricorns are ambitious, even if they are the stay-at-home partner in your relationship. They will be extremely active, have a strong sense of responsibility to their partner, and take commitments seriously. However, they might look elsewhere if the relationship becomes too dutiful. They also need romance, fun, lightness, humor, and adventure!

Generation gaps are not unusual in Capricorn romances, when the older Capricorn partner works hard all through life and seeks pleasurable rewards with a young partner, or the young Capricorn gets a taste of luxury and instant status from an older lover. This is one sign that grows more interested in romance as they age! Younger Capricorns often tend to put business way ahead of pleasure.

Capricorn is impressed by those who entertain well, have "class," and can advance their status in life. Keep improving yourself and cultivate important people. Stay on the conservative side. Extravagant or frivolous loves don't last—Capricorn keeps a weather eye on the bottom line. Even the wildest Capricorns, such as Elvis Presley, Rod Stewart, or David Bowie, show a conservative streak in their personal lives. It's also important to demonstrate a strong sense of loyalty to your family, especially older members. This reassures Capricorn, who'll be happy to grow old along with you!

The Aquarius Lover

Aquarius is one of the most independent, least domestic signs. Finding time alone with this sign may be one of your greatest challenges. They are everybody's buddy, usually surrounded by people they collect—some of whom may be old lovers who are now "just friends." However, it is unlikely that old passions will be rekindled if you manage to become Aquarius's number-one best friend as well as lover, and if you get actively involved in other important aspects of Aquarius's life, such as the political or charitable causes they believe in.

Aquarius needs a supportive backup person who encourages them but is not overly possessive when their natural charisma attracts admirers by the dozen. Take a leaf from Joanne Woodward, whose marriage to perennial Aquarius heartthrob Paul Newman has lasted more than 30 years. Encourage them to develop their original ideas. Don't rain on their parade if they decide suddenly to market their spaghetti sauce and donate the proceeds to their favorite charity, or drive racing cars. Share their goals and be their fan, or you'll never see them.

You may be called on to give them grounding where needed. Aquarius needs someone who can keep track of their projects. But always remember, it's basic friendship—with the tolerance and common ideals that implies—that will hold you together.

The Pisces Lover

They are great fantasists and extremely creative lovers, so use your imagination to add drama and spice to your times together. You can let your fantasies run wild with this sign—and they'll go you one better! They enjoy variety in lovemaking, so try never to let it become routine.

To keep a Pisces hooked, don't hold the string too tight! This is a sensitive, creative sign that may appear to need someone to manage their lives or point the direction out of their Neptunian fog, but if you fall into that role, expect your Pisces to rebel against any strong-arm tactics. Pisces is more susceptible to a play for sympathy than a play for power. They are suckers for a sob story, the most empathetic sign of the zodiac. More than one Pisces has been seduced and held by someone who plays the underdog role.

Long-term relationships work best if you can bring Pisces down to earth and, at the same time, encourage their creative fantasies. Deter them from escapism into alcohol or substance abuse by helping them to get counseling, if needed. Pisces will seek a soulmate who provides positive energy, self-confidence, and a safe harbor from the storms of life.

CHAPTER 3

A User-Friendly Guide to Astrology

Astrology is like a fascinating foreign country with a language all its own and territory that's easy to get lost in. This chapter is a brief introduction to the basics of astrology, to help you find your way around in later travels. Bear in mind, as you discover the difference between signs, houses, and constellations, that the information we share so readily was in ancient times a carefully guarded secret of scholar–priests entrusted with timing sacred ceremonies. While it takes years of study and practice to become an expert, you can derive pleasure and self-knowledge by learning how astrology works. Whether you're planning a brief visit or a long study, this user-friendly guide can give you the basic lay of the land, an overview that will help you get off on the road to understanding your own horoscope.

What Do We Mean by a "Sign"?

Signs are the "real estate" of astrology. They are segments of territory located on the *zodiac,* an imaginary 360-degree belt circling the earth. This belt is divided into twelve equal 30-degree portions, which are the *signs*.

There's a lot of confusion about the difference between the *signs* and the *constellations* of the zodiac. *Constellations* are patterns of stars that originally marked the twelve divisions of the zodiac, like sign posts. Though each *sign* is named after the constellation which once marked the same area, over hundreds of years, the earth's orbit has shifted, so that from our point of view here on earth, the constellations have "moved" and are no longer valid sign posts. However the 30-degree territory that belonged to each sign remains the same. (Most Western astrologers use the 12-equal-part division of the zodiac. But some methods of astrology do still use the constellations instead of the signs.)

Most people think of themselves in terms of their sun sign. A *sun sign* refers to the sign the sun is orbiting through at a given moment (from our point of view here on earth). For instance, "I'm an Aries" means that the sun was passing through Aries when that person was born. However, there are nine other planets (plus asteroids, fixed stars, and sensitive points) which also form our total astrological personality, and some or many of these will be located in other signs. No one is completely "Aries," with all their astrological components in one sign! (Please note that in astrology, the sun and moon are usually referred to as "planets," though of course they're not.)

What Makes a Sign Special?

What makes the sign of Aries associated with go-getters and Taureans savvy with money? And Geminis talk a blue streak and Sagittarians footloose? It is important to note that characteristics associated with the signs are not accidental. They are derived from combinations of four basic components: a sign's element, quality, polarity, and place on the zodiac.

For example, take the element of fire: It's hot, passionate. Then add an active cardinal mode. Give it a jolt of positive energy and place it first in line. And doesn't that sound like the active, me-first, driving, hotheaded, energetic Aries?

Then take the element of earth, practical, sensual, the

27

place where things grow. Add the fixed, stable mode. Give it energy that reacts to its surroundings, that settles in. Put it after Aries. Now you've got a good idea of how sensual, earthy Taurus operates.

Another way to grasp the idea is to pretend you're doing a magical puzzle based on the numbers that can divide into twelve (the number of signs): 4, 3, and 2. There are four "building blocks" or elements, three ways a sign operates (qualities) and two polarities. These alternate in turn around the zodiac, with a different combination coming up for each sign. Here's how they add up.

THE FOUR ELEMENTS

These describe the physical concept of the sign. Is it fiery (dynamic), earthy (practical), airy (mental), water (emotional)? There are three zodiac signs of each of the four elements: fire (Aries, Leo, Sagittarius), earth (Taurus, Virgo, Capricorn), air (Gemini, Libra, Aquarius), water (Cancer, Scorpio, Pisces). These are the same elements that make up our planet: earth, air, fire and water. But astrology uses the elements as *symbols* that link our body and psyche to the rhythms of the planets. Fire signs spread warmth and enthusiasm. They are able to fire up or motivate others. They have hot tempers. These are people who make ideas catch fire and spring into existence. Earth signs are the builders of the zodiac who follow through after the initiative of fire signs to make things happen. These people are solid, practical realists who enjoy material things and sensual pleasures. They are interested in ideas that can be used to achieve concrete results. Air signs are mental people, great communicators. Following the consolidating earth signs, they'll reach out to inspire others through the use of words, social contacts, discussion, and debate. Water signs complete each four-sign series, adding the ingredients of emotion, compassion, and imagination. Water-sign people are nonverbal communicators who attune themselves to their surroundings and react through the medium of feelings.

A SIGN'S QUALITY

The second consideration when defining a sign is how it will operate. Will it take the initiative, or move slowly and deliberately, or adapt easily? Its *quality* (or modality) will tell. There are three qualities and four signs of each quality: cardinal, fixed, and mutable.

Cardinal signs are the start-up signs that begin each season (Aries, Cancer, Libra, Capricorn). These people love to be active, involved in projects. They are usually on the fast track to success, impatient to get things under way. *Fixed signs* (Taurus, Leo, Scorpio, Aquarius) move steadily, always in control. They happen in the middle of a season, after the initial character of the season is established. Fixed signs are naturally more centered. They tend to move more deliberately, doing things slowly but thoroughly. They govern parts of your horoscope where you take root and integrate your experiences. *Mutable signs* (Gemini, Virgo, Sagittarius, Pisces) embody the principle of distribution. These are the signs that break up the cycle, prepare the way for a change by distributing the energy to the next group. Mutables are flexible, adaptable, communicative. They can move in many directions easily, darting around obstacles.

A SIGN'S POLARITY

In addition to an element and a quality, each sign has a polarity, either a positive or negative electrical charge that generates energy around the zodiac like a giant battery. Polarity refers to opposites, which you could also define as masculine/feminine, yin/yang, active/reactive. Alternating around the zodiac, the six fire and air signs are positive, active, masculine, and yang in polarity. These signs are open, expanding outward. The six earth and water signs are reactive, negative, and yin—in other words, nurturing and receptive in polarity, which allows the energy to develop and take shape. All positive energy would be like a car without brakes. All negative energy would be like a stalled vehicle, going nowhere. Both polarities are needed in balanced proportion.

Finally we must consider the order of the signs. This

is vital to the balance of the zodiac and the transmission of energy throughout the zodiac. Each sign is quite different from its neighbors on either side. Yet each seems to grow out of its predecessor like links in a chain, transmitting a synthesis of energy gathered along the chain to the following sign, beginning with the fire-powered active positive cardinal sign of Aries and ending with watery mutable, reactive Pisces.

The Layout of a Horoscope Chart

A horoscope chart is a graphic map of the heavens at a given moment in time. It looks somewhat like a wheel divided with twelve spokes. The territory marked off by each "spoke" is a section called a *house*. The houses are extremely important in astrological interpretation because each house is associated with a different area of life and is influenced (or *ruled*) by a sign and a planet assigned to that house.

In addition, the house is colored by the sign passing over the spoke (or cusp) at the moment of the horoscope. The sequence of the houses begins at the left center spoke (or the 9 position if you were reading a clock) and follows reading counter-clockwise around the chart.

The First House—Home of Aries and Mars

This is the house of "firsts"—the first impression you make, how you initiate matters, the image you choose to project. This is your advertisement to the world. Planets that fall here will intensify the way you come across to others. Often a person's first house will project an entirely different type of personality than the sun sign. For instance, a Capricorn with Leo in the first house will come across as much more flamboyant than the average Capricorn. The sign passing over the cusp of this house at the time of your birth is known as your ascendant or rising sign.

The Second House—Home of Taurus and Venus

This is how you experience the material world—what you value. Here is your contact with the material world—your attitudes about money, possessions, finances, whatever belongs to you, and what you own, as well as your earning and spending capacity. As a Venus-ruled house, it describes your sensuality, your delight in physical pleasures. On a deeper level, this house reveals your sense of self-esteem—how you value yourself.

The Third House—Home of Gemini and Mars

This is how well you communicate with others—are you understood? This house shows how you reach out to others nearby and interact with the immediate environment. Here is how your thinking process works, how you communicate. This house shows your first relationships, your experiences with brothers and sisters, as well as how well you deal with people close to you now, such as your neighbors or pals. It's where you take short trips, write letters, or use the telephone. It shows how your mind works in terms of left-brain logical and analytical functions.

The Fourth House—Home of Cancer and the Moon

This is how you are nurtured and made to feel secure—your roots! At the bottom of the chart, the fourth house, like the home, shows the foundation of life and its psychological underpinnings. Here is where you have the deepest confrontations with who you are and how you make yourself feel secure. It shows your early home environment and the circumstances at the end of your life—your final "home"—as well as the place you call home now. Astrologers look here for information about the parental nurturers in your life.

The Fifth House—Home of Leo and the Sun

This is how you express yourself creatively—your idea of play. The Leo house is where the creative potential develops. Here you express yourself and procreate, in the sense that children are outgrowths of your creative ability. But this house most represents your inner childlike self, who delights in play. If inner security has been established by the time you reach this house, you are now free to have fun, romance, and love affairs, and to give of yourself. This is also the place astrologers look for playful love affairs, flirtations, and brief romantic encounters (rather than long-term commitments).

The Sixth House—Home of Virgo and Mercury

This is how you function in daily life. The sixth house has been called the "repair and maintenance" department. Here is where you get things done, how you look after others and fulfill responsibilities, such as taking care of pets. Here is your daily survival, your "job" routine and organization (as opposed to your career, which is the domain of the tenth house), your diet, and your health and fitness regimens. This house shows how you take care of your body and organize yourself so you can perform efficiently in the world.

The Seventh House—Home of Libra and Venus

This is how you form a partnership. Here is the way you commit to others, as well as your close, intimate, one-on-one relationships (including open enemies—those you "face off" with). This house shows your attitude toward partners and those with whom you enter commitments, contracts, or agreements. Open hostilities, lawsuits, divorces, and marriages happen here. If the first house represents the "I" in your horoscope, the seventh or opposite house is the "not-I"—the complementary partner you attract by the way you come across. If you are having trouble with partnerships, consider what you are attracting by the energies of your first and seventh houses.

The Eighth House—Home of Scorpio and Pluto (also Mars)

This is how you merge with something greater than yourself. Here is where you deal with issues of power and control, where you share with others and merge your energy with another to become something greater. Here are your attitudes toward sex, shared resources, and taxes (what you share with the government). Because this house involves what belongs to others, there can be power struggles or there can be a deep psychological transformation as you bond with another. Here you transcend yourself with the occult, dreams, drugs, or psychic experiences that reflect the collective unconscious.

The Ninth House—Home of Sagittarius and Jupiter

This is how you search for wisdom and higher knowledge. As the third house represents the "lower mind," its opposite on the wheel, the ninth house, is the "higher mind"—the abstract, intuitive, spiritual mind that asks big questions like why are we here, how everything fits together, what it all means. The ninth house shows what you believe in. After the third house explored what was close at hand, the ninth stretches out to explore more exotic territory, either by traveling, broadening mentally with higher education, or stretching spiritually with religious activity. Here is where you write a book or an extensive thesis, where you pontificate, philosophize, or preach.

The Tenth House—Home of Capricorn and Saturn

This is your public image and how you handle authority. This house is located directly overhead at the "high noon" position. This is the most "visible" house in the chart, the one where the world sees you. It deals with your public image, your career (but not your routine "job"), and your reputation. Here is where you go public and take on responsibilities (as opposed to the fourth house, where you stay home). This will affect the career you choose and your "public relations." This house is also associated with your father figure or whoever else was the authority figure in your life.

The Eleventh House—Home of Aquarius and Uranus

This is your support system, how you relate to society and your goals. This house is where you define what you really want, the kinds of friends you have, your teammates, your political affiliations, and the kind of groups you identify with as an equal. Here is where you could become a socially conscious humanitarian—or a party-going social butterfly. It's where you look to others to stimulate you and discover your kinship to the rest of humanity. The sign on this house can help you understand what you gain and lose from friendships, how concerned you are with social approval, and with what others think.

The Twelfth House—Home of Pisces and Neptune

Here is where the boundaries between yourself and others become blurred, where you become selfless. In your trip around the zodiac, you've gone from the "I" of self-assertion in the first house to the final house symbolizing the dissolution that happens before rebirth, a place where the accumulated experiences are processed in the unconscious. Spiritually oriented astrologers look to this house for your past lives and karma. Places where we go to be alone and do spiritual or reparatory work belong here, such as retreats, religious institutions, hospitals. Here is also where we withdraw from society—or are forced to withdraw because of antisocial activity. Selfless giving through charitable acts is part of this house. In your daily life, the twelfth house reveals your deepest intimacies and your best-kept secrets, especially those you hide from yourself and keep repressed deep in the unconscious. It is where we surrender a sense of a separate self to a deep feeling of wholeness, such as selfless service in religion or any activity that involves merging with the greater whole. Many sports stars have important planets in the twelfth house that enable them to find an inner, almost mystical, strength that transcends their limits.

Who's Home in Your Houses?

Houses are stronger or weaker depending on how many planets are inhabiting them and the condition of those planets. If there are many planets in a given house, it follows that the activities of that house will be especially important in your life. If the planet that rules the house is also located there, this too adds power to the house.

CHAPTER 4

The Planets—Players in Your Personal Drama

Once you understand the basic territory of astrology—what defines a sign and the layout of a horoscope chart—you're ready to meet the cast of characters who make the chart come alive. Nothing happens without the planets, which relate to each other to create the action in a chart.

The ten planets in your chart will play starring or supporting roles, depending on their position in your horoscope. A planet in the first house, particularly one that's close to your rising sign, is sure to be a featured player. Planets that are grouped together usually operate together like a team, playing off each other, rather than expressing their energy singularly. A planet that stands alone, away from the others, is usually outstanding and sometimes steals the show.

Each planet has two signs where it is especially at home. These are called its *dignities*. The most favorable place for a planet is in the sign or signs it rules; the next best place is in a sign where it is *exalted,* or especially harmonious. On the other hand, there are places in the horoscope where a planet has to work harder to play its role. These places are called the planet's *detriment* and *fall*. The sign opposite a planet's rulership, which embodies the opposite area of life, is its detriment. The sign opposite its exaltation is called its fall. Though the terms may suggest unfortunate circumstances for the planet, that is not always the case. In fact, a planet that is debilitated can actually be more complete, because it must

36

stretch itself to meet the challenges of living in a more difficult sign. Like world leaders who've had to struggle for greatness, this planet may actually develop great strength and character.

Here's a list of the best places for each planet to be, in the signs they rule. Note that, as new planets were discovered in this century, they replaced the traditional rulers of signs that best complimented their energies.

ARIES—Mars
TAURUS—Venus, in its most sensual form
GEMINI—Mercury, in its communicative role
CANCER—the moon
LEO—the sun
VIRGO—Mercury, in its critical capacity
LIBRA—Venus, in its aesthetic, judgmental form
SCORPIO—Pluto, replacing the sign's original ruler, Mars
SAGITTARIUS—Jupiter
CAPRICORN—Saturn
AQUARIUS—Uranus, replacing Saturn, its original ruler
PISCES—Neptune, replacing Jupiter, its original ruler

A person who has many planets in exalted signs is lucky indeed, for here is where the planet can accomplish the most, and be its most influential and creative.

SUN—Exalted in Aries, where its energy creates action
MOON—Exalted in Taurus, where instincts and reactions operate on a highly creative level
MERCURY—Exalted in Virgo, which it also rules, and where it can reach analytical heights
VENUS—Exalted in Pisces, a sign whose sensitivity encourages love and creativity
MARS—Exalted in Capricorn, a sign that puts energy to work
JUPITER—Exalted in Cancer, where it encourages nurturing and growth
SATURN—At home in Libra, where it steadies the scales of justice and promotes balanced, responsible judgment

37

URANUS—Powerful in Scorpio, where it promotes transformation

NEPTUNE—Especially favored in Cancer, where it gains the security to transcend to a higher state

PLUTO—Exalted in Pisces, where it dissolves the old cycle to make way for transition to the new

The Sun is Always Center Stage

Your sun sign is where you directly express yourself, displaying the part of you that shines brightest, even when you're accompanied by strong costars, or you're dressed modestly, or sharing a house with several other planets. When you know a person's sun sign, you already know some very useful generic qualities. Then, after you add the other planets, you'll have an accurate profile of that person and will be more able to predict how that individual will act in a given situation. The sun's just one actor on the stage, but a very powerful one—a good reason why sun-sign astrology works for so many people.

The sun rules the sign of Leo, gaining strength through the pride, dignity, and confidence of the fixed-fire personality. It is exalted in "me-first" Aries. In its detriment, Aquarius, the sun-ego is strengthened through group participation and social consciousness, rather than through self-centeredness. Note how many Aquarius people are involved in politics, social work, public life, following the demands of their sun sign to be spokesperson for a group. In its fall, Libra, the sun needs the strength of a partner—an "other"—to enhance balance and self-expression.

Like your sun sign, each of the other nine planet's personalities is colored by the sign it is passing through at the time. For example, Mercury, the planet that rules the way you communicate, will express itself in a dynamic, headstrong Aries way if it was passing through the sign of Aries when you were born. You would communicate in a much different way if it were passing through the slower, more patient sign of Taurus. Here's a rundown of the planets and how they behave in every sign.

The Moon—The Oscar Nominee

The Moon's role is to dig beneath the surface to reflect your needs, your longings, and the kind of childhood conditioning you had. In a man's chart, the moon position also describes his female, receptive, emotional side, and the woman in his life who will have the deepest effect. (Venus reveals the kind of woman who attracts him physically).

The sign the moon was passing through at your birth reflects your instinctive emotional nature and the things that appeal to you subconsciously. Since accurate moon tables are too extensive for this book, check through these descriptions to find the moon sign that feels most familiar—or better yet, have your chart calculated by a computer service to get your accurate moon placement.

The moon rules maternal Cancer and is exalted in Taurus—both comforting, home-loving signs where the natural emotional energies of the moon are easily and productively expressed. But when the moon is in the opposite signs—in its Capricorn detriment and its Scorpio fall—it leaves the comfortable nest and deals with emotional issues of power and achievement in the outside world. Those of you with the moon in these signs will find your emotional role more challenging in life.

Moon in Aries

Emotionally, you are independent and ardent. You are an idealistic, impetuous person who falls in and out of love easily. You respond to a challenge, but could cool down once your quarry is captured. To avoid continuous "treat 'em rough" situations, you should work on cultivating patience and tolerance. Be wary of responding to excitement for its own sake.

Moon in Taurus

This is a strong position for the moon, so emotional satisfaction will be an important factor in your life. You are a huggy, sentimental soul who is very fond of the good life and gravitates toward solid, secure relationships. You like frequent displays of affection and creature comforts—all the tangible trappings of a cozy atmosphere. You are sensual and steady emotionally, but very stubborn and determined. You can't be pushed and tend to protect your turf.

Moon in Gemini

You crave mental stimulation and variety in life, which you usually get through either a varied social life, the excitement of flirtation, and/or multiple professional involvements. You may marry more than once and have a rather chaotic emotional life due to your difficulty with commitment and settling down. Be sure to find a partner who is as outgoing as you are. You will have to learn at some point to focus your energies because you tend to be somewhat fragmented—you may do two things at once, or have two careers, homes, or even two lovers. If you can find a creative way to express your many-faceted nature, you'll be ahead of the game.

Moon in Cancer

This is the most powerful lunar position, which is sure to have a deep imprint on your character. Your needs are very much associated with your reaction to the needs of others. You are very sensitive and self-protective, though some of you may mask this with a hard shell. This placement also gives an excellent memory and an uncanny ability to psyche out the needs of others. All of the lunar phases will affect you, especially full moons and eclipses, so be sure to mark them on your calendar. You are happiest at home and may work at home or turn your office into a second home, where you can nurture and comfort people (you may tend to "mother the world"). This psychic, intuitive moon might draw you to occult work in some way. Or you may professionally provide food and shelter to others.

Moon in Leo

This is a warm, passionate moon that takes everything to heart. You are attracted to all that is noble, generous, and aristocratic in life and may be a bit of a snob. You have an innate ability to take command emotionally, but you need strong support, loyalty, and loud applause from those you love. You are possessive of your loved ones and your turf, and you will roar if anyone threatens to take over your territory.

Moon in Virgo

You are rather cool until you decide if others measure up. But once someone or something meets your ideal standards, you hold up your end of the arrangement perfectly. You may, in fact, drive yourself too hard to attain some notion of perfection. Try to be a bit easier on yourself and others. Don't always act the critic! You love to be the teacher and are drawn to situations where you can change others for the better. But sometimes you must learn to accept others for what they are and enjoy what you have.

Moon in Libra

This is a partnership-oriented placement—you may find it difficult to be alone or to do things alone. But you must learn to lean on yourself first. When you have learned emotional balance, you can have excellent relationships. Avoid extremes in your love life—you thrive in a rather conservative, traditional, romantic relationship, where your partner provides attention and flattery—but not possessiveness. You'll be your most charming in an elegant, harmonious atmosphere.

Moon in Scorpio

This is a moon that enjoys and responds to intense, passionate feelings. You may go to extremes and have a very dramatic emotional life, full of ardor, suspicion, jealousy, and obsession. It would be much healthier to channel your need for power and control into meaningful work. This is a good position for anyone in the fields of medicine, police work, research, the occult, psychoanalysis, or intuitive work, because life-and-death situations are not as likely to faze you. However, you do take personal disappointments very hard.

Moon in Sagittarius

You take life's ups and downs with good humor and the proverbial grain of salt. You'll love 'em and leave 'em, and take off on a great adventure at a moment's notice. "Born free" could be your slogan, for you can't stand to be possessed emotionally by anyone. Attracted by the exotic, you have wanderlust mentally and physically. You may be too much in search of new mental and spiritual stimulation to ever settle down.

Moon in Capricorn

Are you ever accused of being too cool and calculating? You have an earthy side, but you take prestige and position very seriously. Your strong drive to succeed extends to your romantic life, where you will be devoted to improving your lifestyle and rising to the top. A structured situation where you can advance methodically makes you feel wonderfully secure. You may be attracted to someone older or very much younger or from a different social world. It may be difficult to look at the lighter side of emotional relationships, but the "up" side of this moon in its detriment is that you tend to be very dutiful and responsible to those you care for.

Moon in Aquarius

You are a people collector with many friends of all backgrounds. You are happiest surrounded by people and may feel slightly uneasy when left alone. Though intense emotions could be unsettling, you usually stay friends with those with whom you get involved. You're tolerant and understanding, but sometimes you can be emotionally unpredictable. You don't like anything to be too rigid and you may resist working on schedule. You may even have a very unconventional love life. With plenty of space, you will be able to sustain relationships, but you'll blow away from possessive demanding types.

Moon in Pisces

You are very responsive and empathetic to others, especially if they have problems, but be on guard against attracting too many people with sob stories. You'll be happiest if you can find a way to express your creative imagination in the arts or in the spiritual or healing professions. You may tend to escape to a fantasy world or be attracted to exotic places or people. You need an emotional anchor, as you are very sensitive to the moods of others. You are happiest near water, working in a field that gives you emotional variety. But steer clear of too much escapism (especially in alcohol) or reclusiveness. Keep a firm foothold in reality.

Mercury—The Scriptwriter

Mercury shows how you think and speak, and how logically your mind works. It stays close to the sun—never more than a sign away—and very often it shares the same sign as the sun, reinforcing the sun's communicative talents. Mercury functions easily in the naturally analytical signs Gemini and Virgo, which it rules. Yet Mercury in Sagittarius and Pisces, where logic often takes second place to visionary ideas, and where Mercury is debilitated, can provide visionary thinking and poetic expression. But this planet must be properly harnessed. Check your sun sign and the signs preceding and following it to see which Mercury position most applies to you.

Mercury in Aries

Your mind is very active and assertive. You never hesitate to say what you think; you never shy away from a battle. In fact, you may relish a verbal confrontation. Tact is not your strong point, so you may have to learn not to trip over your tongue.

Mercury in Taurus

You may be a slow learner, but you have good concentration and mental stamina. You want to make your ideas really happen. You'll attack a problem methodically and consider every angle thoroughly, never jumping to conclusions. You'll stick with a subject until you master it.

Mercury in Gemini

You are a wonderful communicator with great facility for expressing yourself both verbally and in writing. You talk and talk, and you love gathering all kinds of information. You probably finish other people's sentences and talk with hand gestures. You can talk to anybody anytime—and you probably have the phone bills to prove it. You read anything from sci-fi to Shakespeare, and you might need an extra room just for your book collection. Though you learn fast, you may lack focus and discipline. Watch a tendency to jump from subject to subject.

Mercury in Cancer

You rely on intuition more than logic. Your mental processes are usually colored by your emotions, so you may seem shy or hesitant to voice your opinions. But this placement gives you the advantage of great imagination and empathy in the way you communicate with others.

Mercury in Leo

You are enthusiastic and very dramatic in the way you express yourself. You like to hold the attention of groups and could be a great public speaker. You think big, preferring to deal with the overall picture rather than the details.

Mercury in Virgo

This is one of the best places for Mercury. It should give you the ability to think critically, pay attention to details, and analyze thoroughly. Your mind focuses on the practical side of things, making you well suited to teaching or editing.

Mercury in Libra

You are a born diplomat who smoothes over ruffled feathers. You may be a talented debater or lawyer, but constantly weighing the pros and cons of situations makes you vacillate when making decisions.

Mercury in Scorpio

Yours is an investigative mind that stops at nothing to get the answers. You may have a sarcastic, stinging wit, and a gift for the cutting remark. But there's always a grain of truth to your verbal sallies, thanks to your penetrating insight.

Mercury in Sagittarius

You are a super salesman with a tendency to expound. Though you are very broad minded, you can be dogmatic when it comes to telling others what's good for them. You won't hesitate to tell the truth as you see it, so watch a tendency toward tactlessness. On the plus side, you have a great sense of humor. This position of Mercury is often considered by astrologers to be at a disadvantage because Sagittarius opposes Gemini, the sign Mercury rules, and squares off with Virgo, another Mercury-ruled sign. What often happens is that Mercury in Sagittarius oversteps its bounds and loses sight of the facts in a situation. Do a reality check before making promises that you may not be able to deliver.

Mercury in Capricorn

This placement endows good mental discipline. You have a love of learning and a very orderly approach to your subjects. You will patiently plod through the facts and figures until you have mastered the tasks. You grasp structured situations easily, but may be short on creativity.

Mercury in Aquarius

With Uranus and Neptune in Aquarius now energizing your Mercury, you're sure to be on the cutting edge of new ideas. An independent, original thinker, you'll have more far-out ideas than the average person and be quick to check out any unusual opportunities. Your opinions are so well researched and grounded in fact that once your mind is made up, it is difficult to change.

Mercury in Pisces

You have the psychic intuitive mind of a natural poet. You should learn to make use of your creative imagination. You think in terms of helping others, but check a tendency to be vague and forgetful of details.

Venus—The Romantic Heroine

Venus is the planet of romantic love, pleasure, and artistry. It shows what you react to, your tastes, and what (or who) turns you on. It is naturally at home in Libra, the sign of partnerships, or Taurus, the sign of physical pleasures, both of which it rules. Yet in Aries, its detriment, Venus, daring and full of energy, is negatively self-serving. In Pisces, where Venus is exalted, this planet can go overboard, loving to the point of self-sacrifice. While Venus in Virgo, its fall, can be the perfectionist in love, it can also offer affectionate service and true support.

You can find your Venus placement on the charts in this book. Look for the year of your birth in the left-hand column, then follow the line across the page until you read the time period of your birthday. The sign heading that column will be your Venus. If you were born on a day when Venus was changing signs, check the signs preceding or following that day. Here are the roles your Venus plays—and the songs it sings.

Venus in Aries

Scarlett O'Hara could embody this placement. You can't stand to be bored, confined, or ordered around. But a good challenge—maybe even a rousing row—turns you on. Confess—don't you pick a fight now and then just to get someone stirred up? You're attracted by the chase, not the catch, which could cause some problems in your love life if the object of your affection becomes too attainable. You like to wear red and be first with the latest fashion. You'll spot a trend before anyone else.

Venus in Taurus

All your senses work in high gear, making this the perfect placement for a "Material Girl." You love to be surrounded by glorious tastes, smells, textures, sounds, and sights—austerity is not for you. Neither is being rushed, for you like time to enjoy your pleasures. Soothing surroundings with plenty of creature comforts are your cup of tea. You like to feel secure in your nest, with no sudden jolts or surprises. You like familiar objects—in fact, you may hate to let anything or anyone go.

Venus in Gemini

You are a lively, sparkling personality who "Loves the Night Life," thriving in constant variety and a frequent change of scenery. A varied social life is important to you, with plenty of stimulation and a chance to engage in some light flirtation. Commitment may be difficult because playing the field is so much fun.

Venus in Cancer

An atmosphere where you feel protected, coddled, and mothered is best for you. You'd love to be surrounded by children in a cozy, homelike situation. You are attracted to those who are tender and nurturing, who make you feel secure and well provided for—your "Heart Belongs to Daddy" (or Mommy). You may be secretive about your emotional life or attracted to clandestine relationships.

Venus in Leo

You're an "Uptown Girl" or boy who loves "Puttin' on the Ritz" to consort with elegant people, dress up, and be the center of attraction. First-class attention in large doses turns you on, and so does the glitter of real gold and the flash of mirrors. You like to feel like a star at all times, surrounded by your admiring audience. But you may be attracted to flatterers and tinsel, while the real gold requires some digging.

Venus in Virgo

Everything neatly in its place? On the surface, you are attracted to an atmosphere where everything is in perfect order, but underneath are some basic, earthy urges. You are attracted to those who appeal to your need to teach, serve, or play out a Pygmalion fantasy. You are at your best when you are busy doing something useful.

Venus in Libra

"I Feel Pretty" could be your theme song. Elegance and harmony are your key words—you can't abide an atmosphere of contention. Your taste tends toward the classic, with light harmonies of color—nothing clashing, trendy, or outrageous. You love doing things with a partner and should be careful to pick one who is decisive, but patient enough to let you weigh the pros and cons. Steer clear of argumentative types.

Venus in Scorpio

Hidden mysteries intrigue you—in fact, anything that is too open and above board is a bit of a bore. You surely have a stack of whodunits by the bed, along with an erotic magazine or two. You like to solve puzzles, and you may also be fascinated with the occult, crime, or scientific research. Intense, "All or Nothing at All" situations add spice to your life, and you love to ferret out the secrets of others. But you could get burned by your flair for living on the edge. The color black, spicy food, dark wood furniture, and heady perfume all get you in the right mood.

Venus in Sagittarius

"Like a Rolling Stone" sums up your Venus personality. If you are not actually a world traveler, your surroundings are sure to reflect your love of faraway places. You like a casual outdoor atmosphere and a dog or two to pet. There should be plenty of room for athletic equipment and suitcases. You're attracted to kindred souls who love to travel and who share your freedom-loving philosophy of life. Athletics, as well as spiritual or New Age pursuits, could be your other interests.

Venus in Capricorn

"Diamonds Are a Girl's Best Friend" could be the theme song of this ambitious Venus. You want substance in life and you are attracted to whatever will help you get where you are going. Status objects turn you on, and so do those who have a serious, responsible, businesslike approach, or who remind you of a beloved parent. It is characteristic of this placement to be attracted to someone of a different generation. Antiques, traditional clothing, and dignified behavior favor you.

Venus in Aquarius

"Just Friends, Lovers No More" is often what happens to this Venus. You like to be in a group, particularly one pushing a worthy cause. You feel quite at home surrounded by people, remaining detached from any intense commitment. Original ideas and unpredictable people fascinate you. You don't like everything to be planned out in advance, preferring spontaneity and delightful surprises.

Venus in Pisces

"Why Not Take all of Me?" pleads this Venus, who loves to give of yourself—and you find plenty of takers. Stray animals and people appeal to your heart and your pocketbook, but be careful to look at their motives realistically once in a while. You are extremely vulnerable to sob stories of all kinds. Fantasy, theater, and psychic or spiritual activities also speak to you.

Mars—The Conquering Hero

Mars is the mover and shaker in your life. It shows how you pursue your goals and whether you have energy to burn or proceed in a slow, steady pace. Or perhaps you are nervous, restless, and unable to sit still. Your Mars placement will also show how you get angry: Do you explode, do a slow burn, or hold everything inside, then get revenge later?

In Aries, which it rules, and Scorpio, which it corules, Mars is at its most powerful. Yet this drive can be self-serving and impetuous. In Libra, the sign of its detriment, Mars demands cooperation in a relationship. In Capricorn, where it is exalted, Mars becomes an ambitious achiever headed for the top. But in Cancer, the sign of its fall, Mars's aggression becomes tempered by feelings, especially those involving self-protection and security, which are always considered first. The end can never justify the means for Mars in Cancer.

To find your Mars, turn to the chart on page 86. Find your birth year in the left-hand column and trace the line across horizontally until you come to the column headed by the month of your birth. There you will find an abbreviation of your Mars sign. If the description of your Mars sign doesn't ring true, read the description of the sign preceding and following it. You may have been born on a day when Mars was changing signs, and your Mars would then be in the adjacent sign.

Mars in Aries

In the sign it rules, Mars shows its brilliant, fiery nature. You have an explosive temper and can be quite impatient, but on the other hand you have tremendous courage, energy, and drive. You'll let nothing stand in your way as you race to be first! Obstacles are met head on and broken through by force. However, those that require patience and persistence can have you exploding in rage. You're a great starter, but not necessarily around for the finish.

Mars in Taurus

Slow, steady, concentrated energy gives you the power. You've great stamina and you never give up, as you wear away obstacles with your persistence. Often you come out a winner because you've had the patience to hang in there. When angered, you do a slow burn.

Mars in Gemini

You can't sit still for long; this Mars craves variety. You often have two or more things going on at once—it's all an amusing game to you. Your life can get very complicated, but that only adds spice and stimulation. What drives you into a nervous, hyper state? Boredom, sameness, routine, and confinement. You can do wonderful things with your hands and you have a way with words.

Mars in Cancer

You rarely attack head on—instead, you'll keep things to yourself, make plans in secret, and always cover your actions. This might be interpreted by some as manipulative, but you are only being self-protective. You get furious when anyone knows too much about you, but you do like to know all about others. Your mothering and feeding instincts can be put to good use if you work in the food, hotel, or child-care industry. You may have to overcome your fragile sense of security, which prompts you not to take risks and to get physically upset when criticized. Don't take things so personally!

Mars in Leo

You have a very dominant personality that takes center stage—modesty is not one of your traits, nor is taking a back seat. You prefer giving the orders and have been known to make a dramatic scene if they are not obeyed. Properly used, this Mars confers leadership ability, endurance, and courage.

Mars in Virgo

You are the fault finder of the zodiac, who notices every little detail. Mistakes of any kind make you very nervous. You may worry even if everything is going smoothly. You may not express your anger directly, but you sure can nag. You have definite likes and dislikes and you are sure you can do the job better than anyone else. You are certainly more industrious and detail oriented than other signs. Your Mars energy is often most positively expressed in some kind of teaching role.

Mars in Libra

This Mars will have a passion for beauty, justice, and art. Generally, you will avoid confrontations at all costs, preferring to spend your energy finding a diplomatic solution or weighing the pros and cons. Your other techniques are using passive aggression or charm to get people to do what you want.

Mars in Scorpio

This is a powerful placement, so intense that it demands careful channeling into worthwhile activities. Otherwise, you could become obsessed with your sexuality or might use your need for power and control to manipulate others. You are strong willed, shrewd, and very private about your affairs, and you'll usually have a secret agenda behind your actions. Your great stamina, focus, and discipline would be excellent assets for careers in the military or medical fields, especially research or surgery. When angry, you don't get mad—you get even!

Mars in Sagittarius

This expansive Mars often propels people into sales, travel, athletics, or philosophy. Your energies function well when you are on the move. You have a hot temper and are inclined to say what you think before you consider the consequences. You shoot for high goals—and talk endlessly about them—but you may be weak on groundwork. This Mars needs a solid foundation. Watch a tendency to take unnecessary risks.

Mars in Capricorn

This is an ambitious Mars with an excellent sense of timing. You have the drive for success and the discipline to achieve it. You have an eye for those who can be of use to you, and you may dismiss people ruthlessly when you're angry. But you drive yourself hard and deliver full value. This is a good placement for an executive. You'll aim for status and a high material position in life, and keep climbing despite the odds. A great Mars to have!

Mars in Aquarius

This is the most rebellious Mars. You seem to have a drive to assert yourself against the status quo. You may enjoy provoking people, shocking them out of traditional views. Or this placement could express itself in an off-beat sex life—somehow you often find yourself in unconventional situations. You enjoy being a leader of an active group that pursues forward-looking studies, politics, or goals.

Mars in Pisces

This Mars is a good actor who knows just how to appeal to the sympathies of others. You create and project wonderful fantasies or use your sensitive antennae to crusade for those less fortunate. You get what you want through creating a veil of illusion and glamour. This is a good Mars for someone in the creative fields—a dancer, performer, or photographer—or for someone in the motion-picture industry. Many famous film stars have this placement. Watch a tendency to manipulate by making others feel sorry for you.

Jupiter—The Jolly Giant

Jupiter is often viewed as the "Santa Claus" of the horoscope, a jolly happy planet that brings good luck, gifts, success, and opportunities. Jupiter also embodies the functions of the higher mind, where you do complex, expansive thinking and deal with the big overall picture rather than the specifics (the role of Mercury). This big, bright, swirling mass of gases is associated with the kind of windfall you get without too much hard work. You're optimistic under Jupiter's influence—anything seems possible. You'll travel, expand your mind with higher education, and publish to share your knowledge widely. But a strong Jupiter has its down side, too. Jupiter's influence is neither discriminating nor disciplined. It represents the principle of growth without judgment, and could result in extravagance, weight gain, laziness, and carelessness if not kept in check.

Be sure to look up your Jupiter in the tables in this book. When the current position of Jupiter is favorable, you may get that lucky break. At any rate, it's a great time to try new things, take risks, travel, or get more education. Opportunities seem to open up at this time, so take advantage of them. Once a year, Jupiter changes signs. That means you are due for an expansive time every twelve years, when Jupiter travels through your sun sign. You'll also have "up" periods every four years, when Jupiter is in the same element as your sun sign.

Jupiter in Aries

You are the soul of enthusiasm and optimism. Your luckiest times are when you are getting started on an exciting project or selling an ideal that you really believe in, but don't be arrogant with those who do not share your enthusiasm. You follow your impulses, often ignoring budget or other common sense limitations. To produce real, solid benefits, you'll need patience and follow-through wherever this Jupiter falls in your horoscope.

Jupiter in Taurus

You'll spend on beautiful material things, especially items made of natural materials, such as rare woods, pure fabrics, or precious gems. You can't have too much comfort or too many sensual pleasures. Watch a tendency to overindulge in good food, or to overpamper yourself with nothing but the best. Spartan living is not for you! You may be especially lucky in matters of real estate.

Jupiter in Gemini

You are the great talker of the zodiac, and you may be a great writer, too. But restlessness could be your weak point. You jump around, talk too much, and could be a jack of all trades. Keeping a secret is especially difficult, so you'll also have to watch a tendency to spill the beans. Since you love to be at the center of a beehive of activity, you'll have a vibrant social life. Your best opportunities will come through your talent for language—speaking, writing, communicating, and selling.

Jupiter in Cancer

You are luckiest in situations where you can find emotional closeness or deal with basic security needs, such as food, nurturing, or shelter. You may be a great collector and you may simply love to accumulate things—you are the one who stashed things away for a rainy day. You probably have a very good memory and love children—in fact, you may have many children to care for. The food, hotel, child-care, or shipping business hold good opportunities for you.

Jupiter in Leo

You are a natural showman who loves to live in a larger-than-life way. Yours is a personality full of color that always find its way into the limelight. You can't have too much attention or applause. Show biz is a natural place for you, and so is any area where you can play to a crowd. Exercising your flair for drama, your natural playfulness, and your romantic nature brings you good fortune. But watch a tendency to be overly extravagant or to monopolize center stage.

Jupiter in Virgo

You actually love those minute details others find boring. To you, they make all the difference between the perfect and the ordinary. You are the fine craftsman who spots every flaw. You expand your awareness by finding the most efficient methods and by being of service to others. Many will be drawn to medical or teaching fields. You'll also have luck in publishing, crafts, nutrition, and service professions. Watch out for a tendency to overwork.

Jupiter in Libra

This is an other-directed Jupiter that develops best with a partner, for the stimulation of others helps you grow.

You are also most comfortable in harmonious, beautiful situations, and you work well with artistic people. You have a great sense of fair play and an ability to evaluate the pros and cons of a situation. You usually prefer to play the role of diplomat rather than adversary.

Jupiter in Scorpio

You love the feeling of power and control, of taking things to their limit. You can't resist a mystery, and your shrewd, penetrating mind sees right through to the heart of most situations and people. You have luck in work that provides for solutions to matters of life and death. You may be drawn to undercover work, behind-the-scenes intrigue, psychotherapy, the occult, and sex-related ventures. Your challenge will be to develop a sense of moderation and tolerance for other beliefs—this Jupiter can be fanatical. You may have luck in handling other people's money—insurance, taxes, and inheritance can bring you a windfall.

Jupiter in Sagittarius

Independent, outgoing, and idealistic, you'll shoot for the stars. This Jupiter compels you to travel far and wide, both physically and mentally, via higher education. You may have luck while traveling in an exotic place. You also have luck with outdoor ventures, exercise, and animals, particularly horses. Since you tend to be very open about your opinions, watch a tendency to be tactless and to exaggerate. Instead, use your wonderful sense of humor to make your point.

Jupiter in Capricorn

Jupiter is much more restrained in Capricorn, the sign of rules and authority. Here, Jupiter can make you overwork and heighten your ambition or sense of duty. You'll expand in areas that advance your position, putting you farther up the social or corporate ladder. You are lucky working within the establishment in a very structured situation, where you can show off your ability to organize and reap rewards for your hard work.

Jupiter in Aquarius

This is another freedom-loving Jupiter, with great tolerance and originality. You are at your best when you are working for a humanitarian cause and in the company of many supporters. This is a good Jupiter for a political career, for you'll relate to all kinds of people on all social levels. You have an abundance of original ideas, but you are best off away from routine and any situation that imposes rigid rules. You need mental stimulation!

Jupiter in Pisces

You are a giver whose feelings and pocketbook are easily touched by others, so choose your companions with care. You could be the original sucker for a hard-luck story—better find a worthy hospital or charity to appreciate your selfless support. You have a great creative imagination and may attract good fortune in fields related to oil, perfume, pharmaceuticals, petroleum, dance, footwear, and alcohol. But beware of overindulgence in alcohol—focus on a creative outlet instead.

Saturn—The "Heavy"

Jupiter speeds you up with lucky breaks, then along comes Saturn to slow you down with the disciplinary brakes. Saturn has unfairly been called a malefic planet, one of the bad guys of the zodiac. On the contrary, Saturn is one of our best friends, the kind who tells you what's wrong with you for your own good. Under a Saturn transit, we grow up, take responsibility for our lives, and emerge from whatever test this planet has in store, far wiser, more capable, and mature.

When Saturn hits a critical point in your horoscope, you can count on an experience that will make you slow down, pull back, and reexamine your life. It is a call to eliminate what is not working and to shape up. By the end of its 28-year trip around the zodiac, Saturn will have tested you in all areas of your life. The major tests usually happen in seven-year cycles, when Saturn passes over the angles of your chart—your rising sun, midheaven, descendant, and nadir. This is when the real life-changing experiences happen. But you are also in for a testing period whenever Saturn passes a planet in your chart or stresses that planet from a distance. Therefore it is useful to check your planetary positions with the travel schedule of Saturn in order to prepare in advance, or at least to brace yourself.

When Saturn returns to its location at the time of your birth, at approximately age 28, you'll have your first Saturn return. At this time, a person usually takes stock or settles down to find his mission in life and assume full adult duties and responsibilities.

Another way Saturn helps us is to reveal the karmic lessons from previous lives and give us the chance to overcome them. So look at Saturn's challenges as much-needed opportunities for self-improvement. Under a Jupiter influence, you'll have more fun, but Saturn gives you solid, long-lasting results.

Look up your natal Saturn in the tables in this book for clues on where you need work.

Saturn in Aries

Saturn here puts the brakes on Aries' natural drive and enthusiasm. You don't let anyone push you around and you know what's best for yourself. Following orders is not your strong point, and neither is diplomacy. You tend to be quick to go on the offensive in relationships, attacking first, before anyone attacks you. Because no one quite lives up to your standards, you often wind up doing everything yourself. You'll have to learn to cooperate and tone down self-centeredness.

Saturn in Taurus

A big issue is getting control of the cash flow. There will be lean periods that can be frightening, but you have the patience and endurance to stick them out and the methodical drive to prosper in the end. Learn to take a philosophical attitude like Ben Franklin, who also had this placement and who said, "A penny saved is a penny earned."

Saturn in Gemini

You are a serious student of life who may have difficulty communicating or sharing your knowledge. You may be shy, speak slowly, or have fears about communicating, like Eleanor Roosevelt. You dwell in the realms of science, theory, or abstract analysis, even when you are dealing with the emotions, like Sigmund Freud, who also had this placement.

Saturn in Cancer

Your tests come with establishing a secure emotional base. In doing so, you may have to deal with some very basic fears centering on your early home environment. Most of your Saturn tests will have emotional roots in those early childhood experiences. You may have difficulty remaining objective in terms of what you try to achieve, so it will be especially important for you to deal with negative feelings such as guilt, paranoia, jealousy, resentment, and suspicion. Galileo and Michelangelo also navigated these murky waters.

Saturn in Leo

This is an authoritarian Saturn, a strict, demanding parent who may deny the pleasure principle in your zeal to see that rules are followed. Though you may feel guilty about taking the spotlight, you are very ambitious and loyal. You have to watch a tendency toward rigidity, as well as a leaning toward overwork and holding back affection. Joseph Kennedy and Billy Graham share this placement.

Saturn in Virgo

This is a cautious, exacting Saturn, intensely hard on yourself. Most of all, you give yourself the roughest time with your constant worries about every little detail, often making yourself sick. You may have difficulties setting priorities and getting the job done. Your tests will come in learning tolerance and understanding of others. Charles de Gaulle and Nathaniel Hawthorne had this meticulous Saturn.

Saturn in Libra

Saturn is exalted here, which makes this planet an ally. You may choose very serious, older partners in life, perhaps stemming from a fear of dependency. You need to learn to stand solidly on your own before you commit to another. You are extremely cautious as you deliberate every involvement—with good reason. It is best that you find an occupation that makes good use of your sense of duty and honor. Steer clear of fly-by-night situations. Khrushchev and Mao Tse-tung had this placement, too.

Saturn in Scorpio

You have great staying power. This Saturn tests you in situations involving the control of others. You may feel drawn to some kind of intrigue or undercover work, like J. Edgar Hoover. Or there may be an air of mystery surrounding your life and death, like Marilyn Monroe and Robert Kennedy, who had this placement. There are lessons to be learned from your sexual involvements—often sex is used for manipulation or is somehow out of the ordinary. The Roman emperor Caligula and the transvestite Christine Jorgensen are extreme cases.

Saturn in Sagittarius

Your challenges and lessons will come from tests of your spiritual and philosophical values, as happened to Martin Luther King and Gandhi. You are high minded and sincere with the reflective, moral placement. Uncompromising in your ethical standards, you could become a benevolent despot.

Saturn in Capricorn

With the help of Saturn at maximum strength, your judgment will improve with age. And, like Spencer Tracy's screen image, you'll be the gray-haired hero with a strong sense of responsibility. You advance in life slowly but steadily, always with a strong hand at the helm and an eye for the advantageous situation. Negatively, you may be a loner, prone to periods of melancholy.

Saturn in Aquarius

Do you care too much about what others think? Do you feel like an outsider, as Greta Garbo did? You may fear being different from others and therefore slight your own unique, forward-looking gifts, or, like Lord Byron and Howard Hughes, you may take the opposite tack and rebel in the extreme. You can apply discipline to accomplish great humanitarian goals, as Albert Schweitzer did.

Saturn in Pisces

Your fear of the unknown and the irrational may lead you to the safety and protection of an established institution. Some of you may avoid looking too deeply inside at all costs. Jesse James, who had this placement, spent his life on the run. Or you might go in the opposite, more positive direction by developing a discipline that puts you more in control of your feelings. Some of you will take refuge in work with hospitals, charities, or religious institutions.

Queen Victoria, who had this placement, symbolized an era when charitable institutions of all kinds were founded. Discipline applied to artistic work, especially poetry and dance, or spiritual work, such as yoga or meditation, might be helpful.

Uranus, Neptune, and Pluto—The Character Roles

These three outer planets are slow moving but powerful forces in your life. Since they stay in a sign at least seven years, you'll share the sign placement with everyone you went to school with and perhaps your brothers and sisters. However, the area of life (house) where the planet operates in your chart is what makes its influence unique to you. When one of these distant planets changes signs, there is a definite shift in the atmosphere, bringing the feeling of the end of an era.

Since these planets are so far away from the sun—too distant to be seen by the naked eye—they pick up signals from the universe at large. These planetary receivers literally link the sun with distant energies, and then perform a similar function in your horoscope by linking your central character with intuitive, spiritual, transformative forces from the cosmos. Each planet has a special domain and will reflect this in the area of your life where it falls.

Uranus—The Revolutionary, the Techie

Uranus is the brilliant, highly unpredictable genius who shakes us out of our rut and propels us forward. There is nothing ordinary about this quirky green planet that seems to be traveling on its side, surrounded by a swarm of at least fifteen moons. Is it any wonder that astrologers assigned it to Aquarius, the most eccentric and gregarious sign? Uranus seems to wend its way around the sun, marching to its own tune.

Uranus energy is electrical, happening in sudden flashes. It is not influenced by karma or past events, nor does it regard tradition, sex, or sentiment. The Uranian key words are "surprise" and "awakening." Suddenly, there's that flash of inspiration, that bright idea, that totally new approach that turns around whatever scheme you were undertaking. The Uranus place in your life is where you awaken and become your own person, and it is probably the most unconventional place in your chart.

Look up the sign of Uranus at the time of your birth and see where you follow your own tune.

Uranus in Aries

BIRTH DATES:
March 30, 1927–November 4, 1927
January 13, 1928—June 6, 1934
October 10, 1934—March 28, 1935

Your generation is original, creative, and pioneering. It developed the computer, the airplane, and the cyclotron. You let nothing hold you back from exploring the unknown and you have a powerful mixture of fire and electricity behind you. Women of your generation were among the first to be liberated. You are the unforgettable style setters, with a surprise in store for everyone. Like Yoko Ono, Grace Kelly, and Jacqueline Onassis, your life may be jolted by sudden and violent changes.

Uranus in Taurus

BIRTH DATES:
June 6, 1934–October 10, 1934
March 28, 1935–August 7, 1941
October 5, 1941–May 15, 1942

You are probably self-employed or would like to be. You have original ideas about making money, and you brace yourself for sudden changes of fortune. This Uranus can cause shakeups, particularly in finances, but it can also make you a born entrepreneur.

Uranus in Gemini

BIRTH DATES:
August 7, 1941–October 5, 1941
May 15, 1942–August 30, 1948
November 12, 1948–June 10, 1949

You were the first children to be influenced by television and in your adult years, your generation stocks up on answering machines, cordless phones, car phones, computers, and fax machines—any new way you can communicate. You have an inquiring mind, but your interests are rather short lived. This Uranus can be easily fragmented if there is no structure and focus.

Uranus in Cancer

BIRTH DATES:
August 30, 1948–November 12, 1948
June 10, 1949–August 24, 1955
January 28, 1956–June 10, 1956

This generation came at a time when divorce was becoming commonplace, so your home image is unconventional. You may have an unusual relationship with your parents; you may have come from a broken home or an unconventional one. You'll have unorthodox ideas about parenting, intimacy, food, and shelter. You may also be interested in dreams, psychic phenomena, and memory work.

Uranus in Leo

BIRTH DATES:
August 24, 1955–January 28, 1956
June 10, 1956–November 1, 1961
January 10, 1962–August 10, 1962

This generation understood how to use electronic media. Many of your group are now leaders in the high-tech industries, and you also understand how to use the new media to promote yourself. Like Isadora Duncan, you may have a very eccentric kind of charisma and a life that is sparked by unusual love affairs. Your children, too, may have traits that are out of the ordinary. Where this planet falls in your chart, you'll have a love of freedom, be a bit of an egomaniac, and show the full force of your personality in a unique way, like tennis great Martina Navratilova.

Uranus in Virgo

BIRTH DATES:
November 1, 1961–January 10, 1962
August 10, 1962–September 28, 1968
May 20, 1969–June 24, 1969

You'll have highly individual work methods, and many of you will be finding newer, more practical ways to use computers. Like Einstein, who had this placement, you'll break the rules brilliantly. Your generation came at a time of student rebellions, the civil rights movement, and the general acceptance of health foods. Chances are, you're concerned about pollution and cleaning up the environment. You may also be involved with nontraditional healing methods. Heavyweight champ Mike Tyson has this placement.

Uranus in Libra

BIRTH DATES:
September 28, 1968–May 20, 1969
June 24, 1969–November 21, 1974
May 1, 1975–September 8, 1975.

Your generation is likely to have unconventional relationships. Born during the time when women's liberation was a major issue, many of your generation came from broken homes and have no clear image of what a committed relationship entails. There may be sudden splits and experiments before you settle down. Your generation will be much involved in legal and political reforms and in changing artistic and fashion looks.

Uranus in Scorpio

BIRTH DATES:
November 21, 1974–May 1, 1975
September 8, 1975–February 17, 1981
March 20, 1981–November 16, 1981

Interest in transformation, meditation, and life after death signaled the beginning of New Age consciousness. Your generation recognizes no boundaries, no limits, and no external controls. You'll have new attitudes toward death and dying, psychic phenomena, and the occult. Like Mae West and Casanova, you'll shock 'em sexually, too.

Uranus in Sagittarius

BIRTH DATES:
February 17, 1981–March 20, 1981
November 16, 1981–February 15, 1988
Mary 27, 1988–December 2, 1988

Could this generation be the first to travel in outer space? The last generation with this placement included Charles Lindbergh—at that time, the first Zeppelins and the Wright Brothers were conquering the skies. Uranus here forecasts great discoveries, mind expansion, and long-distance travel. Like Galileo and Martin Luther, this generation will generate new theories about the cosmos and man's relation to it.

Uranus in Capricorn

BIRTH DATES:
December 20, 1903–January 30, 1912
September 4, 1912–November 12, 1912

February 15, 1988–May 27, 1988
December 2, 1988–April 1, 1995
June 9, 1995–January 12, 1996

This generation will challenge traditions with the help of electronic gadgets. In these years, we got organized with the help of technology put to practical use. Great leaders, movers and shakers of history like Julius Caesar and Henry VIII, were born under this placement.

Uranus in Aquarius

BIRTH DATES:
January 30, 1912–September 4, 1912
November 12, 1912–April 1, 1919
August 16, 1919–January 22, 1920
April 1, 1995–June 9, 1995
January 12, 1996–March 10, 2003

The last generation with this placement produced great innovative minds such as Leonard Bernstein and Orson Welles. The next will become another radical breakthrough generation, much concerned with global issues that involve all humanity. Intuition, innovation, and sudden changes will surprise everyone when Uranus is in its home sign. This will be a time of experimentation on every level.

Uranus in Pisces

BIRTH DATES:
April 1, 1919–August 16, 1919
January 22, 1920–March 31, 1927
November 4, 1927–January 12, 1928

In this century, Uranus in Pisces focused attention on the rise of electronic entertainment—radio and the cinema, and the secretiveness of Prohibition. This produced a generation of idealists exemplified by Judy Garland's theme, "Somewhere Over the Rainbow."

Neptune—The Glamour Girl

Under Neptune's influence, you see what you want to see. Neptune is the planet of illusion, dissolution (it dissolves hard reality), and makeup. Neptune is not interested in the world at face value—it dons tinted glasses or blurs the facts with the haze of an intoxicating substance.

But Neptune also encourages you to create, to let your fantasies and daydreams run free, to break through your ordinary perceptions and go to another level of reality, where you can experience either confusion or ecstasy. Neptune's force can pull you off course, like this planet affects its neighbor, Uranus, but only if you allow this to happen. Those who use Neptune wisely can translate their daydreams into poetry, theater, design, or inspired moves in the business world, avoiding the tricky "con artist" side of this planet.

Find your Neptune listed here:

Neptune in Cancer

BIRTH DATES:
July 19, 1901–December 25, 1901
May 21, 1902–September 23, 1914
December 14, 1914–July 19, 1915
March 19, 1916–May 2, 1916

Dreams of the homeland, idealistic patriotism, and glamorization of the nurturing assets of women characterized this time. You who were born here have unusual psychic ability and deep insights into the basic needs of others.

Neptune in Leo

BIRTH DATES:
September 23, 1914–December 14, 1914
July 19, 1915–March 19, 1916

May 2, 1916–September 21, 1928
February 19, 1929–July 24, 1929

Neptune here brought us the glamour and high living of the 1920s and the big spenders of that time, when Neptunian temptations of gambling, seduction, theater, and lavish entertaining distracted from the realities of the age. Those born in that generation also made great advances in the arts.

Neptune in Virgo

BIRTH DATES:
September 21, 1928–February 19, 1929
July 24, 1929–October 3, 1942
April 17, 1943–August 2, 1943

Neptune in Virgo encompassed the Great Depression and World War II, while those born at this time later spread the gospel of health and fitness. This generation's devotion to spending hours at the office inspired the term "workaholic." Health-care concerns of the elderly will come to the forefront of national consciousness as this generation ages, changing the way we think about growing old.

Neptune in Libra

BIRTH DATES:
October 3, 1942–April 17, 1943
August 2, 1943–December 24, 1955
March 12, 1956–October 19, 1956
June 15, 1957–August 6, 1957

Neptune in Libra was the romantic generation who would later be concerned with relating. As this generation matured, there was a new trend toward marriage and commitment. Racial and sexual equality became important issues, as they redesigned traditional male and female roles to suit modern times.

Neptune in Scorpio

BIRTH DATES:

December 24, 1955–March 12, 1956

October 19, 1956–June 15, 1957

August 6, 1957–January 4, 1970

May 3, 1970–November 6, 1970

Neptune in Scorpio brought in a generation that would become interested in transformative power. Born in an era that glamorized sex, drugs, rock and roll, and Eastern religion, they matured in a more sobering time of AIDS, cocaine abuse, and New Age spirituality. As they evolve, they will become active in healing the planet from the results of the abuse of power.

Neptune in Sagittarius

BIRTH DATES:

January 4, 1970–May 3, 1970

November 6, 1970–January 19, 1984

June 23, 1984–November 21, 1984

Neptune in Sagittarius was the time when space travel became a reality. The Neptune influence glamorized new approaches to mysticism, religion, and mind expansion. This generation will take a new approach to spiritual life, with emphasis on visions, mysticism, and clairvoyance.

Neptune in Capricorn

BIRTH DATES:

January 19, 1984–June 23, 1984

November 21, 1984–January 29, 1998

Neptune in Capricorn, which began in 1984 and would stay until 1998, brought a time when delusions about material power were first glamorized, then dashed on the rocks of reality. It was also a time when the psychic and occult worlds spawned a new category of business enterprise and sold services on television.

Neptune in Aquarius

BIRTH DATES:
Starting January 29, 1998 through the end of the century

This should be a time of breakthroughs, when the creative influence of Neptune reaches a universal audience. This is a time of dissolving barriers, when we truly become one world.

Pluto—The Private Eye

Pluto deals with the underworld of our personality, digging out our secrets to effect a total transformation as it brings deep subconscious feelings to the surface. Nothing escapes—or is sacred—with Pluto. When this tiny planet zaps a strategic point in your horoscope, your life changes so dramatically that there's no going back.

While Mars governs the visible power, Pluto is the power behind the scenes, where you can transform, heal, and affect the unconscious needs of the masses. Pluto governs your need to control, as well as your attitudes toward death and immortality. Much of the strength of your Pluto will depend on its position in your chart and the aspects it makes to other planets.

Because Pluto was discovered only recently, the signs of its exaltation and fall are debated. However, it was given the rulership of Scorpio. As it passed through Scorpio from 1984 to 1995 under the rule of Pluto, we were able to witness this planet's fullest effect. Because of its eccentric path, the length of time Pluto stays in any given sign can vary from 13 to 32 years.

Pluto in Gemini

BIRTH DATES:
Late 1800s–May 28, 1914

This was a time of mass suggestion and breakthroughs in communications, when many brilliant writers, such as Ernest Hemingway and F. Scott Fitzgerald, were born. Henry Miller, D. H. Lawrence, and James Joyce scandalized society by using explicit sexual images and language in their literature. "Muckraking" journalists exposed corruption. Pluto-ruled Scorpio President Theodore Roosevelt said, "Speak softly, but carry a big stick." This generation had an intense need to communicate and made major breakthroughs in knowledge. A compulsive restlessness and a thirst for a variety of experiences characterizes many of this generation.

Pluto in Cancer

BIRTH DATES:
May 28, 1914–June 14, 1939

Pluto in Cancer suggests great emotional (Cancer) power. During this time period dictators and mass media arose to manipulate the emotions of the masses. Women's rights were obtained as Pluto transited this lunar-ruled sign, transforming the position of women in society. Deep sentimental feelings, acquisitiveness, and possessiveness characterize these times and the people who were born then.

Pluto in Leo

BIRTH DATES:
June 14, 1939–August 19, 1957

The performing arts, under Leo's rule, never wielded more power over the masses than during this era. Pluto in Leo transforms via creative self-expression, exemplified by the almost shamanistic rock and roll stars such

74

as Mick Jagger and John Lennon, who were born at this time. (So were Bill and Hillary Clinton.) People born with Pluto in Leo often tend to be self-centered and love to "do their own thing"—for better or for worse.

Pluto in Virgo

BIRTH DATES:
August 19, 1957–October 5, 1971
April 17, 1972–July 30, 1972

This became the "yuppie" generation that sparked a mass clean-up shape-up movement toward fitness, health, and obsessive careerism. It's a much more sober, serious, driven generation than the fun-loving Pluto in Leos. During this time, inventions took on a practical turn, as answering machines, fax machines, car phones, and home office equipment have all transformed the workplace.

Pluto in Libra

BIRTH DATES:
October 5, 1971–April 17, 1972
July 30, 1972–August 28, 1984

A mellower generation, people born at this time are concerned with partnerships, working together, and finding diplomatic solutions to problems. Marriage is important to this generation, who redefine it along more traditional, but equal-partnership lines. This was a time of women's liberation, gay rights, ERA, and legal battles over abortion, all of which transformed our ideas about relationships.

Pluto in Scorpio

BIRTH DATES:
August 28, 1984–January 17, 1995

Pluto was in its ruling sign for a comparatively short period of time. In 1989, it was at its perihelion, or the closest point to the sun and Earth. We have all felt this transforming power somewhere in our lives. This was a time of record achievements, destructive sexually transmitted diseases, nuclear power controversies, and explosive political issues. Pluto destroys in order to create new understanding—think of it as a phoenix rising from the ashes, which should be some consolation for those of you who have felt Pluto's force before 1995. Sexual shockers were par for the course during these intense years, when black clothing, transvestites, body piercing, tattoos, and sexually explicit advertising pushed the boundaries of good taste.

Pluto in Sagittarius

BIRTH DATES:
January 17, 1995–January 27, 2008

During our current Pluto transit through Sagittarius, we are being pushed to expand our horizons and find deeper meaning in life. For many of us, this will mean traveling the globe via our modems as we explore the vastness of the Internet. It signals a time of spiritual transformation and religion will exert much power in politics as well. Since Sagittarius is the sign that rules travel, there's a good possibility that Pluto, the planet of extremes, will make space travel a reality for some of us. Discovery of life on Mars, traveling here as minute life forms on meteors, could transform our ideas about where we came from. At this writing, a giant telescope in Puerto Rico has been reactivated to search the faraway galaxies for pulsing hints of life.

New dimensions in electronic publishing, concern with animal rights and the environment, and an increasing emphasis on extreme forms of religion are signs of Pluto in Sagittarius. Look for charismatic religious leaders to arise now. We'll also be developing far-reaching philosophies designed to elevate our lives with a new sense of purpose.

Look Up Your Planets

The following tables are provided so that you can look up the signs of seven major planets—Venus, Mars, Saturn, Jupiter, Uranus, Neptune, and Pluto. We do not have room for tables for the moon and Mercury, which change signs often.

How to Use the Venus Table

Find the year of your birth in the vertical column on the left, then follow across the page until you find the correct date. Your Venus sign is at the top of that column.

VENUS SIGNS 1901–2000

	Aries	Taurus	Gemini	Cancer	Leo	Virgo
1901	3/29–4/22	4/22–5/17	5/17–6/10	6/10–7/5	7/5–7/29	7/29–8/23
1902	5/7–6/3	6/3–6/30	6/30–7/25	7/25–8/19	8/19–9/13	9/13–10/7
1903	2/28–3/24	3/24–4/18	4/18–5/13	5/13–6/9	6/9–7/7	7/7–8/17
						9/6–11/8
1904	3/13–5/7	5/7–6/1	6/1–6/25	6/25–7/19	7/19–8/13	8/13–9/6
1905	2/3–3/6	3/6–4/9	7/8–8/6	8/6–9/1	9/1–9/27	9/27–10/21
	4/9–5/28	5/28–7/8				
1906	3/1–4/7	4/7–5/2	5/2–5/26	5/26–6/20	6/20–7/16	7/16–8/11
1907	4/27–5/22	5/22–6/16	6/16–7/11	7/11–8/4	8/4–8/29	8/29–9/22
1908	2/14–3/10	3/10–4/5	4/5–5/5	5/5–9/8	9/8–10/8	10/8–11/3
1909	3/29–4/22	4/22–5/16	5/16–6/10	6/10–7/4	7/4–7/29	7/29–8/23
1910	5/7–6/3	6/4–6/29	6/30–7/24	7/25–8/18	8/19–9/12	9/13–10/6
1911	2/28–3/23	3/24–4/17	4/18–5/12	5/13–6/8	6/9–7/7	7/8–11/8
1912	4/13–5/6	5/7–5/31	6/1–6/24	6/24–7/18	7/19–8/12	8/13–9/5
1913	2/3–3/6	3/7–5/1	7/8–8/5	8/6–8/31	9/1–9/26	9/27–10/20
	5/2–5/30	5/31–7/7				
1914	3/14–4/6	4/7–5/1	5/2–5/25	5/26–6/19	6/20–7/15	7/16–8/10
1915	4/27–5/21	5/22–6/15	6/16–7/10	7/11–8/3	8/4–8/28	8/29–9/21
1916	2/14–3/9	3/10–4/5	4/6–5/5	5/6–9/8	9/9–10/7	10/8–11/2
1917	3/29–4/21	4/22–5/15	5/16–6/9	6/10–7/3	7/4–7/28	7/29–8/21
1918	5/7–6/2	6/3–6/28	6/29–7/24	7/25–8/18	8/19–9/11	9/12–10/5
1919	2/27–3/22	3/23–4/16	4/17–5/12	5/13–6/7	6/8–7/7	7/8–11/8
1920	4/12–5/6	5/7–5/30	5/31–6/23	6/24–7/18	7/19–8/11	8/12–9/4
1921	2/3–3/6	3/7–4/25	7/8–8/5	8/6–8/31	9/1–9/25	9/26–10/20
	4/26–6/1	6/2–7/7				
1922	3/13–4/6	4/7–4/30	5/1–5/25	5/26–6/19	6/20–7/14	7/15–8/9
1923	4/27–5/21	5/22–6/14	6/15–7/9	7/10–8/3	8/4–8/27	8/28–9/20
1924	2/13–3/8	3/9–4/4	4/5–5/5	5/6–9/8	9/9–10/7	10/8–11/12
1925	3/28–4/20	4/21–5/15	5/16–6/8	6/9–7/3	7/4–7/27	7/28–8/21

Libra	Scorpio	Sagittarius	Capricorn	Aquarius	Pisces
8/23–9/17	9/17–10/12	10/12–1/16	1/16–2/9 11/7–12/5	2/9–3/5 12/5–1/11	3/5–3/29
10/7–10/31	10/31–11/24	11/24–12/18	12/18–1/11	2/6–4/4	1/11–2/6 4/4–5/7
8/17–9/6 11/8–12/9	12/9–1/5			1/11–2/4	2/4–2/28
9/6–9/30	9/30–10/25	1/5–1/30 10/25–11/18	1/30–2/24 11/18–12/13	2/24–3/19 12/13–1/7	3/19–4/13
10/21–11/14	11/14–12/8	12/8–1/1/06			1/7–2/3
8/11–9/7	9/7–10/9 12/15–12/25	10/9–12/15 12/25–2/6	1/1–1/25	1/25–2/18	2/18–3/14
9/22–10/16	10/16–11/9	11/9–12/3	2/6–3/6 12/3–12/27	3/6–4/2 12/27–1/20	4/2–4/27
11/3–11/28	11/28–12/22	12/22–1/15			1/20–2/4
8/23–9/17	9/17–10/12	10/12–11/17	1/15–2/9 11/17–12/5	2/9–3/5 12/5–1/15	3/5–3/29
10/7–10/30	10/31–11/23	11/24–12/17	12/18–12/31	1/1–1/15 1/29–4/4	1/16–1/28 4/5–5/6
11/19–12/8	12/9–12/31		1/1–1/10	1/11–2/2	2/3–2/27
9/6–9/30	1/1–1/4 10/1–10/24	1/5–1/29 10/25–11/17	1/30–2/23 11/18–12/12	2/24–3/18 12/13–12/31	3/19–4/12
10/21–11/13	11/14–12/7	12/8–12/31		1/1–1/6	1/7–2/2
8/11–9/6	9/7–10/9 12/6–12/30	10/10–12/5 12/31	1/1–1/24	1/25–2/17	2/18–3/13
9/22–10/15	10/16–11/8	1/1–2/6 11/9–12/2	2/7–3/6 12/3–12/26	3/7–4/1 12/27–12/31	4/2–4/26
11/3–11/27	11/28–12/21	12/22–12/31		1/1–1/19	1/20–2/13
8/22–9/16	9/17–10/11	1/1–1/14 10/12–11/6	1/15–2/7 11/7–12/5	2/8–3/4 12/6–12/31	3/5–3/28
10/6–10/29	10/30–11/22	11/23–12/16	12/17–12/31	1/1–4/5	4/6–5/6
11/9–12/8	12/9–12/31		1/1–1/9	1/10–2/2	2/3–2/26
9/5–9/30	1/1–1/3 9/31–10/23	1/4–1/28 10/24–11/17	1/29–2/22 11/18–12/11	2/23–3/18 12/12–12/31	3/19–4/11
10/21–11/13	11/14–12/7	12/8–12/31		1/1–1/6	1/7–2/2
8/10–9/6	9/7–10/10 11/29–12/31	10/11–11/28	1/1–1/24	1/25–2/16	2/17–3/12
9/21–10/14	10/15–11/7	1/2–2/6 11/8–12/1	2/7–3/5 12/2–12/25	3/6–3/31 12/26–12/31	4/1–4/26
11/13–11/26	11/27–12/21	12/22–12/31		1/1–1/19	1/20–2/12
8/22–9/15	9/16–10/11	1/1–1/14 10/12–11/6	1/15–2/7 11/7–12/5	2/8–3/3 12/6–12/31	3/4–3/27

VENUS SIGNS 1901–2000

	Aries	Taurus	Gemini	Cancer	Leo	Virgo
1926	5/7–6/2	6/3–6/28	6/29–7/23	7/24–8/17	8/18–9/11	9/12–10/5
1927	2/27–3/22	3/23–4/16	4/17–5/11	5/12–6/7	6/8–7/7	7/8–11/9
1928	4/12–5/5	5/6–5/29	5/30–6/23	6/24–7/17	7/18–8/11	8/12–9/4
1929	2/3–3/7	3/8–4/19	7/8–8/4	8/5–8/30	8/31–9/25	9/26–10/19
	4/20–6/2	6/3–7/7				
1930	3/13–4/5	4/6–4/30	5/1–5/24	5/25–6/18	6/19–7/14	7/15–8/9
1931	4/26–5/20	5/21–6/13	6/14–7/8	7/9–8/2	8/3–8/26	8/27–9/19
1932	2/12–3/8	3/9–4/3	4/4–5/5	5/6–7/12	9/9–10/6	10/7–11/1
			7/13–7/27	7/28–9/8		
1933	3/27–4/19	4/20–5/28	5/29–6/8	6/9–7/2	7/3–7/26	7/27–8/20
1934	5/6–6/1	6/2–6/27	6/28–7/22	7/23–8/16	8/17–9/10	9/11–10/4
1935	2/26–3/21	3/22–4/15	4/16–5/10	5/11–6/6	6/7–7/6	7/7–11/8
1936	4/11–5/4	5/5–5/28	5/29–6/22	6/23–7/16	7/17–8/10	8/11–9/4
1937	2/2–3/8	3/9–4/13	7/7–8/3	8/4–8/29	8/30–9/24	9/25–10/18
	4/14–6/3	6/4–7/6				
1938	3/12–4/4	4/5–4/28	4/29–5/23	5/24–6/18	6/19–7/13	7/14–8/8
1939	4/25–5/19	5/20–6/13	6/14–7/8	7/9–8/1	8/2–8/25	8/26–9/19
1940	2/12–3/7	3/8–4/3	4/4–5/5	5/6–7/4	9/9–10/5	10/6–10/31
			7/5–7/31	8/1–9/8		
1941	3/27–4/19	4/20–5/13	5/14–6/6	6/7–7/1	7/2–7/26	7/27–8/20
1942	5/6–6/1	6/2–6/26	6/27–7/22	7/23–8/16	8/17–9/9	9/10–10/3
1943	2/25–3/20	3/21–4/14	4/15–5/10	5/11–6/6	6/7–7/6	7/7–11/8
1944	4/10–5/3	5/4–5/28	5/29–6/21	6/22–7/16	7/17–8/9	8/10–9/2
1945	2/2–3/10	3/11–4/6	7/7–8/3	8/4–8/29	8/30–9/23	9/24–10/18
	4/7–6/3	6/4–7/6				
1946	3/11–4/4	4/5–4/28	4/29–5/23	5/24–6/17	6/18–7/12	7/13–8/8
1947	4/25–5/19	5/20–6/12	6/13–7/7	7/8–8/1	8/2–8/25	8/26–9/18
1948	2/11–3/7	3/8–4/3	4/4–5/6	5/7–6/28	9/8–10/5	10/6–10/31
			6/29–8/2	8/3–9/7		
1949	3/26–4/19	4/20–5/13	5/14–6/6	6/7–6/30	7/1–7/25	7/26–8/19
1950	5/5–5/31	6/1–6/26	6/27–7/21	7/22–8/15	8/16–9/9	9/10–10/3
1951	2/25–3/21	3/22–4/15	4/16–5/10	5/11–6/6	6/7–7/7	7/8–11/9

Libra	Scorpio	Sagittarius	Capricorn	Aquarius	Pisces
10/6–10/29	10/30–11/22	11/23–12/16	12/17–12/31	1/1–4/5	4/6–5/6
11/10–12/8	12/9–12/31	1/1–1/7	1/8	1/9–2/1	2/2–2/26
9/5–9/28	1/1–1/3	1/4–1/28	1/29–2/22	2/23–3/17	3/18–4/11
	9/29–10/23	10/24–11/16	11/17–12/11	12/12–12/31	
10/20–11/12	11/13–12/6	12/7–12/30	12/31	1/1–1/5	1/6–2/2
8/10–9/6	9/7–10/11	10/12–11/21	1/1–1/23	1/24–2/16	2/17–3/12
	11/22–12/31				
9/20–10/13	1/1–1/3	1/4–2/6	2/7–3/4	3/5–3/31	4/1–4/25
	10/14–11/6	11/7–11/30	12/1–12/24	12/25–12/31	
11/2–11/25	11/26–12/20	12/21–12/31		1/1–1/18	1/19–2/11
8/21–9/14	9/15–10/10	1/1–1/13	1/14–2/6	2/7–3/2	3/3–3/26
		10/11–11/5	11/6–12/4	12/5–12/31	
10/5–10/28	10/29–11/21	11/22–12/15	12/16–12/31	1/1–4/5	4/6–5/5
11/9–12/7	12/8–12/31		1/1–1/7	1/8–1/31	2/1–2/25
9/5–9/27	1/1–1/2	1/3–1/27	1/28–2/21	2/22–3/16	3/17–4/10
	9/28–10/22	10/23–11/15	11/16–12/10	12/11–12/31	
10/19–11/11	11/12–12/5	12/6–12/29	12/30–12/31	1/1–1/5	1/6–2/1
8/9–9/6	9/7–10/13	10/14–11/14	1/1–1/22	1/23–2/15	2/16–3/11
	11/15–12/31				
9/20–10/13	1/1–1/3	1/4–2/5	2/6–3/4	3/5–3/30	3/31–4/24
	10/14–11/6	11/7–11/30	12/1–12/24	12/25–12/31	
11/1–11/25	11/26–12/19	12/20–12/31		1/1–1/18	1/19–2/11
8/21–9/14	9/15–10/9	1/1–1/12	1/13–2/5	2/6–3/1	3/2–3/26
		10/10–11/5	11/6–12/4	12/5–12/31	
10/4–10/27	10/28–11/20	11/21–12/14	12/15–12/31	1/1–4/4	4/6–5/5
11/9–12/7	12/8–12/31		1/1–1/7	1/8–1/31	2/1–2/24
9/3–9/27	1/1–1/2	1/3–1/27	1/28–2/20	2/21–3/16	3/17–4/9
	9/28–10/21	10/22–11/15	11/16–12/10	12/11–12/31	
10/19–11/11	11/12–12/5	12/6–12/29	12/30–12/31	1/1–1/4	1/5–2/1
8/9–9/6	9/7–10/15	10/16–11/7	1/1–1/21	1/22–2/14	2/15–3/10
	11/8–12/31				
9/19–10/12	1/1–1/4	1/5–2/5	2/6–3/4	3/5–3/29	3/30–4/24
	10/13–11/5	11/6–11/29	11/30–12/23	12/24–12/31	
11/1–11/25	11/26–12/19	12/20–12/31		1/1–1/17	1/18–2/10
8/20–9/14	9/15–10/9	1/1–1/12	1/13–2/5	2/6–3/1	3/2–3/25
		10/10–11/5	11/6–12/5	12/6–12/31	
10/4–10/27	10/28–11/20	11/21–12/13	12/14–12/31	1/1–4/5	4/6–5/4
11/10–12/7	12/8–12/31		1/1–1/7	1/8–1/31	2/1–2/24

VENUS SIGNS 1901–2000

	Aries	Taurus	Gemini	Cancer	Leo	Virgo
1952	4/10–5/4	5/5–5/28	5/29–6/21	6/22–7/16	7/17–8/9	8/10–9/3
1953	2/2–3/3	3/4–3/31	7/8–8/3	8/4–8/29	8/30–9/24	9/25–10/18
	4/1–6/5	6/6–7/7				
1954	3/12–4/4	4/5–4/28	4/29–5/23	5/24–6/17	6/18–7/13	7/14–8/8
1955	4/25–5/19	5/20–6/13	6/14–7/7	7/8–8/1	8/2–8/25	8/26–9/18
1956	2/12–3/7	3/8–4/4	4/5–5/7	5/8–6/23	9/9–10/5	10/6–10/31
			6/24–8/4	8/5–9/8		
1957	3/26–4/19	4/20–5/13	5/14–6/6	6/7–7/1	7/2–7/26	7/27–8/19
1958	5/6–5/31	6/1–6/26	6/27–7/22	7/23–8/15	8/16–9/9	9/10–10/3
1959	2/25–3/20	3/21–4/14	4/15–5/10	5/11–6/6	6/7–7/8	7/9–9/20
					9/21–9/24	9/25–11/9
1960	4/10–5/3	5/4–5/28	5/29–6/21	6/22–7/15	7/16–8/9	8/10–9/2
1961	2/3–6/5	6/6–7/7	7/8–8/3	8/4–8/29	8/30–9/23	9/24–10/17
1962	3/11–4/3	4/4–4/28	4/29–5/22	5/23–6/17	6/18–7/12	7/13–8/8
1963	4/24–5/18	5/19–6/12	6/13–7/7	7/8–7/31	8/1–8/25	8/26–9/18
1964	2/11–3/7	3/8–4/4	4/5–5/9	5/10–6/17	9/9–10/5	10/6–10/31
			6/18–8/5	8/6–9/8		
1965	3/26–4/18	4/19–5/12	5/13–6/6	6/7–6/30	7/1–7/25	7/26–8/19
1966	5/6–6/31	6/1–6/26	6/27–7/21	7/22–8/15	8/16–9/8	9/9–10/2
1967	2/24–3/20	3/21–4/14	4/15–5/10	5/11–6/6	6/7–7/8	7/9–9/9
					9/10–10/1	10/2–11/9
1968	4/9–5/3	5/4–5/27	5/28–6/20	6/21–7/15	7/16–8/8	8/9–9/2
1969	2/3–6/6	6/7–7/6	7/7–8/3	8/4–8/28	8/29–9/22	9/23–10/17
1970	3/11–4/3	4/4–4/27	4/28–5/22	5/23–6/16	6/17–7/12	7/13–8/8
1971	4/24–5/18	5/19–6/12	6/13–7/6	7/7–7/31	8/1–8/24	8/25–9/17
1972	2/11–3/7	3/8–4/3	4/4–5/10	5/11–6/11	9/9–10/5	10/6–10/30
			6/12–8/6	8/7–9/8		
1973	3/25–4/18	4/18–5/12	5/13–6/5	6/6–6/29	7/1–7/25	7/26–8/19
1974						
	5/5–5/31	6/1–6/25	6/26–7/21	7/22–8/14	8/15–9/8	9/9–10/2
1975	2/24–3/20	3/21–4/13	4/14–5/9	5/10–6/6	6/7–7/9	7/10–9/2
					9/3–10/4	10/5–11/9

Libra	Scorpio	Sagittarius	Capricorn	Aquarius	Pisces
9/4–9/27	1/1–1/2	1/3–1/27	1/28–2/20	2/21–3/16	3/17–4/9
	9/28–10/21	10/22–11/15	11/16–12/10	12/11–12/31	
10/19–11/11	11/12–12/5	12/6–12/29	12/30–12/31	1/1–1/5	1/6–2/1
8/9–9/6	9/7–10/22	10/23–10/27	1/1–1/22	1/23–2/15	2/16–3/11
	10/28–12/31				
9/19–10/13	1/1–1/6	1/7–2/5	2/6–3/4	3/5–3/30	3/31–4/24
	10/14–11/5	11/6–11/30	12/1–12/24	12/25–12/31	
11/1–11/25	11/26–12/19	12/20–12/31		1/1–1/17	1/18–2/11
8/20–9/14	9/15–10/9	1/1–1/12	1/13–2/5	2/6–3/1	3/2–3/25
		10/10–11/5	11/6–12/6	12/7–12/31	
10/4–10/27	10/28–11/20	11/21–12/14	12/15–12/31	1/1–4/6	4/7–5/5
11/10–12/7	12/8–12/31		1/1–1/7	1/8–1/31	2/1–2/24
9/3–9/26	1/1–1/2	1/3–1/27	1/28–2/20	2/21–3/15	3/16–4/9
	9/27–10/21	10/22–11/15	11/16–12/10	12/11–12/31	
10/18–11/11	11/12–12/4	12/5–12/28	12/29–12/31	1/1–1/5	1/6–2/2
8/9–9/6	9/7–12/31		1/1–1/21	1/22–2/14	2/15–3/10
9/19–10/12	1/1–1/6	1/7–2/5	2/6–3/4	3/5–3/29	3/30–4/23
	10/13–11/5	11/6–11/29	11/30–12/23	12/24–12/31	
11/1–11/24	11/25–12/19	12/20–12/31		1/1–1/16	1/17–2/10
8/20–9/13	9/14–10/9	1/1–1/12	1/13–2/5	2/6–3/1	3/2–3/25
		10/10–11/5	11/6–12/7	12/8–12/31	
10/3–10/26	10/27–11/19	11/20–12/13	2/7–2/25	1/1–2/6	4/7–5/5
			12/14–12/31	2/26–4/6	
11/10–12/7	12/8–12/31		1/1–1/6	1/7–1/30	1/31–2/23
9/3–9/26	1/1	1/2–1/26	1/27–2/20	2/21–3/15	3/16–4/8
	9/27–10/21	10/22–11/14	11/15–12/9	12/10–12/31	
10/18–11/10	11/11–12/4	12/5–12/28	12/29–12/31	1/1–1/4	1/5–2/2
8/9–9/7	9/8–12/31		1/1–1/21	1/22–2/14	2/15–3/10
9/18–10/11	1/1–1/7	1/8–2/5	2/6–3/4	3/5–3/29	3/30–4/23
	10/12–11/5	11/6–11/29	11/30–12/23	12/24–12/31	
	11/25–12/18	12/19–12/31		1/1–1/16	1/17–2/10
10/31–11/24					
8/20–9/13	9/14–10/8	1/1–1/12	1/13–2/4	2/5–2/28	3/1–3/24
		10/9–11/5	11/6–12/7	12/8–12/31	
			1/30–2/28	1/1–1/29	
10/3–10/26	10/27–11/19	11/20–12/13	12/14–12/31	3/1–4/6	4/7–5/4
			1/1–1/6	1/7–1/30	1/31–2/23
11/10–12/7	12/8–12/31				

VENUS SIGNS 1901–2000

	Aries	Taurus	Gemini	Cancer	Leo	Virgo
1976	4/8–5/2	5/2–5/27	5/27—6/20	6/20–7/14	7/14–8/8	8/8–9/1
1977	2/2–6/6	6/6–7/6	7/6–8/2	8/2–8/28	8/28–9/22	9/22–10/17
1978	3/9–4/2	4/2–4/27	4/27–5/22	5/22–6/16	6/16–7/12	7/12–8/6
1979	4/23–5/18	5/18–6/11	6/11–7/6	7/6–7/30	7/30–8/24	8/24–9/17
1980	2/9–3/6	3/6–4/3	4/3–5/12 6/5–8/6	5/12–6/5 8/6–9/7	9/7–10/4	10/4–10/30
1981	3/24–4/17	4/17–5/11	5/11–6/5	6/5–6/29	6/29–7/24	7/24–8/18
1982	5/4–5/30	5/30–6/25	6/25–7/20	7/20–8/14	8/14–9/7	9/7–10/2
1983	2/22–3/19	3/19–4/13	4/13–5/9	5/9–6/6	6/6–7/10 8/27–10/5	7/10–8/27 10/5–11/9
1984	4/7–5/2	5/2–5/26	5/26–6/20	6/20–7/14	7/14–8/7	8/7–9/1
1985	2/2–6/6	6/7–7/6	7/6–8/2	8/2–8/28	8/28–9/22	9/22–10/16
1986	3/9–4/2	4/2–4/26	4/26–5/21	5/21–6/15	6/15–7/11	7/11–8/7
1987	4/22–5/17	5/17–6/11	6/11–7/5	7/5–7/30	7/30–8/23	8/23–9/16
1988	2/9–3/6	3/6–4/3	4/3–5/17 5/27–8/6	5/17–5/27 8/28–9/22	9/7–10/4 9/22–10/16	10/4–10/29
1989	3/23–4/16	4/16–5/11	5/11–6/4	6/4–6/29	6/29–7/24	7/24–8/18
1990	5/4–5/30	5/30–6/25	6/25–7/20	7/20–8/13	8/13–9/7	9/7–10/1
1991	2/22–3/18	3/18–4/13	4/13–5/9	5/9–6/6	6/6–7/11 8/21–10/6	7/11–8/21 10/6–11/9
1992	4/7–5/1	5/1–5/26	5/26–6/19	6/19–7/13	7/13–8/7	8/7–8/31
1993	2/2–6/6	6/6–7/6	7/6–8/1	8/1–8/27	8/27–9/21	9/21–10/16
1994	3/8–4/1	4/1–4/26	4/26–5/21	5/21–6/15	6/15–7/11	7/11–8/7
1995	4/22–5/16	5/16–6/10	6/10–7/5	7/5–7/29	7/29–8/23	8/23–9/16
1996	2/9–3/6	3/6–4/3	4/3–8/7	8/7–9/7	9/7–10/4	10/4–10/29
1997	3/23–4/16	4/16–5/10	5/10–6/4	6/4–6/28	6/28–7/23	7/23–8/17
1998	5/3–5/29	5/29–6/24	6/24–7/19	7/19–8/13	8/13–9/6	9/6–9/30
1999	2/21–3/18	3/18–4/12	4/12–5/8	5/8–6/5	6/5–7/12 8/15–10/7	7/12–8/15 10/7–11/9
2000	4/6–5/1	5/1–5/25	5/25–6/13	6/13–7/13	7/13–8/6	8/6–8/31

Libra	Scorpio	Sagittarius	Capricorn	Aquarius	Pisces
9/1–9/26	9/26–10/20	1/1–1/26	1/26–2/19	2/19–3/15	3/15–4/8
		10/20–11/14	11/14–12/8	12/9–1/4	
10/17–11/10	11/10–12/4	12/4–12/27	12/27–1/20/78		1/4–2/2
8/6–9/7	9/7–1/7			1/20–2/13	2/13–3/9
9/17–10/11	10/11–11/4	1/7–2/5	2/5–3/3	3/3–3/29	3/29–4/23
		11/4–11/28	11/28–12/22	12/22–1/16/80	
10/30–11/24	11/24–12/18	12/18–1/11/81			1/16–2/9
8/18–9/12	9/12–10/9	10/9–11/5	1/11–2/4	2/4–2/28	2/28–3/24
			11/5–12/8	12/8–1/23/82	
10/2–10/26	10/26–11/18	11/18–12/12	1/23–3/2	3/2–4/6	4/6–5/4
			12/12–1/5/83		
11/9–12/6	12/6–1/1/84			1/5–1/29	1/29–2/22
9/1–9/25	9/25–10/20	1/1–1/25	1/25–2/19	2/19–3/14	3/14–4/7
		10/20–11/13	11/13–12/9	12/10–1/4	
10/16–11/9	11/9–12/3	12/3–12/27	12/28–1/19		1/4–2/2
8/7–9/7	9/7–1/7			1/20–2/13	2/13–3/9
9/16–10/10	10/10–11/3	1/7–2/5	2/5–3/3	3/3–3/28	3/28–4/22
		11/3–11/28	11/28–12/22	12/22–1/15	
10/29–11/23	11/23–12/17	12/17–1/10			1/15–2/9
8/18–9/12	9/12–10/8	10/8–11/5	1/10–2/3	2/3–2/27	2/27–3/23
			11/5–12/10	12/10–1/16/90	
10/1–10/25	10/25–11/18	11/18–12/12	1/16–3/3	3/3–4/6	4/6–5/4
			12/12–1/5		
11/9–12/6	12/6–12/31	12/31–1/25/92		1/5–1/29	1/29–2/22
8/31–9/25	9/25–10/19	10/19–11/13	1/25–2/18	2/18–3/13	3/13–4/7
			11/13–12/8	12/8–1/3/93	
10/16–11/9	11/9–12/2	12/2–12/26	12/26–1/19		1/3–2/2
8/7–9/7	9/7–1/7			1/19–2/12	2/12–3/8
9/16–10/10	10/10–11/13	1/7–2/4	2/4–3/2	3/2–3/28	3/28–4/22
		11/3–11/27	11/27–12/21	12/21–1/15	
10/29–11/23	11/23–12/17	12/17–1/10/97			1/15–2/9
8/17–9/12	9/12–10/8	10/8–11/5	1/10–2/3	2/3–2/27	2/27–3/23
			11/5–12/12	12/12–1/9	
9/30–10/24	10/24–11/17	11/17–12/11	1/9–3/4	3/4–4/6	4/6–5/3
11/9–12/5	12/5–12/31	12/31–1/24		1/4–1/28	1/28–2/21
8/31–9/24	9/24–10/19	10/19–11/13	1/24–2/18	2/18–3/12	3/13–4/6
			11/13–12/8	12/8	

How to Use the Mars, Jupiter, and Saturn Tables

Find the year of your birth on the left side of each column. The dates when the planet entered each sign are listed on the right side of each column. (Signs are abbreviated to the first three letters.) Your birthday should fall on or between each date listed, and your planetary placement should correspond to the earlier sign of that period.

MARS SIGN 1901–2000

Year	Month	Day	Sign		Year	Month	Day	Sign
1901	MAR	1	Leo		1905	JAN	13	Scp
	MAY	11	Vir			AUG	21	Sag
	JUL	13	Lib			OCT	8	Cap
	AUG	31	Scp			NOV	18	Aqu
	OCT	14	Sag			DEC	27	Pic
	NOV	24	Cap		1906	FEB	4	Ari
1902	JAN	1	Aqu			MAR	17	Tau
	FEB	8	Pic			APR	28	Gem
	MAR	19	Ari			JUN	11	Can
	APR	27	Tau			JUL	27	Leo
	JUN	7	Gem			SEP	12	Vir
	JUL	20	Can			OCT	30	Lib
	SEP	4	Leo			DEC	17	Scp
	OCT	23	Vir		1907	FEB	5	Sag
	DEC	20	Lib			APR	1	Cap
1903	APR	19	Vir			OCT	13	Aqu
	MAY	30	Lib			NOV	29	Pic
	AUG	6	Scp		1908	JAN	11	Ari
	SEP	22	Sag			FEB	23	Tau
	NOV	3	Cap			APR	7	Gem
	DEC	12	Aqu			MAY	22	Can
1904	JAN	19	Pic			JUL	8	Leo
	FEB	27	Ari			AUG	24	Vir
	APR	6	Tau			OCT	10	Lib
	MAY	18	Gem			NOV	25	Scp
	JUN	30	Can		1909	JAN	10	Sag
	AUG	15	Leo			FEB	24	Cap
	OCT	1	Vir			APR	9	Aqu
	NOV	20	Lib			MAY	25	Pic

	JUL	21	Ari		AUG	19	Can
	SEP	26	Pic		OCT	7	Leo
	NOV	20	Ari	1916	MAY	28	Vir
1910	JAN	23	Tau		JUL	23	Lib
	MAR	14	Gem		SEP	8	Scp
	MAY	1	Can		OCT	22	Sag
	JUN	19	Leo		DEC	1	Cap
	AUG	6	Vir	1917	JAN	9	Aqu
	SEP	22	Lib		FEB	16	Pic
	NOV	6	Scp		MAR	26	Ari
	DEC	20	Sag		MAY	4	Tau
1911	JAN	31	Cap		JUN	14	Gem
	MAR	14	Aqu		JUL	28	Can
	APR	23	Pic		SEP	12	Leo
	JUN	2	Ari		NOV	2	Vir
	JUL	15	Tau	1918	JAN	11	Lib
	SEP	5	Gem		FEB	25	Vir
	NOV	30	Tau		JUN	23	Lib
1912	JAN	30	Gem		AUG	17	Scp
	APR	5	Can		OCT	1	Sag
	MAY	28	Leo		NOV	11	Cap
	JUL	17	Vir		DEC	20	Aqu
	SEP	2	Lib	1919	JAN	27	Pic
	OCT	18	Scp		MAR	6	Ari
	NOV	30	Sag		APR	15	Tau
1913	JAN	10	Cap		MAY	26	Gem
	FEB	19	Aqu		JUL	8	Can
	MAR	30	Pic		AUG	23	Leo
	MAY	8	Ari		OCT	10	Vir
	JUN	17	Tau		NOV	30	Lib
	JUL	29	Gem	1920	JAN	31	Scp
	SEP	15	Can		APR	23	Lib
1914	MAY	1	Leo		JUL	10	Scp
	JUN	26	Vir		SEP	4	Sag
	AUG	14	Lib		OCT	18	Cap
	SEP	29	Scp		NOV	27	Aqu
	NOV	11	Sag	1921	JAN	5	Pic
	DEC	22	Cap		FEB	13	Ari
1915	JAN	30	Aqu		MAR	25	Tau
	MAR	9	Pic		MAY	6	Gem
	APR	16	Ari		JUN	18	Can
	MAY	26	Tau		AUG	3	Leo
	JUL	6	Gem		SEP	19	Vir

	NOV	6	Lib		APR	7	Pic
	DEC	26	Scp		MAY	16	Ari
1922	FEB	18	Sag		JUN	26	Tau
	SEP	13	Cap		AUG	9	Gem
	OCT	30	Aqu		OCT	3	Can
	DEC	11	Pic		DEC	20	Gem
1923	JAN	21	Ari	1929	MAR	10	Can
	MAR	4	Tau		MAY	13	Leo
	APR	16	Gem		JUL	4	Vir
	MAY	30	Can		AUG	21	Lib
	JUL	16	Leo		OCT	6	Scp
	SEP	1	Vir		NOV	18	Sag
	OCT	18	Lib		DEC	29	Cap
	DEC	4	Scp	1930	FEB	6	Aqu
1924	JAN	19	Sag		MAR	17	Pic
	MAR	6	Cap		APR	24	Ari
	APR	24	Aqu		JUN	3	Tau
	JUN	24	Pic		JUL	14	Gem
	AUG	24	Aqu		AUG	28	Can
	OCT	19	Pic		OCT	20	Leo
	DEC	19	Ari	1931	FEB	16	Can
1925	FEB	5	Tau		MAR	30	Leo
	MAR	24	Gem		JUN	10	Vir
	MAY	9	Can		AUG	1	Lib
	JUN	26	Leo		SEP	17	Scp
	AUG	12	Vir		OCT	30	Sag
	SEP	28	Lib		DEC	10	Cap
	NOV	13	Scp	1932	JAN	18	Aqu
	DEC	28	Sag		FEB	25	Pic
1926	FEB	9	Cap		APR	3	Ari
	MAR	23	Aqu		MAY	12	Tau
	MAY	3	Pic		JUN	22	Gem
	JUN	15	Ari		AUG	4	Can
	AUG	1	Tau		SEP	20	Leo
1927	FEB	22	Gem		NOV	13	Vir
	APR	17	Can	1933	JUL	6	Lib
	JUN	6	Leo		AUG	26	Scp
	JUL	25	Vir		OCT	9	Sag
	SEP	10	Lib		NOV	19	Cap
	OCT	26	Scp		DEC	28	Aqu
	DEC	8	Sag	1934	FEB	4	Pic
1928	JAN	19	Cap		MAR	14	Ari
	FEB	28	Aqu		APR	22	Tau

	JUN	2	Gem		AUG	19	Vir
	JUL	15	Can		OCT	5	Lib
	AUG	30	Leo		NOV	20	Scp
	OCT	18	Vir	1941	JAN	4	Sag
	DEC	11	Lib		FEB	17	Cap
1935	JUL	29	Scp		APR	2	Aqu
	SEP	16	Sag		MAY	16	Pic
	OCT	28	Cap		JUL	2	Ari
	DEC	7	Aqu	1942	JAN	11	Tau
1936	JAN	14	Pic		MAR	7	Gem
	FEB	22	Ari		APR	26	Can
	APR	1	Tau		JUN	14	Leo
	MAY	13	Gem		AUG	1	Vir
	JUN	25	Can		SEP	17	Lib
	AUG	10	Leo		NOV	1	Scp
	SEP	26	Vir		DEC	15	Sag
	NOV	14	Lib	1943	JAN	26	Cap
1937	JAN	5	Scp		MAR	8	Aqu
	MAR	13	Sag		APR	17	Pic
	MAY	14	Scp		MAY	27	Ari
	AUG	8	Sag		JUL	7	Tau
	SEP	30	Cap		AUG	23	Gem
	NOV	11	Aqu	1944	MAR	28	Can
	DEC	21	Pic		MAY	22	Leo
1938	JAN	30	Ari		JUL	12	Vir
	MAR	12	Tau		AUG	29	Lib
	APR	23	Gem		OCT	13	Scp
	JUN	7	Can		NOV	25	Sag
	JUL	22	Leo	1945	JAN	5	Cap
	SEP	7	Vir		FEB	14	Aqu
	OCT	25	Lib		MAR	25	Pic
	DEC	11	Scp		MAY	2	Ari
1939	JAN	29	Sag		JUN	11	Tau
	MAR	21	Cap		JUL	23	Gem
	MAY	25	Aqu		SEP	7	Can
	JUL	21	Cap		NOV	11	Leo
	SEP	24	Aqu		DEC	26	Can
	NOV	19	Pic	1946	APR	22	Leo
1940	JAN	4	Ari		JUN	20	Vir
	FEB	17	Tau		AUG	9	Lib
	APR	1	Gem		SEP	24	Scp
	MAY	17	Can		NOV	6	Sag
	JUL	3	Leo		DEC	17	Cap

1947	JAN	25	Aqu		MAR	20	Tau
	MAR	4	Pic		MAY	1	Gem
	APR	11	Ari		JUN	14	Can
	MAY	21	Tau		JUL	29	Leo
	JUL	1	Gem		SEP	14	Vir
	AUG	13	Can		NOV	1	Lib
	OCT	1	Leo		DEC	20	Scp
	DEC	1	Vir	1954	FEB	9	Sag
1948	FEB	12	Leo		APR	12	Cap
	MAY	18	Vir		JUL	3	Sag
	JUL	17	Lib		AUG	24	Cap
	SEP	3	Scp		OCT	21	Aqu
	OCT	17	Sag		DEC	4	Pic
	NOV	26	Cap	1955	JAN	15	Ari
1949	JAN	4	Aqu		FEB	26	Tau
	FEB	11	Pic		APR	10	Gem
	MAR	21	Ari		MAY	26	Can
	APR	30	Tau		JUL	11	Leo
	JUN	10	Gem		AUG	27	Vir
	JUL	23	Can		OCT	13	Lib
	SEP	7	Leo		NOV	29	Scp
	OCT	27	Vir	1956	JAN	14	Sag
	DEC	26	Lib		FEB	28	Cap
1950	MAR	28	Vir		APR	14	Aqu
	JUN	11	Lib		JUN	3	Pic
	AUG	10	Scp		DEC	6	Ari
	SEP	25	Sag	1957	JAN	28	Tau
	NOV	6	Cap		MAR	17	Gem
	DEC	15	Aqu		MAY	4	Can
1951	JAN	22	Pic		JUN	21	Leo
	MAR	1	Ari		AUG	8	Vir
	APR	10	Tau		SEP	24	Lib
	MAY	21	Gem		NOV	8	Scp
	JUL	3	Can		DEC	23	Sag
	AUG	18	Leo	1958	FEB	3	Cap
	OCT	5	Vir		MAR	17	Aqu
	NOV	24	Lib		APR	27	Pic
1952	JAN	20	Scp		JUN	7	Ari
	AUG	27	Sag		JUL	21	Tau
	OCT	12	Cap		SEP	21	Gem
	NOV	21	Aqu		OCT	29	Tau
	DEC	30	Pic	1959	FEB	10	Gem
1953	FEB	8	Ari		APR	10	Can

	JUN	1	Leo		NOV	14	Cap
	JUL	20	Vir		DEC	23	Aqu
	SEP	5	Lib	1966	JAN	30	Pic
	OCT	21	Scp		MAR	9	Ari
	DEC	3	Sag		APR	17	Tau
1960	JAN	14	Cap		MAY	28	Gem
	FEB	23	Aqu		JUL	11	Can
	APR	2	Pic		AUG	25	Leo
	MAY	11	Ari		OCT	12	Vir
	JUN	20	Tau		DEC	4	Lib
	AUG	2	Gem	1967	FEB	12	Scp
	SEP	21	Can		MAR	31	Lib
1961	FEB	5	Gem		JUL	19	Scp
	FEB	7	Can		SEP	10	Sag
	MAY	6	Leo		OCT	23	Cap
	JUN	28	Vir		DEC	1	Aqu
	AUG	17	Lib	1968	JAN	9	Pic
	OCT	1	Scp		FEB	17	Ari
	NOV	13	Sag		MAR	27	Tau
	DEC	24	Cap		MAY	8	Gem
1962	FEB	1	Aqu		JUN	21	Can
	MAR	12	Pic		AUG	5	Leo
	APR	19	Ari		SEP	21	Vir
	MAY	28	Tau		NOV	9	Lib
	JUL	9	Gem		DEC	29	Scp
	AUG	22	Can	1969	FEB	25	Sag
	OCT	11	Leo		SEP	21	Cap
1963	JUN	3	Vir		NOV	4	Aqu
	JUL	27	Lib		DEC	15	Pic
	SEP	12	Scp	1970	JAN	24	Ari
	OCT	25	Sag		MAR	7	Tau
	DEC	5	Cap		APR	18	Gem
1964	JAN	13	Aqu		JUN	2	Can
	FEB	20	Pic		JUL	18	Leo
	MAR	29	Ari		SEP	3	Vir
	MAY	7	Tau		OCT	20	Lib
	JUN	17	Gem		DEC	6	Scp
	JUL	30	Can	1971	JAN	23	Sag
	SEP	15	Leo		MAR	12	Cap
	NOV	6	Vir		MAY	3	Aqu
1965	JUN	29	Lib		NOV	6	Pic
	AUG	20	Scp		DEC	26	Ari
	OCT	4	Sag	1972	FEB	10	Tau

	MAR	27	Gem	1978	JAN	26	Can
	MAY	12	Can		APR	10	Leo
	JUN	28	Leo		JUN	14	Vir
	AUG	15	Vir		AUG	4	Lib
	SEP	30	Lib		SEP	19	Scp
	NOV	15	Scp		NOV	2	Sag
	DEC	30	Sag		DEC	12	Cap
1973	FEB	12	Cap	1979	JAN	20	Aqu
	MAR	26	Aqu		FEB	27	Pic
	MAY	8	Pic		APR	7	Ari
	JUN	20	Ari		MAY	16	Tau
	AUG	12	Tau		JUN	26	Gem
	OCT	29	Ari		AUG	8	Can
	DEC	24	Tau		SEP	24	Leo
1974	FEB	27	Gem		NOV	19	Vir
	APR	20	Can	1980	MAR	11	Leo
	JUN	9	Leo		MAY	4	Vir
	JUL	27	Vir		JUL	10	Lib
	SEP	12	Lib		AUG	29	Scp
	OCT	28	Scp		OCT	12	Sag
	DEC	10	Sag		NOV	22	Cap
1975	JAN	21	Cap		DEC	30	Aqu
	MAR	3	Aqu	1981	FEB	6	Pic
	APR	11	Pic		MAR	17	Ari
	MAY	21	Ari		APR	25	Tau
	JUL	1	Tau		JUN	5	Gem
	AUG	14	Gem		JUL	18	Can
	OCT	17	Can		SEP	2	Leo
	NOV	25	Gem		OCT	21	Vir
1976	MAR	18	Can		DEC	16	Lib
	MAY	16	Leo	1982	AUG	3	Scp
	JUL	6	Vir		SEP	20	Sag
	AUG	24	Lib		OCT	31	Cap
	OCT	8	Scp		DEC	10	Aqu
	NOV	20	Sag	1983	JAN	17	Pic
1977	JAN	1	Cap		FEB	25	Ari
	FEB	9	Aqu		APR	5	Tau
	MAR	20	Pic		MAY	16	Gem
	APR	27	Ari		JUN	29	Can
	JUN	6	Tau		AUG	13	Leo
	JUL	17	Gem		SEP	30	Vir
	SEP	1	Can		NOV	18	Lib
	OCT	26	Leo	1984	JAN	11	Scp

	AUG	17	Sag		JUL	12	Tau
	OCT	5	Cap		AUG	31	Gem
	NOV	15	Aqu		DEC	14	Tau
	DEC	25	Pic	1991	JAN	21	Gem
1985	FEB	2	Ari		APR	3	Can
	MAR	15	Tau		MAY	26	Leo
	APR	26	Gem		JUL	15	Vir
	JUN	9	Can		SEP	1	Lib
	JUL	25	Leo		OCT	16	Scp
	SEP	10	Vir		NOV	29	Sag
	OCT	27	Lib	1992	JAN	9	Cap
	DEC	14	Scp		FEB	18	Aqu
1986	FEB	2	Sag		MAR	28	Pic
	MAR	28	Cap		MAY	5	Ari
	OCT	9	Aqu		JUN	14	Tau
	NOV	26	Pic		JUL	26	Gem
1987	JAN	8	Ari		SEP	12	Can
	FEB	20	Tau	1993	APR	27	Leo
	APR	5	Gem		JUN	23	Vir
	MAY	21	Can		AUG	12	Lib
	JUL	6	Leo		SEP	27	Scp
	AUG	22	Vir		NOV	9	Sag
	OCT	8	Lib		DEC	20	Cap
	NOV	24	Scp	1994	JAN	28	Aqu
1988	JAN	8	Sag		MAR	7	Pic
	FEB	22	Cap		APR	14	Ari
	APR	6	Aqu		MAY	23	Tau
	MAY	22	Pic		JUL	3	Gem
	JUL	13	Ari		AUG	16	Can
	OCT	23	Pic		OCT	4	Leo
	NOV	1	Ari		DEC	12	Vir
1989	JAN	19	Tau	1995	JAN	22	Leo
	MAR	11	Gem		MAY	25	Vir
	APR	29	Can		JUL	21	Lib
	JUN	16	Leo		SEP	7	Scp
	AUG	3	Vir		OCT	20	Sag
	SEP	19	Lib		NOV	30	Cap
	NOV	4	Scp	1996	JAN	8	Aqu
	DEC	18	Sag		FEB	15	Pic
1990	JAN	29	Cap		MAR	24	Ari
	MAR	11	Aqu		MAY	2	Tau
	APR	20	Pic		JUN	12	Gem
	MAY	31	Ari		JUL	25	Can

	SEP	9	Leo		NOV	27	Lib
	OCT	30	Vir	1999	JAN	26	Scp
1997	JAN	3	Lib		MAY	5	Lib
	MAR	8	Vir		JUL	5	Scp
	JUN	19	Lib		SEP	2	Sag
	AUG	14	Scp		OCT	17	Cap
	SEP	28	Sag		NOV	26	Aqu
	NOV	9	Cap	2000	JAN	4	Pic
	DEC	18	Aqu		FEB	12	Ari
1998	JAN	25	Pic		MAR	23	Tau
	MAR	4	Ari		MAY	3	Gem
	APR	13	Tau		JUN	16	Can
	MAY	24	Gem		AUG	1	Leo
	JUL	6	Can		SEP	17	Vir
	AUG	20	Leo		NOV	4	Lib
	OCT	7	Vir		DEC	23	Scp

JUPITER SIGN 1901–2000

1901	JAN	19	Cap		OCT	26	Ari
1902	FEB	6	Aqu	1917	FEB	12	Tau
1903	FEB	20	Pic		JUN	29	Gem
1904	MAR	1	Ari	1918	JUL	13	Can
	AUG	8	Tau	1919	AUG	2	Leo
	AUG	31	Ari	1920	AUG	27	Vir
1905	MAR	7	Tau	1921	SEP	25	Lib
	JUL	21	Gem	1922	OCT	26	Scp
	DEC	4	Tau	1923	NOV	24	Sag
1906	MAR	9	Gem	1924	DEC	18	Cap
	JUL	30	Can	1926	JAN	6	Aqu
1907	AUG	18	Leo	1927	JAN	18	Pic
1908	SEP	12	Vir		JUN	6	Ari
1909	OCT	11	Lib		SEP	11	Pic
1910	NOV	11	Scp	1928	JAN	23	Ari
1911	DEC	10	Sag		JUN	4	Tau
1913	JAN	2	Cap	1929	JUN	12	Gem
1914	JAN	21	Aqu	1930	JUN	26	Can
1915	FEB	4	Pic	1931	JUL	17	Leo
1916	FEB	12	Ari	1932	AUG	11	Vir
	JUN	26	Tau	1933	SEP	10	Lib

1934	OCT	11	Scp		OCT	5	Sag
1935	NOV	9	Sag	1960	MAR	1	Cap
1936	DEC	2	Cap		JUN	10	Sag
1937	DEC	20	Aqu		OCT	26	Cap
1938	MAY	14	Pic	1961	MAR	15	Aqu
	JUL	30	Aqu		AUG	12	Cap
	DEC	29	Pic		NOV	4	Aqu
1939	MAY	11	Ari	1962	MAR	25	Pic
	OCT	30	Pic	1963	APR	4	Ari
	DEC	20	Ari	1964	APR	12	Tau
1940	MAY	16	Tau	1965	APR	22	Gem
1941	MAY	26	Gem		SEP	21	Can
1942	JUN	10	Can		NOV	17	Gem
1943	JUN	30	Leo	1966	MAY	5	Can
1944	JUL	26	Vir		SEP	27	Leo
1945	AUG	25	Lib	1967	JAN	16	Can
1946	SEP	25	Scp		MAY	23	Leo
1947	OCT	24	Sag		OCT	19	Vir
1948	NOV	15	Cap	1968	FEB	27	Leo
1949	APR	12	Aqu		JUN	15	Vir
	JUN	27	Cap		NOV	15	Lib
	NOV	30	Aqu	1969	MAR	30	Vir
1950	APR	15	Pic		JUL	15	Lib
	SEP	15	Aqu		DEC	16	Scp
	DEC	1	Pic	1970	APR	30	Lib
1951	APR	21	Ari		AUG	15	Scp
1952	APR	28	Tau	1971	JAN	14	Sag
1953	MAY	9	Gem		JUN	5	Sc
1954	MAY	24	Can		SEP	11	Sag
1955	JUN	13	Leo	1972	FEB	6	Cap
	NOV	17	Vir		JUL	24	Sag
1956	JAN	18	Leo		SEP	25	Cap
	JUL	7	Vir	1973	FEB	23	Aqu
	DEC	13	Lib	1974	MAR	8	Pic
1957	FEB	19	Vir	1975	MAR	18	Ari
	AUG	7	Lib	1976	MAR	26	Tau
1958	JAN	13	Scp		AUG	23	Gem
	MAR	20	Lib		OCT	16	Tau
	SEP	7	Scp	1977	APR	3	Gem
1959	FEB	10	Sag		AUG	20	Can
	APR	24	Scp		DEC	30	Gem

1978	APR	12	Can		1989	MAR	11	Gem
	SEP	5	Leo			JUL	30	Can
1979	FEB	28	Can		1990	AUG	18	Leo
	APR	20	Leo		1991	SEP	12	Vir
	SEP	29	Vir		1992	OCT	10	Lib
1980	OCT	27	Lib		1993	NOV	10	Scp
1981	NOV	27	Scp		1994	DEC	9	Sag
1982	DEC	26	Sag		1996	JAN	3	Cap
1984	JAN	19	Cap		1997	JAN	21	Aqu
1985	FEB	6	Aqu		1998	FEB	4	Pic
1986	FEB	20	Pic		1999	FEB	13	Ari
1987	MAR	2	Ari			JUN	28	Tau
1988	MAR	8	Tau			OCT	23	Ari
	JUL	22	Gem		2000	FEB	14	Tau
	NOV	30	Tau			JUN	30	Gem

SATURN SIGN 1903–2000

1903	JAN	19	Aqu			SEP	13	Scp
1905	APR	13	Pic		1926	DEC	2	Sag
	AUG	17	Aqu		1929	MAR	15	Cap
1906	JAN	8	Pic			MAY	5	Sag
1908	MAR	19	Ari			NOV	30	Cap
1910	MAY	17	Tau		1932	FEB	24	Aqu
	DEC	14	Ari			AUG	13	Cap
1911	JAN	20	Tau			NOV	20	Aqu
1912	JUL	7	Gem		1935	FEB	14	Pic
	NOV	30	Tau		1937	APR	25	Ari
1913	MAR	26	Gem			OCT	18	Pic
1914	AUG	24	Can		1938	JAN	14	Ari
	DEC	7	Gem		1939	JUL	6	Tau
1915	MAY	11	Can			SEP	22	Ari
1916	OCT	17	Leo		1940	MAR	20	Tau
	DEC	7	Can		1942	MAY	8	Gem
1917	JUN	24	Leo		1944	JUN	20	Can
1919	AUG	12	Vir		1946	AUG	2	Leo
1921	OCT	7	Lib		1948	SEP	19	Vir
1923	DEC	20	Scp		1949	APR	3	Leo
1924	APR	6	Lib			MAY	29	Vir

96

1950	NOV	20	Lib		1977	JUN	5	Leo
1951	MAR	7	Vir		1977	NOV	17	Vir
	AUG	13	Lib		1978	JAN	5	Leo
1953	OCT	22	Scp			JUL	26	Vir
1956	JAN	12	Sag		1980	SEP	21	Lib
	MAY	14	Scp		1982	NOV	29	Scp
	OCT	10	Sag		1983	MAY	6	Lib
1959	JAN	5	Cap			AUG	24	Scp
1962	JAN	3	Aqu		1985	NOV	17	Sag
1964	MAR	24	Pic		1988	FEB	13	Cap
	SEP	16	Aqu			JUN	10	Sag
	DEC	16	Pic			NOV	12	Cap
1967	MAR	3	Ari		1991	FEB	6	Aqu
1969	APR	29	Tau		1993	MAY	21	Pic
1971	JUN	18	Gem			JUN	30	Aqu
1972	JAN	10	Tau		1994	JAN	28	Pic
	FEB	21	Gem		1996	APR	7	Ari
1973	AUG	1	Can		1998	JUN	9	Tau
1974	JAN	7	Gem			OCT	25	Ari
	APR	18	Can		1999	MAR	1	Tau
1975	SEP	17	Leo		2000	AUG	10	Gem
1976	JAN	14	Can			OCT	16	Tau

CHAPTER 5

How to Decode the Symbols (Glyphs) on Your Chart

Astrology has its own special symbolic language, which has evolved over thousands of years. For beginners, it looks like a mysterious code . . . and it is! When you first try to decipher your chart, you may recognize the tiny moon and the symbol for your sign. Perhaps you'll also recognize Mars and Venus, since they are often used as male and female gender symbols outside of astrology. But the other marks could look as strange as Japanese to the uninitiated. Those little characters, called glyphs (or sigils) were created centuries ago, and any astrologer from Russia to Argentina could read your chart and know what it means. So a chart set up in Moscow can be interpreted by an astrologer in New York. And, since there are only 12 signs and 10 planets (not counting a few asteroids and other space creatures some astrologers use), it's a lot easier than learning to read Japanese!

You may well ask why you should bother to put in the effort at all. There are several good reasons. First, it's interesting. The glyphs are much more than little drawings—they are magical codes that contain within them keys to the meanings of the planets. Cracking the code can teach you immediately, in a visual way, much about the deeper meaning of a planet or sign.

If you ever get your horoscope chart done by computer, the printout will be written in glyphs. Though many charts have a list of the planets in plain English, many do not, leaving you mystified if you can't read the glyphs. You might pick out the symbol for the sun and the trident of Neptune . . . but then there's Jupiter (is that a number 4?) and Mercury, who looks like Venus wearing a hat.

Here's a code-cracker for the glyphs, beginning with the glyphs for the planets. To those who already know their glyphs . . . don't just skim over the chapter! There are hidden meanings to discover, so test your glyph-ese.

The Glyphs for the Planets

Almost all the glyphs of the planets are combinations of the most basic forms: the circle, the half-circle or arc, and the cross. Artists and glyph designers have stylized these forms over the years, but the basic concept is always visible. Each component of the glyph has a special meaning in relation to the others, which combines to create the meaning of the completed symbol.

For instance, the circle, which has no beginning or end, is one of the oldest symbols of spirit or spiritual forces. All of the early diagrams of the heavens—the spiritual territory—are shown in circular form. The semicircle or arc symbolizes the receptive, finite soul, which contains spiritual potential in the curving line. The vertical line symbolizes movement from heaven to earth. The horizontal line describes temporal movement, here and now, in time and space. Superimposed together, the vertical and horizontal planes symbolize manifestation in the material world.

The Sun Glyph ☉

The sun is always shown by this powerful solar symbol, a circle with a point in the center. It is you, your spiritual center, your infinite personality incarnating the point into the finite cycles of birth and death.

This symbol was brought into common use in the 16th century, after a German occultist and scholar, Cornelius Agrippa (1486–1535) wrote a book called *Die Occulta*

Philosophia, which became accepted as the standard work in its field. Agrippa collected many medieval astrological and magical symbols in this book, which astrologers later copied and continued to use.

The Moon Glyph ☽

This is surely the easiest symbol to spot on a chart. The moon glyph is a left-facing arc stylized into the crescent moon, which perfectly captures the reactive, receptive, emotional nature of the moon. As part of a circle, the arc symbolizes the potential fulfillment of the entire circle. It is the life force that is still incomplete.

The Mercury Glyph ☿

This is the "Venus with a hat" glyph. With another stretch of the imagination, can't you see the winged cap of Mercury the messenger? The upturned crescent could be antennae that tune in and transmit messages from the sun, signifying that Mercury is the way you communicate, the way your mind works. The upturned arc is receiving energy into the spirit or solar circle, which will later be translated into action on the material plane, symbolized by the cross. All the elements are equally sized because Mercury is neutral—it doesn't play favorites! This planet symbolizes objective, detached, unemotional thinking.

The Venus Glyph ♀

Here the relationship is between two elements—the circle, or spirit, above the cross of matter. Spirit is elevated over matter, pulling it upward. Venus asks, "What is beautiful? What do you like best, what do you love to have done to you?" Venus determines both your ideal of beauty and what feels good sensually. It governs your own allure and power to attract, as well as what attracts and pleases you.

The Mars Glyph ♂

In this glyph, the cross of matter is stylized into an arrowhead pointed up and outward, propelled by the circle of spirit. You can deduce that Mars embodies your spiritual energy projected into the outer world. It's your assertiveness, your initiative, your aggressive drive; it's what you like to do to others; it's your temper. If you know someone's Mars, you know whether they'll blow up when angry or do a slow burn. Your task is to use your outgoing Mars energy wisely and well.

The Jupiter Glyph ♃

Jupiter is the basic cross of the matter, with a large stylized crescent perched on the left side of the horizontal, temporal plane. You might think of the crescent as an open hand—one meaning of Jupiter is "luck," or what's handed to you. You don't work for what you get from Jupiter—it comes to you if you're open to it.

The Jupiter glyph might also remind you of a jumbo jet with a huge tail fin, about to take off. This is the planet of travel, mental and spiritual, and of expanding your horizons via new ideas, new spiritual dimensions, and new places. Jupiter embodies the optimism and enthusiasm of the traveler about to embark on an exciting adventure.

The Saturn Glyph ♄

Flip Jupiter over and you've got Saturn. (This might not be immediately apparent, because Saturn is usually stylized into an "h" form like the one shown here.) But the principle it expresses is the opposite of Jupiter's expansive tendencies. Saturn pulls you back to earth—the receptive arc is pushed down underneath the cross of matter. Before there are any rewards or expansion, the duties and obligations of the material world must be considered. Saturn says, "Stop, wait, and finish your chores before you take off!"

Saturn's glyph also resembles the sickle of old Father Time. Saturn was first known as Chronos, the Greek god of time, for time brings all matter to an end. When it was thought to be the most distant planet (before the discovery of Uranus), Saturn was believed to be the place where time stopped. After the soul, having departed from earth, journeyed back to the outer reaches of the universe, it finally stopped at Saturn, at "the end of time."

The Uranus Glyph ♅

The glyph for Uranus is often stylized to form a capital "H" after Sir William Herschel, the planet's discoverer. But the more esoteric version curves the two pillars of the H into crescent antennae, or ears, or like satellite discs receiving signals from space. These are perched on the horizontal material line of the cross (matter) and pushed from below by the circle of the spirit. To many sci-fi fans, Uranus looks like an orbiting satellite.

Uranus channels the highest energy of all, the white electrical light of the universal spiritual sun, the force that holds the cosmos together. This pure electrical energy is gathered from all over the universe. Because it doesn't follow an ordinary celestial drumbeat, it can't be controlled or predicted, which is also true of those who are strongly influenced by this eccentric planet. In the symbol, this energy is manifested through the balance of polarities (the two opposite arms of the glyph) like the two polarized wires of a lightbulb.

The Neptune Glyph ♆

Neptune's glyph is usually stylized to look like a trident, the weapon of the Roman god Neptune. However, on a more esoteric level, it shows the large upturned crescent of the soul pierced through by the cross of matter. Neptune nails down, or materializes, soul energy, bringing impulses from the soul level into manifestation. That is why Neptune is associated with imagination or "imagining in," making an image of the soul. Neptune works through feeling, sensitivity, and mystical capacity to bring the divine into the earthly realm.

The Pluto Glyph ♀

Pluto is written two ways. One is a composite of the letters "PL," the first two letters of the word Pluto and coincidentally the initials of Percival Lowell, one of the planet's discoverers. The other, more esoteric symbol is a small circle above a large open crescent that surmounts the cross of matter. This depicts Pluto's power to regenerate—you might imagine from this glyph a new little spirit emerging from the sheltering cup of the soul. Pluto rules the forces of life and death—after a Pluto experience, you are transformed or reborn in some way.

Sci-fi fans might visualize this glyph as a small satellite (the circle) being launched. It was shortly after Pluto's discovery that we learned how to harness the nuclear forces that made space exploration possible. Pluto rules the transformative power of atomic energy, which totally changed our lives and from which there was no turning back.

The Glyphs for the Signs

On an astrological chart, the glyph for the sign will appear after that of the planet. When you see the moon glyph followed by a number and the glyph for the sign, this means that the moon was passing over a certain degree of an astrological sign at the time of the chart. On the dividing points between the segments, or "houses," on your chart, you'll find the symbol for the sign that rules the house.

Since sun-sign symbols do not always bring together the same basic components of the planetary glyphs, where do their meanings come from? Many have been passed down from ancient Egyptian and Chaldean civilizations with few modifications. Others have been adapted over the centuries. In deciphering many of the glyphs, you'll often find that many symbols reveal a dual nature of the sign, which is not always apparent in sun-sign descriptions. For instance, the Gemini glyph is similar to the Roman numeral for two, and reveals this sign's longing to discover a twin soul. The Cancer glyph may be interpreted as resembling either nurturing breasts or the self-protective claws of the crab. Libra's glyph embodies the duality of the spirit balanced with material reality. The Sagittarius glyph shows that the aspirant must also carry along the earthly animal nature in his quest. The Capricorn sea goat is another symbol with dual emphasis. The goat climbs high yet is always pulled back by the deep waters of the unconscious. Aquarius embodies the double waves of mental detachment, balanced by the desire for connection with others in a friendly way. And finally, the two fishes of Pisces, which are forever tied together, show the duality of the soul and the spirit that must be reconciled.

The Aries Glyph ♈

Since the symbol for Aries is the ram, this glyph's most obvious association is with a ram's horns, which characterize one aspect of the Aries personality—an aggressive, me-first, leaping-head-first attitude. But the symbol may have other meanings for you, too. Some astrologers liken it to a fountain of energy, which Aries people also embody. The first sign of the zodiac bursts on the scene eagerly, ready to go. Another analogy is to the eyebrows and nose of the human head, which Aries rules, and the thinking power that is initiated in the brain. Another interesting theory is that the symbol represents spirit descending from a higher realm into the mind of man, which would be the point of the V shape in the Aries glyph.

The origin of this symbol links it to the Egyptian god Amun, represented by a ram. As Amon-Ra, this god was believed to embody the creator of the universe, the leader of all the other gods. This relates easily to the position of Aries as the leader (or first sign) of the zodiac, which begins at the spring equinox, a time of the year when nature is renewed.

The Taurus Glyph ♉

This is another easy glyph to draw and identify. It takes little imagination to decipher the bull's head with long, curving horns. Like the bull, the archetypal Taurus is slow to anger but ferocious when provoked, as well as stubborn, steady, and sensual. Another association is the Taurus-ruled larynx (and thyroid) of the throat area and the Eustachian tubes (the "horns" of the glyph) running up to the ears, which coincide with the relationship of Taurus to the voice, song, and music. Many famous singers, musicians, and composers have prominent Taurus influences.

Many ancient religions involved a bull as the central figure in fertility rites or initiations, usually symbolizing the victory of man over his animal nature. Another possible origin is in the sacred bull of Egypt, who embodied the incarnate form of Osiris, god of death and resurrection. In early Christian imagery, the Taurean bull, representing St. Luke, appears in many art forms along with the Lion (Leo and St. Mark), the Man (Aquarius and St. Matthew) and the Eagle (Scorpio and St. John).

The Gemini Glyph ♊

The standard glyph immediately calls to mind the Roman numeral for two and the symbol for Gemini, the "twins." In almost all images for this sign, the relationship between two persons is emphasized. This is the sign of communication and human contact, and it manifests the desire to share. Many of the figurative images for Gemini show twins with their arms around each other, emphasizing that they are sharing the same ideas and the same ground. In the glyph, the top line indicates mental communication, while the bottom line indicates shared physical space.

The most famous Gemini legend is that of the twin sons, Castor and Pollux, one of whom had a mortal father, while the other was the son of Zeus, king of the gods. When it came time for the mortal twin to die, his grief-stricken brother pleaded with Zeus, who agreed to let them spend half the year on earth, in mortal form, and half in immortal life, with the gods on Mt. Olympus. This reflects a basic concept of humankind, which possesses an immortal soul yet is also subject to the limits of mortality.

The Cancer Glyph ♋

Two convenient images relate to the Cancer glyph. The easiest to picture is the curving claws of the Cancer symbol, the crab. Like the crab, Cancer's element is water. This sensitive sign also has a hard protective shell to protect its tender interior. It must be wily to escape predators, scampering sideways and hiding shyly under the rocks. The crab also responds to the cycles of the moon, as do all shellfish. The other image is that of two female breasts, which Cancer rules, showing that this is a sign that nurtures and protects others as well as itself. In ancient Egypt, Cancer was also represented by the scarab beetle, a symbol of regeneration and eternal life.

The Leo Glyph ♌

Lions have belonged to the sign of Leo since earliest times and it is not difficult to imagine the king of beasts with his sweeping mane and curling tail from this glyph. The upward sweep of the glyph easily describes the positive energy of Leos—the flourishing tail and the flamboyant qualities. Another analogy, which is a stretch, is that of a heart leaping up with joy and enthusiasm, also very typical of Leo. Notice that the Leo glyph seems to be an extension of Cancer's glyph, with a significant difference. In the Cancer glyph, the figures are folding inward, protectively, while the Leo glyph expresses energy outwardly, with no duality in the symbol (or in

Leo). In early Christian imagery, the Leo lion represented St. Mark.

The Virgo Glyph ♍

You can read much into this mysterious glyph. For instance, it could represent the initials of "Mary Virgin," or a young woman holding a staff of wheat, or stylized female genitalia, all common interpretations. The "M" shape might also remind you that Virgo is ruled by Mercury. The cross beneath the symbol could indicate the grounded, practical nature of this earth sign.

The earliest zodiacs link Virgo with the Egyptian goddess Isis, who gave birth to the god Horus after her husband Osiris had been killed, in the archetype of a miraculous conception. There are many statues of Isis nursing her baby son, which are reminiscent of medieval Virgin and Child motifs. This sign has also been associated with the image of the Holy Grail, where the Virgo symbol was substituted with a chalice.

The Libra Glyph ♎

It is not difficult to read the standard image for Libra, the scales, into this glyph. There is another meaning, however, that is equally relevant: the setting sun as it descends over the horizon. Libra's natural position on the zodiac wheel is the descendent or sunset position (as Aries' natural position is the ascendant, or rising sign). Both images relate to Libra's personality. Libra is always weighing pros and cons for a balanced decision. In the sunset image, the sun (male) hovers over the horizontal Earth (female) before setting. Libra is the space between these lines, harmonizing yin and yang, spiritual and material, the ideal and real worlds. The glyph has also been linked to the kidneys, which are ruled by Libra.

The Scorpio Glyph ♏

With its barbed tail, this glyph is easy to identify with the sign of the Scorpion. It also represents the male sexual parts, over which the sign rules. However, some earlier symbols for Scorpio, such as the Egyptian, represent it as an erect serpent. You can also draw the conclusion that Mars is ruled by the arrowhead.

Another image for Scorpio, not identifiable in this glyph, is the eagle. Scorpios can go to extremes, soaring like the eagle or self-destructing like the Scorpion. In early Christian imagery, which often used zodiacal symbols, the Scorpio eagle was chosen to symbolize the intense apostle St. John the Evangelist.

The Sagittarius Glyph ♐

This glyph is one of the easiest to spot and draw—an upward pointing arrow lifting up a cross. The arrow is pointing skyward, while the cross represents the four elements of the material world, which the arrow must convey. Elevating materiality into spirituality is an important Sagittarius quality, which explains why this sign is associated with higher learning, religion, philosophy, and travel—the aspiring professions. Sagittarius can also send barbed arrows of frankness in the pursuit of truth. (This is also the sign of the super-salesman.)

Sagittarius is symbolically represented by the centaur, a mythological creature who is half-man, half horse, aiming his arrow toward the skies. Though Sagittarius is motivated by spiritual aspiration, it also must balance the powerful appetites of the animal nature. The centaur Chiron, a figure in Greek mythology, became a wise teacher after many adventures and world travels.

The Capricorn Glyph ♑

One of the most difficult symbols to draw, this glyph may take some practice. It is a representation of the seagoat: a mythical animal that is a goat with a curving fish's tail. The goat part of Capricorn wants to leave the waters of the emotions and climb to the elevated areas of life. But the first part is the unconscious, the deep chaotic psychic level that draws the goat back. Capricorn is often trying to escape the deep, feeling part of life by submerging himself in work, steadily climbing to the top. To some people, the glyph represents a seated figure with a bent knee, a reminder that Capricorn governs the knee area of the body.

An interesting aspect of this figure is how the sharp pointed horns of the symbol, which represent the penetrating, shrewd, conscious side of Capricorn, contrast with the swishing tail, which represents its serpentine, unconscious, emotional force. One Capricorn legend, which dates from Roman times, tells of the earthy fertility god, Pan, who tried to save himself from uncontrollable sexual desires by jumping into the Nile. His upper body then turned into a goat, while the lower part became a fish. Later, Jupiter gave him a safe haven in the skies, as a constellation.

The Aquarius Glyph ≈

This ancient water symbol can be traced back to an Egyptian hieroglyph representing streams of life force. Symbolized by the water bearer, Aquarius is distributor of the waters of life—the magic liquid of regeneration. The two waves can also be linked to the positive and negative charges of the electrical energy that Aquarius rules, a sort of universal wavelength. Aquarius is tuned in intuitively to higher forces via this electrical force. The duality of the glyph could also refer to the dual nature of Aquarius, a sign that runs hot and cold, is friendly but also detached in the mental world of air signs.

In Greek legends, Aquarius is represented by Ganymede, who was carried to heaven by an eagle in order to become the cup bearer of Zeus, and to supervise the annual flooding of the Nile. The sign became associated with aviation and notions of flight.

The Pisces Glyph ⋊⋉

Here is an abstraction of the familiar image of Pisces, two fishes swimming in opposite directions, bound together by a cord. The fishes represent spirit, which yearns for the freedom of heaven, while the soul remains attached to the desires of the temporal world. During life on earth, the spirit and the soul are bound together and when they complement each other, instead of pulling in opposite directions, this facilitates the creative expression for which Pisceans are known. The ancient version of this glyph, taken from the Egyptians, had no connecting line, which was added in the fourteenth century.

Another interpretation is that the left fish indicates the direction of involution or the beginning of the cycle; the right-hand fish, the direction of evolution, the way to completion of a cycle. It's an appropriate meaning for Pisces, the last sign of the zodiac.

CHAPTER 6

Answers to Your Questions

Here are the answers to some questions frequently asked by regular readers of this book. You may have been wondering about them, too.

QUESTION: *Why don't other stars in the cosmos influence our horoscopes?*
Most astrologers find that ten planets—considering the sun and moon as "planets"—give us quite enough information to delineate a horoscope. However, a growing number of astrologers are finding that other celestial bodies, such as asteroids and certain fixed stars, add an extra dimension and special nuances to the horoscope. Certain stars are said to bring specific lessons on life's journey when they are also linked with one of the key planets in a horoscope. These lessons are expressed by the mythology the star represents.

The fixed stars were used by the ancient astrologers and now are enjoying a renaissance thanks to a group of scholars dedicated to reinterpreting their mythology and adapting ancient techniques for modern times. Those interested in fixed stars will find much fascinating information in *Brady's Book of Fixed Stars* by Bernadette Brady (Samuel Weiser, 1998).

QUESTION: *If I was born on a Mercury retrograde, does it make a difference?*
Many highly original and creative thinkers were born with Mercury in retrograde, or apparent backward motion, such as Oscar Wilde, Norman Mailer, Dylan

Thomas, Bruce Springsteen, Hillary Clinton, Harry S. Truman, and Mae West. You might find the three Mercury retrograde periods each year easier to cope with than other people. However, it is the whole chart and the aspects to your natal Mercury that must be considered before drawing any conclusions.

QUESTION: *I'm very different from my twin brother. Since we were born only twenty minutes apart, how do you account for that?*
If you have your exact time of birth, you might be able to find out for yourself by having an accurate horoscope chart made. Even a few minutes difference in time of birth can change the emphasis in a chart because of the movement of the earth. A different rising sign, which sets up the "houses" of your chart, moves over the horizon every two hours. And the moon moves about 13 degrees in a day. A change of degree or a rising sign can make a big difference.

If you have the exact degree of your moon and rising sign and your brother's moon and rising sign, you might be interested in comparing Sabian Symbols, which are symbolic meanings for each degree; they can be quite enlightening. There are several books on the Sabian Symbols, such as *The Sabian Symbols as an Oracle* by Lynda and Richard Hill (White Horse Books, 1995), a very readable recent addition to these interpretations.

Another possible reason for your differences is that you may each operate on a different level of your similar horoscopes. Or because you react to each other, you may each choose to manifest other facets of your charts. For example, one twin with a Cancer sun sign may manifest the creative, perceptive facets of her chart and become a child psychologist. Her sister may become a sharp businesswoman, running a hotel or real estate business, choosing the more practical side of her chart.

QUESTION: *If you were born on a day when the sun was changing signs, does that mean that you* *have characteristics of the preceding or following sign?*

If you were born on a day when the Sun or moon was changing signs, then it is very important to get your exact time of birth and to have an accurate horoscope chart cast. When there is a sign change, there are many shifts in energy. Between one sign and the next, there is a difference in element, modality, and polarity. Therefore, you are not likely to be partly one sign and partly another. If you do manifest characteristics of the adjacent sign, it may be due to other planets in that sign or to your rising sign.

QUESTION: *How do I answer my religious friends and family who disapprove of my interest in astrology?*

Astrology has a long history of being attacked by religious and scientific skeptics, most of whom know little about real astrology. (There's even an Internet mailing list especially for those who wish to ventilate their anti-astrology feelings.) Point out that there has never been any conflict between astrology and religion; there are no anti-astrology writings in the Bible. In fact, the three Wise Men or Magi were astrologers. In medieval times, astrology was integrated with religion. Many famous European cathedrals, such as Chartres and Canterbury, have astrology motifs, and there's a very ancient zodiac from the floor of a synagogue in New York's Jewish Museum. There is no dogma to astrology that might counter religious beliefs—astrology is not a belief system, it is a technique. In other words, you are not getting into anything dangerous with astrology, which may be what your friends fear.

Many religious people feel threatened by astrologers because they confuse modern-day astrology with that practiced by charlatans of the past or because they feel that someone interested in astrology will turn away from religion. However, as anyone who has delved seriously into astrology can attest, the study of astrology tends to bring one closer to a spiritual understanding of the interchange between a universal design, the material world, and man's place in it. Astrology can, in a very practical way, help man keep in balance with the forces of the universe.

QUESTION: *Can I find the answer to a question based on a horoscope for the time it is asked?*

This belongs to a specific discipline within astrology called *horary astrology*. It works according to specific rules and is practiced by specialists within the field. If you would like to find an answer this way, be sure to consult an astrologer who specializes in horary techniques. There is also an astrology program called "Nostradamus" (by Air Software; see our resource list in the Internet chapter), which was created for horary work.

CHAPTER 7

Your Daily Agenda:

Make the Most of the Millennium!

Set your schedule on a successful course by letting astrology help you coordinate your activities with the most beneficial times. For instance, if you know the dates that the tricky planet Mercury will be creating havoc with communications, you'll be sure to back up the hard drive on your computer, keep duplicates of your correspondence, record those messages, and read between the lines of contracts. When Venus is in your sign, you'll get a new hairstyle, entertain a VIP client, and circulate where you'll be seen and admired.

To find out for yourself if there's truth to the saying "timing is everything," mark your own calendar for love, career moves, vacations, and important events by using the following information and the tables in this chapter and the one titled "Look Up Your Planets," as well as the moon sign listings under your daily forecast. Here are the happenings to note on your agenda:

- Dates of your sun sign (high-energy period)
- The month previous to your sun sign (love energy period)
- Dates of planets in your sign this year
- Full and new moons (pay special attention when these fall in your sun sign)
- Eclipses

- Moon in your sun sign every month, as well as moon in the opposite sign (listed in daily forecast)
- Mercury retrogrades
- Other retrograde periods

When to Switch on the Power!

Every birthday starts a cycle of solar energy for you. You should feel a new surge of vitality as the powerful sun enters your sign. This is the time when predominant energies are most favorable to you—so go for it! Start new projects, make your big moves. You'll get the recognition you deserve now, because your sun sign is most prominent. Look in the tables in this book to see if other planets will also be passing through your sun sign at this time. Venus (love, beauty), Mars (energy, drive), or Mercury (communication, mental sharpness) reinforce the sun and give an extra boost to your life in the areas they affect. Venus will rev up your social and love life, making you seem especially attractive. Mars gives you extra energy and drive, while Mercury fuels your brain power and helps you communicate. Jupiter signals an especially lucky period of expansion.

There are two "down" times related to the sun. During the month before your birthday period, when you are winding up your annual cycle, you could be feeling especially vulnerable and depleted, so get extra rest, watch your diet, and don't overstress yourself. Use this time to gear up for a big "push" when the sun enters your sign.

Another "down" time is when the sun is the opposite sign (six months from your birthday) and the prevailing energies are very different from yours. You may feel at odds with the world and things might not come easily. You'll have to work harder for recognition, because people are not on your wavelength. However, this could be a good time to work on a team, in cooperation with others, or behind the scenes.

Phase in and Phase out with the Moon

Working with the phases of the moon is as easy as looking up at the night sky. At the new moon, when both sun and moon are in the same sign, it's the best time to begin new ventures, especially the activities that are favored by that sign. You'll have powerful energies pulling you in the same direction. You'll be focused outward, toward action. Postpone breaking off, terminating, deliberating, or reflecting, activities that require introspection and passive work.

Get your project under way during the first quarter, then go public at the full moon, a time of high intensity, when feelings come out into the open. This is your time to shine—to express yourself. Be aware, however, that because pressures are being released, other people are also letting off steam and confrontations are possible. So try to avoid arguments. Traditionally, astrologers often advise against surgery at this time, for it could produce heavier bleeding.

From the last quarter to the new moon is a winding-down phase, a time to cut off unproductive relationships, do serious thinking, and perform inwardly directed activities.

You'll feel some new and full moons more strongly than others, especially the new moons that fall in your sun sign and the full moons in your opposite sign. Because that particular full moon happens at your low-energy time of year, it is likely to be an especially stressful time in a relationship, when hidden problems or unexpressed emotions could surface.

The Year 2000 Full and New Moons

New Moon in Capricorn—January 6
Full Moon in Leo—January 20 (eclipse 11:45 p.m. EST)
New Moon in Aquarius—February 5 (eclipse 8:03 a.m. EST)
Full Moon in Virgo—February 19

New Moon in Pisces—March 6
Full Moon in Virgo—March 20
New Moon in Aries—April 4
Full Moon in Libra—April 18
New Moon in Taurus—May 4
Full Moon in Scorpio—May 18
New Moon in Gemini—June 2
Full Moon in Sagittarius—June 16
New Moon in Cancer—July 1 (eclipse 3:34 p.m. EDT)
Full Moon in Capricorn—July 16 (eclipse 9:55 a.m. EDT)
New Moon in Leo—July 30 (eclipse 10:25 p.m. EDT)
Full Moon in Aquarius—August 15
New Moon in Virgo—August 29
Full Moon in Pisces—September 13
New Moon in Libra—September 27
Full Moon in Aries—October 13
New Moon in Scorpio—October 27
Full Moon in Taurus—November 11
New Moon in Sagittarius—November 25
Full Moon in Gemini—December 11
New Moon in Capricorn—December 25 (eclipse 12:22 p.m. EST)

Six Eclipses this Year!

There are six eclipses this year (last year, there were only four), which means you can expect changes that will be sure to influence your life, especially if you are a Capricorn, Cancer, Leo, or Aquarius. Both solar and lunar eclipses are times when our natural rhythms are altered, depending on where the eclipse falls in your horoscope and how many planets you have in the sign of the eclipse. If it falls on or close to your birthday, you're going to have important changes in your life, perhaps a turning point.

Lunar eclipses happen when the earth is on a level plane with the sun and moon and moves exactly between them during the time of the full moon, breaking the powerful monthly cycle of opposition of these two forces. We might say the earth "short circuits" the connection between them. The effect can be either confusion or clarity, as our subconscious energies, which normally react to the pull of opposing sun and moon, are turned off. As we are temporarily freed from the subconscious attachments, we might have objective insights that could help us change any destructive emotional patterns, such as addictions, which normally occur at this time. This momentary "turn off" could help us turn our lives around. On the other hand, this break in the normal cycle could cause a bewildering disorientation that intensifies our insecurities.

The solar eclipse occurs at the new moon and this time the moon blocks the sun's energies as it passes exactly between the sun and the earth. This means the objective, conscious force, represented by the sun, will be temporarily darkened. Subconscious lunar forces, activating our deepest emotions, will now dominate, putting us in a highly subjective state. Emotional truths can be revealed or emotions can run wild, as our objectivity is cut off and hidden patterns surface. If your sign is affected, you may find yourself beginning a period of work on a deep inner level; you may have psychic experiences or a surfacing of deep feelings.

You'll start feeling the energies of an upcoming eclipse a few days after the previous new or full moon. The energy continues to intensify until the actual eclipse, then disperses for three or four days. So plan ahead at least a week or more before an eclipse and allow several days afterward for the natural rhythms to return. Try not to make major moves during this period (it's not a great time to get married, change jobs, or buy a home).

Eclipses in 2000

Lunar Eclipse in Leo—January 20 (11:45 p.m. EST)
Solar Eclipse in Aquarius—February 5 (8:03 a.m. EST)
Solar Eclipse in Cancer—July 1 (3:34 p.m. EDT)

Lunar Eclipse in Capricorn—July 16 (9:55 a.m. EDT)
Solar Eclipse in Leo—July 30 (10:25 p.m. EDT)
Solar Eclipse in Capricorn—December 25 (12:22 p.m. EST)

Moon Sign Timing

You can forecast the daily emotional "weather" to determine your monthly high and low days, or to synchronize your activities with the cycles and the sign of the moon. Take note of the moon's daily sign under your daily forecast at the end of the book. Here are some of the activities favored and moods you are likely to encounter under each sign.

Moon in Aries

Get moving! The new moon in Aries is an ideal time to start new projects. Everyone is pushy and raring to go, rather impatient and short tempered. Leave details and follow-up for later. Competitive sports or martial arts are great ways to let off steam. Quiet types could use some assertiveness, but it's a great day for dynamos. Be careful not to step on too many toes.

Moon in Taurus

It's time to do solid, methodical tasks. This is the time to tackle follow-through or backup work, laying the foundations for success. Make investments, buy real estate, do appraisals, make some hard bargains. Attend to your property—get out in the country or spend some time in your garden. Enjoy creature comforts, music, a good dinner, and sensual lovemaking. Forget about starting a diet.

Moon in Gemini

Talk means action today. Telephone, write letters, fax! Make new contacts, and be sure to stay in touch with steady customers as well. You can handle lots of tasks at once. It's a great day for mental activity of any kind. Don't try to pin people down—they too are feeling restless, so keep it light. Flirtations and socializing are good. Watch gossip—and don't give away secrets.

Moon in Cancer

This is a moody, sensitive, emotional time. People respond to personal attention and mothering. Stay at home, have a family dinner, call your mother. Nostalgia, memories, and psychic powers are heightened. You'll want to hang on to people and things—don't clean out your closets now. You could have some shrewd insights into what others really need and want, so pay attention to dreams, intuition, and gut reactions.

Moon in Leo

Everybody is in a much more confident, enthusiastic, generous mood. It's a good day to ask for a raise, show what you can do, and dress like a star. People will respond to flattery, and are sure to enjoy a bit of drama and theater. You may be feeling extravagant, so treat yourself royally and show off a bit—but don't break the bank! Be careful that you don't promise more than you can deliver!

Moon in Virgo

Do practical, down-to-earth chores, such as reviewing your budget and making repairs. Be an efficiency expert. This is not a day to ask for a raise. Have a health checkup, revamp your diet, buy vitamins or health food. Make your home spotless, taking care of details and piled-up chores. Reorganize your work and life so they run more smoothly, efficiently, and inexpensively. Be prepared for others to be in a critical, fault-finding mood.

Moon in Libra

Relationships of all kinds are favored. Attend to legal matters, negotiate contracts, and arbitrate. Do things with your favorite partner—socialize, be romantic, or buy a special gift or a beautiful object. Decorate yourself or your surroundings, buying new clothes, throwing a party, or having an elegant, romantic evening. Smooth over any ruffled feathers as you avoid confrontations and stick to civilized discussions.

Moon in Scorpio

This is a day to do things with passion. You'll have excellent concentration and focus, but try not to get too intense emotionally, and avoid sharp exchanges with loved ones. Others may tend to go to extremes, get jealous, and overreact. Today is great for troubleshooting, problem-solving, research, scientific work—and making love. Pay attention to psychic vibes.

Moon in Sagittarius

It's a great time for travel and for having philosophical discussions. Set long-range career goals, work out, do sports, or buy athletic equipment. Others will be feeling upbeat, exuberant, and adventurous. Risk taking is favored today—you may feel like taking a gamble, betting on the horses, visiting a local casino, or buying a lottery ticket. Teaching, writing, and spiritual activities also get the green light. Relax outdoors; take care of animals.

Moon in Capricorn

You can accomplish a lot today, so get on the ball! Issues concerning your basic responsibilities, duties, family, and parents could crop up. You'll be expected to deliver on your promises and stick to your schedule now, so weed out the deadwood from your life and attack chores systematically. Get a dental checkup or attend to your aching knees.

Moon in Aquarius

It's a great day for doing things in groups—so take part in clubs, meetings, outings, politics, or parties. Campaign for your candidate, work for a worthy cause, or deal with larger issues that affect the welfare of humanity. Buy a computer or electronic gadget. Watch TV. Wear something outrageous or try something you've never done before. Present an original idea. Don't stick to a rigid schedule—go with the flow. Take a class in meditation, mind control, or yoga.

Moon in Pisces

This can be a very creative day, so let your imagination work overtime. Film, theater, music, or ballet could inspire you. Spend some time alone, resting and reflecting, reading, watching a favorite film, or writing poetry. Daydreams can also be profitable. Help those less fortunate or lend a listening ear to someone who may be feeling blue. Don't overindulge in self-pity or escapism via alcohol, however, for people are especially vulnerable to substance abuse now. Turn your thoughts to romance and someone special.

When the Planets Go Backward

All the planets, except for the sun and moon, have times when they appear to move backward—or retrograde—in the sky, or so it seems from our point of view on earth. At these times, planets do not work as they usually do, so it's best to take a break from that planet's energies in our life and do some work on an inner level.

How to Outwit Mercury Mischief

Mercury goes retrograde most often, and its effects can be especially irritating. When it reaches a short distance ahead of the sun three times a year, it seems to move backward from our point of view. Astrologers often compare retrograde motion to the optical illusion that occurs when we ride on a train that passes another train traveling at a different speed—the second train appears to be moving in reverse.

What this means to you is that the Mercury-ruled areas of your life—analytical thought processes, communications, scheduling, and such—are subject to all kinds of confusion. So be prepared as people change their minds and renege on commitments. Communications equipment can break down, schedules must be changed on short notice, and people are late for appointments or don't show up at all. Traffic is terrible, and major purchases malfunction, don't work out, or get delivered in the wrong color. Letters don't arrive or are delivered to the wrong address. Employees will make errors that have to be corrected later. Contracts don't work out or must be renegotiated.

Since most of us can't put our lives on hold for nine weeks every year (three Mercury retrograde periods), we should learn to tame the trickster and make it work for us. The key is in the prefix "re." This is the time to go back over things in your life. Reflect on what you've done during the previous months, looking for deeper insights, spotting errors you've missed, and taking time to review and reevaluate what has happened. This time is very good for inner spiritual work and meditations. REst and REward yourself—it's a good time to take a vacation, especially if you REvisit a favorite place. REorganize your work and finish up projects that are backed up, or clean out your desk and closets, throwing away what you can't REcycle. If you must sign contracts or agreements, do so with a contingency clause that lets you REevaluate the terms later.

Postpone major purchases or commitments. Don't get married (unless you're remarrying the same person). Try not to rely on other people keeping appointments, contracts or agreements to the letter—it's best to have several alternatives. Double-check and read between the lines. Don't buy anything connected with communications or transportation—and if you must, be sure to cover yourself. Mercury retrograding through your sun sign will intensify its effect on your life.

If Mercury was retrograde when you were born, you may be one of the lucky people who don't suffer the frustrations of this period. If so, your mind probably works in a very intuitive, insightful way.

The sign Mercury is retrograding through can give you an idea of what's in store—as well as the sun signs that will be especially challenged.

Mercury Retrograde Periods in 2000
February 21–March 14
June 23–July 17
October 18–November 8

Fortunately, there are no Venus or Mars retrograde periods this year; however, both planes were retrograde in 1999, so it might be useful to reexamine what to do during these times.

Venus Retrograde—Make Peace!

Retrograding Venus can cause relationships to take a backward step or it can make you extravagant and impractical. It's *not* a good time to redecorate—you'll hate the color of the walls later. Postpone getting a new hairstyle and try not to fall in love either. But if you wish to make amends in an already-troubled relationship, make peaceful overtures then.

There is no Venus retrograde period in the year 2000.

Mars Tips—When to Push and When to Hold Back!

Mars shows how and when to get where you want to go, so timing your moves with Mars on your side can give you a big push. On the other hand, pushing Mars the wrong way can guarantee that you'll run into frustrations in every corner. Your best times to forge ahead are during the weeks when Mars is traveling through your sun sign or your Mars sign (look these up in the chapter on how to find your planets). Also consider times when Mars is in a compatible sign (fire with air signs, or earth with water signs). You'll be sure to have planetary power on your side.

Hold your fire when Mars retrogrades (fortunately this is a "go-ahead" year, when Mars moves forward all year long). This is the time to exercise patience, so let someone else run with the ball, especially if it's the opposing team. You may feel that you're not accomplishing much, but that's the right idea. Slow down and work off any frustrations at the gym. It's also best to postpone buying mechanical devices, which are Mars ruled, and to take extra care when handling sharp objects. Sports, especially those requiring excellent balance, should be played with care—be sure to use the appropriate protective gear and don't take unnecessary chances. This is not the time for daredevil moves! Pace yourself and pay extra attention to your health, since you may be especially vulnerable at this time.

When Other Planets Retrograde

The slower-moving planets, (Saturn, Jupiter, Neptune, Uranus, and Pluto) stay retrograde for months at a time. When Saturn is retrograde, you may feel more like hanging out at the beach than getting things done—it's an uphill battle with self-discipline at this time. Neptune retrograde promotes a dreamy escapism from reality, whereas Uranus retrograde may mean setbacks in areas where there have been sudden changes. Think of this as an adjustment period, a time to think things over and allow new ideas to develop. Pluto retrograde is a time to work on establishing proportion and balance in areas where there have been recent dramatic transformations.

When the planets start moving forward again, there's a shift in the atmosphere. Activities connected with each planet start moving ahead; planets that were stalled get rolling. Make a special note of those days on your calendar and proceed accordingly.

Other Retrogrades in 2000

Pluto turns retrograde in Sagittarius—March 15
Neptune turns retrograde in Aquarius—May 8
Uranus turns retrograde in Aquarius—May 25
Pluto turns direct in Sagittarius—August 20
Saturn turns retrograde in Taurus—September 12
Jupiter turns retrograde in Taurus—September 29
Neptune turns direct in Aquarius—October 15
Uranus turns direct in Aquarius—October 26

CHAPTER 8

What Makes Your Horoscope Special—Your Rising Sign

At the moment you were born, when you assumed an independent physical body, one of the signs of the zodiac (that is, a 30-degree slice of the sky) was just passing over the eastern horizon. In astrology, this is called the rising sign or ascendant, and it is one of the most important factors in your horoscope because it determines the uniqueness of your chart. Other babies who were born later or earlier in the day, in the same hospital as you were born, might have planets in the same signs as you do, but would have a different rising sign because as the earth turns, a different sign rises over the horizon every two hours. Therefore the planets would be in a different place in their horoscopes, emphasizing different areas of their lives.

In a horoscope, the other signs follow the rising sings in sequence, rotating counterclockwise. Therefore, the rising sign sets up the pathway of your chart. It rules the first house, which is your physical body and your appearance, and it also influences your style, tastes, health, and physical environment—where you are most comfortable working and living. The rising sign is one of the most important factors in your chart because it not only shows how you appear outwardly, but it also sets up the path you are to follow through the horoscope. After the rising sign is determined, then each house or area of your chart will be influenced by the signs following in sequence.

When we know the rising sign of a chart, we know where to put each planet—in which area of life it will operate. Without a valid rising sign, your collection of planets would have no "homes." Once the rising sign is established, it becomes possible to analyze a chart accurately. That is why many astrologers insist on knowing the exact time of a client's birth before they analyze a chart.

Your rising sign has an important relationship with your sun sign. Some complement the sun sign; others hide the sun under a totally different mask, as if playing an entirely different role. So it is often difficult to guess the person's sun sign from outer appearances. For example, a Leo with a conservative Capricorn ascendant would come across as much less flamboyant than a Leo with an Aries or Sagittarius ascendant. If the sun sign is reinforced by other planets in the same sign, it can also assert its personality much more strongly. A Leo with Venus and Jupiter also in Leo might counteract the conservative image of the Capricorn ascendant, in the preceding example. However, it is usually the ascendant that is reflected in the first impression.

Rising signs change every two hours with the earth's rotation. Those born early in the morning when the sun was on the horizon, will be most likely to project the image of the sun sign. These people are often called a "double Aries" or a "double Virgo," because the same sun sign and ascendant reinforce each other.

Look up your rising sign on the chart at the end of this chapter. Since rising signs change rapidly, it is important to know your birth time as close to the minute as possible. Even a few minutes' difference could change the rising sign and the setup of your chart. If you are unsure about the exact time, but know within a few hours, check the following descriptions to see which is most like the personality you project.

Aries Rising—Fiery Emotions

You are the most aggressive version of your sun sign, with boundless energy that can be used productively. Watch a tendency to overreact emotionally and blow your top. You come across as openly competitive, a positive asset in business or sports, but be on guard against impatience, which could lead to head injuries. Your walk and bearing could have the telltale head-forward Aries posture. You may wear more bright colors, especially red, than others of your sign. You may also have a tendency to drive your car faster.

Taurus Rising—The Earth Mother

You'll exude a protective nurturing quality, even if you're male, which draws those in need of TLC and support. You're slow moving, with a beautiful (or distinctive) speaking or singing voice that can be especially soothing or melodious. You probably surround yourself with comfort, good food, luxurious surroundings, and sensual pleasures, and you prefer welcoming others into your home to gadding about. You may have a talent for business, especially in trading, appraising, or real estate. This ascendant gives a well-padded physique that gains weight easily.

Gemini Rising—Expressive Talents

You're naturally sociable, with a lighter, more ethereal look than others of your sign, especially if you're female. You love to be with people and you express your ideas and feelings easily; you may have writing or speaking talent. You thrive on variety and a constantly changing scenario, with many different characters, though you may relate at a deeper level than might be suspected and you will be far more sympathetic and caring than you might project. You will probably travel widely and change partners and jobs several times (or juggle two at once). Physically, you should try to cultivate tranquility and create a calmer atmosphere, because your nerves are quite sensitive.

Cancer Rising—Sensitive Antenna

You easily pick up others' needs and feelings—a great gift in business, the arts, and personal relationships—but guard against overreacting or taking things too personally, especially during full-moon periods. Find creative outlets for your natural nurturing gifts, such as helping the less fortunate, particularly children. Your insights would be useful in psychology; your desire to feed and care for others in the restaurant, hotel, or child-care industry. You may be especially fond of wearing romantic old clothes, collecting antiques, and, of course, good food. Since your body will retain fluids, you should pay attention to your diet. Escape to places near water for relaxation.

Leo Rising—Scene Player

You may come across as more poised than you really feel, but you play it to the hilt, projecting a proud royal presence. This ascendant gives you a natural flair for drama, as you project a much more outgoing, optimistic, sunny personality than others of your sign. You take care to please your public by always projecting your best star quality, probably tossing a luxuriant mane of hair or, if you're female, dazzling with a spectacular jewelry collection. Since you may have a strong parental nature, you could well be the regal family matriarch or patriarch.

Virgo Rising—Cool and Calculating

Virgo rising masks your inner nature with a practical, analytical outer image. You seem very neat, orderly, and more particular, than others of your sign. Others in your life may feel they must live up to your high standards. Though at times you may be openly critical, this masks a well-meaning desire to have only the best for your loved ones. Your sharp eye for details could be used in the financial world, or your literary skills could draw you to teaching or publishing. The healing arts, health care, and other service-oriented professions attract many with this Virgo emphasis in their chart. Physically, you may have a very sensitive digestive system.

Libra Rising—The Charmer

Libra rising makes you appear a charmer—a more social, public person than others of your sign. Your private life will extend beyond your home and family to include an active social life. You may tend to avoid confrontations in relationships, preferring to smooth the way or negotiate diplomatically than give in to an emotional reaction. Because you are interested in all aspects of a situation, you may be slow to reach decisions. Physically, you'll have good proportions and pleasing symmetry. You're likely to have pleasing, if not beautiful, facial features. You move gracefully, and you have a winning smile and good taste in your clothes and home decor. Legal, diplomatic, or public relations professions could draw your interest.

Scorpio Rising—Magnetic Power

You project an intriguing air of mystery when Scorpio's secretiveness and sense of underlying power combines with your sign. You can project the image of a master manipulator, always in control and moving comfortably in the world of power. Your physical look comes across as intense and many of you have remarkable eyes, with a direct, penetrating gaze. But you'll never reveal your private agenda and you tend to keep your true feelings under wraps (watch a tendency toward paranoia). You may have an interesting romantic history with secret love affairs. Many of you heighten your air of mystery by wearing black. You're happiest near water and should provide yourself with a seaside retreat.

Sagittarius Rising—The Wanderer

You travel with this ascendant. You may also be a more outdoor, sportive type, with an athletic, casual, outgoing air. Your moods are camouflaged with cheerful optimism or a philosophical attitude. Though you don't hesitate to speak your mind, you can also laugh at your troubles or crack a joke more easily than others of your sign. This ascendant can also draw you to the field of higher education or to a spiritual life. You'll seem to have less attachment to things and people and you may travel widely. Your strong, fast legs are a physical bonus.

Capricorn Rising—Serious Business

This rising sign makes you come across as serious, goal oriented, disciplined, and careful with cash. You are not one of the zodiac's big spenders, though you might splurge occasionally on items with good investment value. You're the traditional, conservative type in dress and environment, and you might come across as quite formal and businesslike. You'll function well in a structured or corporate environment where you can climb to the top (you are always aware of who's the boss). In your personal life, you could be a loner or a single parent who is "father and mother" to your children.

Aquarius Rising—One of a Kind

You come across as less concerned about what others think and could even be a bit eccentric. You're more at ease with groups of people than others in your sign, and you may be attracted to public life. Your appearance may be unique— either unconventional or unimportant to you. Those with the sun in a water sign (Cancer, Scorpio, Pisces) may exercise your nurturing qualities with a large group, an extended family, or a day-care or community center.

Pisces Rising—Romantic Roles

Your creative, nurturing talents are heightened, and so is your ability to project emotional drama. And your dreamy eyes and poetic air bring out the protective instinct in others. You could be attracted to the arts, especially theater, dance, film, or photography, or to psychology or spiritual or charity work. Since you are vulnerable to up-and-down mood swings, it is especially important for you to find interesting, creative work where you can express your talents and boost your self-esteem. Accentuate the positive and be wary of escapist tendencies, particularly involving alcohol or drugs, to which you are supersensitive.

RISING SIGNS—A.M. BIRTHS

	1 AM	2 AM	3 AM	4 AM	5 AM	6 AM	7 AM	8 AM	9 AM	10 AM	11 AM	12 NOON
Jan 1	Lib	Sc	Sc	Sc	Sag	Sag	Cap	Cap	Aq	Aq	Pis	Ar
Jan 9	Lib	Sc	Sc	Sc	Sag	Sag	Sag	Cap	Cap	Aq	Pis	Tau
Jan 17	Sc	Sc	Sc	Sag	Sag	Cap	Cap	Aq	Aq	Pis	Ar	Tau
Jan 25	Sc	Sc	Sag	Sag	Sag	Cap	Cap	Aq	Pis	Ar	Tau	Tau
Feb 2	Sc	Sc	Sag	Sag	Cap	Cap	Aq	Pis	Pis	Ar	Tau	Gem
Feb 10	Sc	Sag	Sag	Sag	Cap	Cap	Aq	Aq	Pis	Ar	Tau	Gem
Feb 18	Sc	Sag	Sag	Cap	Cap	Aq	Pis	Pis	Ar	Tau	Gem	Gem
Feb 26	Sag	Sag	Sag	Cap	Aq	Aq	Pis	Ar	Tau	Tau	Gem	Can
Mar 6	Sag	Sag	Cap	Cap	Aq	Aq	Pis	Pis	Ar	Tau	Gem	Can
Mar 14	Sag	Cap	Cap	Aq	Aq	Pis	Ar	Tau	Tau	Gem	Gem	Can
Mar 22	Sag	Cap	Cap	Aq	Pis	Ar	Ar	Tau	Gem	Gem	Can	Can
Mar 30	Cap	Cap	Aq	Pis	Pis	Ar	Tau	Tau	Gem	Can	Can	Can
Apr 7	Cap	Cap	Aq	Pis	Ar	Ar	Tau	Gem	Gem	Can	Can	Leo
Apr 14	Cap	Aq	Aq	Pis	Ar	Tau	Tau	Gem	Gem	Can	Can	Leo
Apr 22	Cap	Aq	Pis	Ar	Ar	Tau	Gem	Gem	Can	Can	Leo	Leo
Apr 30	Aq	Aq	Pis	Ar	Tau	Tau	Gem	Can	Can	Can	Leo	Leo
May 8	Aq	Pis	Ar	Ar	Tau	Gem	Gem	Can	Can	Leo	Leo	Leo
May 16	Aq	Pis	Ar	Tau	Gem	Gem	Can	Can	Can	Leo	Leo	Vir
May 24	Pis	Ar	Ar	Tau	Gem	Gem	Can	Can	Leo	Leo	Leo	Vir
June 1	Pis	Ar	Tau	Gem	Gem	Can	Can	Can	Leo	Leo	Vir	Vir
June 9	Ar	Ar	Tau	Gem	Gem	Can	Can	Leo	Leo	Leo	Vir	Vir
June 17	Ar	Tau	Gem	Gem	Can	Can	Can	Leo	Leo	Vir	Vir	Vir
June 25	Tau	Tau	Gem	Gem	Can	Can	Leo	Leo	Leo	Vir	Vir	Lib
July 3	Tau	Gem	Gem	Can	Can	Can	Leo	Leo	Vir	Vir	Vir	Lib
July 11	Tau	Gem	Gem	Can	Can	Leo	Leo	Leo	Vir	Vir	Lib	Lib
July 18	Gem	Gem	Can	Can	Can	Leo	Leo	Vir	Vir	Vir	Lib	Lib
July 26	Gem	Gem	Can	Can	Leo	Leo	Vir	Vir	Vir	Lib	Lib	Sc
Aug 3	Gem	Can	Can	Can	Leo	Leo	Vir	Vir	Vir	Lib	Lib	Sc
Aug 11	Gem	Can	Can	Leo	Leo	Leo	Vir	Vir	Lib	Lib	Lib	Sc
Aug 18	Can	Can	Can	Leo	Leo	Vir	Vir	Vir	Lib	Lib	Sc	Sc
Aug 27	Can	Can	Leo	Leo	Leo	Vir	Vir	Lib	Lib	Lib	Sc	Sc
Sept 4	Can	Can	Leo	Leo	Leo	Vir	Vir	Vir	Lib	Lib	Sc	Sc
Sept 12	Can	Leo	Leo	Leo	Vir	Vir	Lib	Lib	Lib	Sc	Sc	Sag
Sept 20	Leo	Leo	Leo	Vir	Vir	Vir	Lib	Lib	Sc	Sc	Sc	Sag
Sept 28	Leo	Leo	Leo	Vir	Vir	Lib	Lib	Lib	Sc	Sc	Sag	Sag
Oct 6	Leo	Leo	Vir	Vir	Vir	Lib	Lib	Sc	Sc	Sc	Sag	Sag
Oct 14	Leo	Vir	Vir	Vir	Lib	Lib	Lib	Sc	Sc	Sag	Sag	Cap
Oct 22	Leo	Vir	Vir	Lib	Lib	Lib	Sc	Sc	Sc	Sag	Sag	Cap
Oct 30	Vir	Vir	Vir	Lib	Lib	Sc	Sc	Sc	Sag	Sag	Cap	Cap
Nov 7	Vir	Vir	Lib	Lib	Lib	Sc	Sc	Sc	Sag	Sag	Cap	Cap
Nov 15	Vir	Vir	Lib	Lib	Sc	Sc	Sc	Sag	Sag	Cap	Cap	Aq
Nov 23	Vir	Lib	Lib	Lib	Sc	Sc	Sag	Sag	Sag	Cap	Cap	Aq
Dec 1	Vir	Lib	Lib	Sc	Sc	Sc	Sag	Sag	Cap	Cap	Aq	Aq
Dec 9	Lib	Lib	Lib	Sc	Sc	Sag	Sag	Sag	Cap	Cap	Aq	Pis
Dec 18	Lib	Lib	Sc	Sc	Sc	Sag	Sag	Cap	Cap	Aq	Aq	Pis
Dec 28	Lib	Lib	Sc	Sc	Sag	Sag	Sag	Cap	Aq	Aq	Pis	Ar

RISING SIGNS—P.M. BIRTHS

	1 PM	2 PM	3 PM	4 PM	5 PM	6 PM	7 PM	8 PM	9 PM	10 PM	11 PM	12 MID-NIGHT
Jan 1	Tau	Gem	Gem	Can	Can	Can	Leo	Leo	Vir	Vir	Vir	Lib
Jan 9	Tau	Gem	Gem	Can	Can	Leo	Leo	Leo	Vir	Vir	Vir	Lib
Jan 17	Gem	Gem	Can	Can	Can	Leo	Leo	Vir	Vir	Vir	Lib	Lib
Jan 25	Gem	Gem	Can	Can	Leo	Leo	Leo	Vir	Vir	Vir	Lib	Lib
Feb 2	Gem	Can	Can	Can	Leo	Leo	Vir	Vir	Vir	Lib	Lib	Sc
Feb 10	Gem	Can	Can	Leo	Leo	Leo	Vir	Vir	Lib	Lib	Lib	Sc
Feb 18	Can	Can	Can	Leo	Leo	Vir	Vir	Vir	Lib	Lib	Sc	Sc
Feb 26	Can	Can	Leo	Leo	Leo	Vir	Vir	Lib	Lib	Lib	Sc	Sc
Mar 6	Can	Leo	Leo	Leo	Vir	Vir	Vir	Lib	Lib	Sc	Sc	Sc
Mar 14	Can	Leo	Leo	Vir	Vir	Vir	Lib	Lib	Lib	Sc	Sc	Sag
Mar 22	Leo	Leo	Leo	Vir	Vir	Lib	Lib	Lib	Sc	Sc	Sc	Sag
Mar 30	Leo	Leo	Vir	Vir	Vir	Lib	Lib	Sc	Sc	Sc	Sag	Sag
Apr 7	Leo	Leo	Vir	Vir	Lib	Lib	Lib	Sc	Sc	Sc	Sag	Sag
Apr 14	Leo	Vir	Vir	Vir	Lib	Lib	Sc	Sc	Sc	Sag	Sag	Cap
Apr 22	Leo	Vir	Vir	Lib	Lib	Lib	Sc	Sc	Sc	Sag	Sag	Cap
Apr 30	Vir	Vir	Vir	Lib	Lib	Sc	Sc	Sc	Sag	Sag	Cap	Cap
May 8	Vir	Vir	Lib	Lib	Lib	Sc	Sc	Sag	Sag	Sag	Cap	Cap
May 16	Vir	Vir	Lib	Lib	Sc	Sc	Sc	Sag	Sag	Cap	Cap	Aq
May 24	Vir	Lib	Lib	Lib	Sc	Sc	Sag	Sag	Sag	Cap	Cap	Aq
June 1	Vir	Lib	Lib	Sc	Sc	Sc	Sag	Sag	Cap	Cap	Aq	Aq
June 9	Lib	Lib	Lib	Sc	Sc	Sag	Sag	Sag	Cap	Cap	Aq	Pis
June 17	Lib	Lib	Sc	Sc	Sc	Sag	Sag	Cap	Cap	Aq	Aq	Pis
June 25	Lib	Lib	Sc	Sc	Sag	Sag	Sag	Cap	Cap	Aq	Pis	Ar
July 3	Lib	Sc	Sc	Sc	Sag	Sag	Cap	Cap	Aq	Aq	Pis	Ar
July 11	Lib	Sc	Sc	Sag	Sag	Sag	Cap	Cap	Aq	Pis	Ar	Tau
July 18	Sc	Sc	Sc	Sag	Sag	Cap	Cap	Aq	Aq	Pis	Ar	Tau
July 26	Sc	Sc	Sag	Sag	Sag	Cap	Cap	Aq	Pis	Ar	Tau	Tau
Aug 3	Sc	Sc	Sag	Sag	Cap	Cap	Aq	Aq	Pis	Ar	Tau	Gem
Aug 11	Sc	Sag	Sag	Sag	Cap	Cap	Aq	Pis	Ar	Tau	Tau	Gem
Aug 18	Sc	Sag	Sag	Cap	Cap	Aq	Pis	Pis	Ar	Tau	Gem	Gem
Aug 27	Sag	Sag	Sag	Cap	Cap	Aq	Pis	Ar	Tau	Tau	Gem	Gem
Sept 4	Sag	Sag	Cap	Cap	Aq	Pis	Pis	Ar	Tau	Gem	Gem	Can
Sept 12	Sag	Sag	Cap	Cap	Aq	Aq	Pis	Ar	Tau	Tau	Gem	Can
Sept 20	Sag	Cap	Cap	Aq	Pis	Pis	Ar	Tau	Gem	Gem	Can	Can
Sept 28	Cap	Cap	Aq	Aq	Pis	Ar	Tau	Tau	Gem	Gem	Can	Can
Oct 6	Cap	Cap	Aq	Pis	Ar	Ar	Tau	Gem	Gem	Can	Can	Leo
Oct 14	Cap	Aq	Aq	Pis	Ar	Tau	Tau	Gem	Gem	Can	Can	Leo
Oct 22	Cap	Aq	Pis	Ar	Ar	Tau	Gem	Gem	Can	Can	Leo	Leo
Oct 30	Aq	Aq	Pis	Ar	Tau	Tau	Gem	Can	Can	Can	Leo	Leo
Nov 7	Aq	Aq	Pis	Ar	Tau	Tau	Gem	Can	Can	Can	Leo	Leo
Nov 15	Aq	Pis	Ar	Tau	Gem	Gem	Can	Can	Can	Leo	Leo	Vir
Nov 23	Pis	Ar	Ar	Tau	Gem	Gem	Can	Can	Leo	Leo	Leo	Vir
Dec 1	Pis	Ar	Tau	Gem	Gem	Can	Can	Can	Leo	Leo	Vir	Vir
Dec 9	Ar	Tau	Tau	Gem	Can	Can	Can	Leo	Leo	Leo	Vir	Vir
Dec 18	Ar	Tau	Gem	Gem	Can	Can	Can	Leo	Leo	Vir	Vir	Vir
Dec 28	Tau	Tau	Gem	Gem	Can	Can	Leo	Leo	Vir	Vir	Vir	Lib

135

CHAPTER 9

Stay Healthy and Fit This Millennium Year

Of all the changes in the past few years, those involving our health care may have the most effect on our future well-being. Rather than depending on medical experts, we'll be taking on more and more responsibility for our own health, beginning with adopting a healthier lifestyle.

Astrology can help you sort out your health priorities and put your life on a healthier course. Since before the last millennium, different parts of the body and their potential illnesses have been associated with specific signs of the zodiac. Today's astrologers use these ancient associations not only to locate potential health problems, but also to help clients harmonize their activities with those favored by each sign.

Using the stars as a guide, you can create your own calendar for a healthier millennium, by focusing on the part of the body associated with each sun sign and the general health concerns related to that sign during the dates when each sign is predominant. By the end of the year, you should be healthier from head to toe.

Capricorn (December 22– January 19)

Capricorn, the sign of Father Time, brings up the subject of aging. If sags and wrinkles are keeping you from looking as young as you feel, you may want to investigate plastic surgery during this period. Many foods have anti-aging qualities and might be worth adding to your diet. Teeth are also ruled by this sign, a reminder to have regular cleanings and dental checkups.

Capricorn is also the sign of the workaholic, so be sure not to overdo in your quest for health. Plan for long-term gains and keep a steady, even pace for lasting results. Grim determination can be counterproductive if you're also trying to relieve tension, so remember to include pleasurable activities in your self-care program. Take up a sport for pure enjoyment, instead of pushing yourself to excel.

Here are some other health-producing things to do during Capricorn: Check your office environment for hidden health saboteurs, like poor air quality, poor lighting, and uncomfortable seating. Get an ergonomically designed chair to protect your back, or buy a specially designed back support cushion if your chair is uncomfortable. If you work at a computer, check your keyboard and the height of the computer screen for ergonomic comfort.

Capricorn rules the skeletal structure, which makes this a great time to look at the state of your posture and the condition of your bones and joints. It's never too early to counteract osteoporosis by adding weight-bearing exercise to your routine. If your joints (especially your knees) are showing early signs of arthritis, you may need to add calcium supplements to your diet. Check your posture, which affects your looks and your health. Remember to protect your knees when you work out or play sports, perhaps adding exercises to strengthen this area.

Aquarius (January 20–February 18)

Aquarius, the sign of high-tech gadgets and new ideas, should inspire you with new ways to get fit and healthy. This sign reminds us that we don't have to follow the crowd to keep fit. There are many ways to adapt your exercise routine to your individual needs. If your schedule makes it difficult to get to the gym or take regular exercise classes, look over the vast selection of exercise videos available and take class anytime you want. Or set up a gym at home with portable home exercise equipment.

New Age health treatments are favored by Aquarius, which makes this an ideal month to consider alternative approaches to health and fitness. Since Aquarius rules the circulatory system, you might benefit from a therapeutic massage, a relaxing whirlpool, or one of the new electronic massage machines. If your budget permits, this is an ideal month to visit one of the many wonderful health spas around the country for a spring tune-up.

Calves and ankles are Aquarius territory and should be emphasized in your exercise program. Be sure your ankles are well supported and protect yourself against sprains.

This is also a good time to consider the air quality around you. Aquarians are often vulnerable to airborne allergies and are highly sensitive to air pollution. Do some air quality control on your environment with an air purifier, ionizer, or humidifier. During flu season, read up on ways to strengthen your immune system.

Aquarius is a sign of reaching out to others, a cue to make your health regime more social—doing your exercises with friends could make staying fit more fun.

Pisces (February 19–March 20)

Perhaps it's no accident that we do spring cleaning during Pisces. The last sign of the zodiac, which rules the lymphatic system, is supersensitive to toxins. This is the ideal time to detox your system with a liquid diet or a supervised fast. This may also help you get rid of water retention, a common Pisces problem.

Feet are Pisces territory. Consider how often you take your feet for granted and how miserable life can be when your feet hurt. Since our feet reflect and affect the health of the entire body, devote some time this month to pampering them. Check your walking shoes or buy new ones tailored especially for your kind of exercise. Investigate orthotics, especially if you walk or run a lot. These custom-molded inserts could make a big difference in your comfort and performance.

The soles of our feet connect with all other parts of our body, just as the sign of Pisces embodies all the previous signs. This is the theory behind reflexology, a therapeutic foot massage technique that treats all areas of the body via the nerve endings on the soles of the feet. For the sake of your feet, as well as your entire body, consider treating yourself to a session with a local practitioner of this technique.

Pisces is the ideal time to start walking outdoors again, enjoying the first signs of Spring. Try doing local errands on foot, as much as possible.

Aries (March 21–April 19)

This Mars-ruled sign is a high-energy time of year. It's time to step up the intensity of your workouts, so you'll be in great shape for summer. Aerobics, competitive sports, and activities that burn calories are all favored. Try a new sport that has plenty of action and challenge, like soccer or bike racing. Be sure you have the proper headgear, since Aries rules the head.

Healthwise, if you've been burning the candle at both ends, or repressing anger, this may show up as headaches. The way to work off steam under Aries is to schedule extra time at the gym, take up a racket sport or ping pong—anything that lets you hit an object hard! If there's a martial arts studio nearby, why not investigate this fascinating form of exercise—you too can do Kung Fu! Or get into spring training with your local baseball team!

Taurus (April 20–May 20)

Spring is in full bloom, and what better time to awaken your senses to the beauty of nature? Planting a garden can be a relaxing antidote to a stressful job. Long walks in the woods, listening to the sounds of returning birds, and smelling the spring flowers help you slow down and enjoy the pleasures of the Earth. If you've been longing for a pet, why not adopt one now from your local animal shelter? Walking your new dog could bring you a new circle of animal-loving friends.

This is a month to enjoy all your senses. Add more beautiful music to your library, try some new recipes, take up a musical instrument, or learn the art of massage. This pleasure-loving time can be one of the most sensual in your love life, so plan a weekend getaway to somewhere special with the one you love.

This is also a time to go to local farmers' markets and add more fresh vegetables to your diet. While we're on the subject of food, you may be tempted to overindulge during the Taurus period, so be sure there are plenty of low-calorie treats available. If you are feeling too lethargic, your thyroid might be sluggish. Taurus is associated with the neck and throat area, which includes the thyroid glands and vocal cords.

Since we often hold tension in our neck area, pause several times during the day for a few stretches and head rolls. If you wake up with a stiff neck, you may be using the wrong kind of pillow. Perhaps a smaller, more flexible pillow filled with flax seeds would make a difference.

Gemini (May 21–June 20)

One of the most social times of year, Gemini is related to the nerves, our body's lines of communication, so this would be a great time to combine socializing with exercise—include friends in your exercise routines. Join a friendly exercise class or jogging group. Or learn a Gemini-type sport, such as tennis or golf, which will develop your timing and manual dexterity, and improve your communication with others.

If your nerves are on edge, you may need more fun and laughter in your life. Getting together with friends, going to parties, and doing things in groups brings more perspective into your life.

Since Gemini is also associated with the lungs, this is an ideal time to quit smoking. Investigate natural ways to relieve tension, such as yoga or meditation. Doing things with your hands—playing the piano, typing, doing craftwork—are also helpful.

Those of you who run, race-walk, or jog may want to try hand weights during the Gemini month, or add upper-body exercises to your daily routine.

Cancer (June 21–July 22)

Good health begins at home, and Cancer is the perfect time to do some healthy housekeeping. Evaluate your home for potential toxins in the water or building material. Could you benefit from air and water purifiers, un-dyed sheets and towels, biodegradable cleaners? How about safer cooking utensils of stainless steel or glass?

This is also a good month for nurturing others and yourself, airing problems and providing the emotional support that should make your home a happier, more harmonious place to live.

Cancer rules digestive difficulties, especially gastric ul-cers. Emotionally caused digestive problems—those stomach-knotting insecurities—can crop up under Can-cer. Baby yourself with some extra pampering if you're feeling blue.

All boating and water sports are ideal Cancer-time activities. Sometimes just a walk by your local pond or sitting for a few moments by a fountain can do wonders to relieve stress and tension.

If you've been feeling emotionally insecure, these feel-ings may be sensitized now, especially near the full moon. Being with loved ones, old friends, and family could supply the kind of support you need. Plan some special family activities that bring everyone close together.

The breast area is ruled by Cancer, a reminder to have regular checkups, according to your age and family history of breast-related illness.

Leo (July 23–August 22)

We're now in the heart of summer, the time when you need to consider your relationship to Leo's ruler, the sun. Tans do look great, but in recent years we've all been warned about the permanent damage the sun can do. So don't leave home without a big hat or an umbrella, along with some sunblock formulated for your skin type.

If you've been faithful to your exercise program, you probably look great in your swimsuit. If not, now's the time to contemplate some spot-reducing exercises to zero in on problem areas. This is prime time for outdoor activity—biking, swimming, team sports—that can supplement your routine. Leos like Arnold Schwartzenegger and Madonna are models of the benefits of weight training. Since this is a time to glorify the body beautiful, why not consider what a body-building regime could do for you?

Leo rules the upper back and heart, so consider your cardiovascular fitness and make your diet healthier for your heart. Are you getting enough aerobic exercise? Also, step up exercises that strengthen the Leo-ruled upper back, such as swimming.

If you have planned a vacation for this month, make it a healthy one, a complete change of pace. Spend time playing with children, expressing the child within yourself. The Leo time is great for creative activities and doing whatever you enjoy most.

Virgo (August 23–September 22)

Virgo is associated with the care of the body in general and the maintenance of the abdomen, digestive system, lower liver, and intestines in particular. This is a trouble-shooting time of year, the perfect weeks to check your progress, schedule medical exams and diagnostic tests, and generally evaluate your health. If you need a change of diet, supplements, or special care, consult the appropriate advisers.

It's also a good time to make your life run more efficiently. It's a great comfort to know that you've got a smooth organization backing you up. Go through your files and closets to eliminate clutter; edit your drawers and toss out whatever is no longer relevant to your life.

In this back-to-school time, many of us are taking self-improvement courses. Consider a course to improve your health—nutrition, macrobiotic cooking, or massage, for example.

Libra (September 23–October 22)

Are your personal scales in balance? If you're overdoing in any area of your life, Libra is an excellent time to address the problem. If you have been working too hard or taking life too seriously, what you may need is a dose of culture, art, music, or perhaps some social activity.

If your body is off balance, consider yoga, spinal adjustments, or a detoxification program. Libra rules the kidneys and lower back, which respond to relaxation and tension-relieving exercises. Make time to entertain friends and to be romantic with the one you love. Harmonize your body with chiropractic work; cleanse your kidneys with plenty of liquids.

Since this is the sign of relationships, you may enjoy working out with a partner or with loved ones. Make morning walks or weekend hikes family affairs. Take a romantic bicycle tour and picnic in the autumn countryside, putting more beauty in all areas of your life.

Libra is also the sign of grace—and what's more graceful than dance? If ballet is not your thing, why not swing to a Latin or African beat? Dancing combines art, music, romance, relaxation, graceful movement, social contact, and exercise. What more can you ask?

Scorpio (October 23–November 21)

If you have been keeping an exercise program all year, you should see a real difference—if not a total transformation—now. Scorpio is the time to transform yourself with a new hair color, get a makeover, change your style. Eliminate what's been holding you back, including self-destructive habits. These weeks of Scorpio should enhance your willpower and determination.

The sign rules the regenerative and eliminative organs, so it's a great time to turn over a new leaf. Sexual activity comes under Scorpio, so this can be a passionate time for love. It's also a good time to examine your attitudes about sex and to put safe sexual practices into your life.

It's no accident that this passionate time is football season, which reminds us that sports are a very healthy way to express or diffuse emotions. If you enjoy winter sports, why not prepare for the ski slopes or ice skating? Scorpio loves intense, life-or-death competition, so be sure your muscles are warmed up before going all out.

Sagittarius (November 22– December 21)

Ruled by a jovial Jupiter, this is holiday time, a time to kick back, socialize with friends, and enjoy a whirl of parties and get togethers. High-calorie temptations abound, so you may want to add an extra workout or two after hitting the buffet table. Or better yet, head for the dance floor instead of the hors d'oeuvres. Most people tend to loosen up on resolve around this time of year . . . there's just too much fun to be had.

If you can, combine socializing with athletic activities. Local football games, bike riding, hikes, and long walks with your dog in tow are just as much fun in cooler weather. Let others know that you'd like a health-promoting gift—sports equipment, a gym membership, or an exercise video—for Christmas. Plan your holiday buffet to lessen temptation with plenty of low-calorie choices.

In your workouts, concentrate on Sagittarius-ruled areas with exercises for the hips, legs, and thighs. This is a sports-loving sign, ideal for downhill or cross-country skiing or roller blading and basketball.

You may find the more spiritual kinds of exercise, such as yoga or tai chi, which work on the mind as well as the body, more appealing now. Once learned, these exercises can be done anywhere. Yoga exercises are especially useful for those who travel, especially those designed to release tension in the neck and back. Isometric-type exercises, which work one muscle group against another, can be done in a car or plane seat. If you travel often, investigate equipment that fits easily in your suitcase, such as water-filled weights, home gym devices, or elastic bands.

This sign of expansiveness offers the ideal opportunity to set your goals for next year. Ask yourself what worked best for you this year and where you want to be at the end of 2001. Most important, in holiday-loving Sagittarius-time, go for the health-promoting activities and sports you truly enjoy. These are the best for you in the long run, for they're the ones you'll keep doing with pleasure.

CHAPTER 10

Astrology Adventures on the Internet:

What's New, What's Exciting, and What's Free!

Would you like a free copy of your chart, some sophisticated software to perform all the astrology calculations and give you a beautiful printout, or a screensaver custom designed for your sign? Then boot up your modem and get ready to tour the thousands of astrology websites lighting up cyberspace.

There's a global community of astrologers online with sites that offer everything from chart services to chat rooms to individual readings. Even better, many of the most exciting sites offer *free* software, *free* charts, and *free* articles to download. You can virtually get an education in astrology from your computer screen, sharing your insights with new astrology-minded pals in a chat room or on a mailing list and later meeting them in person at one of the hundreds of conferences around the world.

So if you're curious to see a copy of your chart (or someone else's), a mini-reading, even a personalized zodiac screen saver, or perhaps order a copy of your favorite astrology book, log on!

One caveat, however: Since the Internet is constantly changing, some of these sites may have changed addresses or content, even though this selection was chosen with an eye to longevity. If this happens, there is usually a referral to the new site at the old address.

Free Charts

Go to this Internet address: *http://www.alabe.com*. Astro-labe Software distributes some of the most creative and easy-to-use programs now available. Guests at this site are rewarded with a free chart of the moment you log on. They will also E-mail a copy of your chart, as well as a mini reading.

For an immediate chart printout, surf to this address: *http://www.astro.ch/,* and check into Astrodienst, home of a world atlas that will give you the accurate longitude and latitude worldwide. Once you have entered your birthday and place of birth, your chart will be displayed, ready to be downloaded to your printer. One handy feature of this particular chart is that the planetary placement is written out in an easy-to-read list alongside the chart (an important feature, if you haven't yet learned the astrology glyphs).

Free Software

Go right to this address: *http://www.alabe.com*. There you will find a demo preview of Astrolabe Software, programs that are favored by many professional astrologers. If you're serious about studying astrology, you'll want to check out the latest demo version of "Solar Fire," one of the most user-friendly astrology programs available. Try the program the pros use before you buy—you'll be impressed!

If you would like a totally functional astrology program, go to this address: *http://www.magitech.com/~cruiser1/astrolog.htm*.

Walter Pullen's amazingly complete ASTROLOG program is offered absolutely free at this site. Here is a program that is ultra-sophisticated, can be adapted for all formats—DOS, WINDOWS, MAC, UNIX—and has some very cool features such as a revolving globe and a constellation map. It's a must for those who want to get involved with astrology without paying the big bucks for a professional-caliber program, or for those who want to add ASTROLOG's unique features to their astrology software library. This program has it all!

Another great resource for software is Astro Computing Services. Their website has free demos of several excellent programs. Note especially their Electronic Astrologer, one of the most effective and reasonably priced programs on the market. Go to *http://www.astrocom.com* for software, books, readings, chart services, and software demos.

Free Social Life

Join a newsgroup or mailing list! You'll never feel lonely again, but you will be very busy reading the letters that overflow your mailbox every day, so be prepared! Of the many new groups, there are several devoted to astrology. The most popular is "alt.astrology." Here's your chance to connect with astrologers worldwide, exchange information, and answer some of the skeptics who frequent this newsgroup. Your mailbox will be jammed with letters from astrologers from everywhere on the planet, sharing charts of current events, special techniques, and personal problems. Check the "Web Fest" site below for astrologers on the Festival mailing list, a popular list for professional astrologers and beginners alike.

Free Screen Saver

Matrix New Age Voices offers a way to put your sign in view with a beautifully designed graphic screensaver, downloadable at this site. There are also many other diversions at this site, so spend some enjoyable hours here. Address: *http://thenewage.com/*.

Astrology Course

Schedule a long visit to *http://www.panplanet.com/,* where you will find the Canopus Academy of Astrology, a site loaded with goodies. For the experienced astrologer there are excellent articles from top astrologers. They've done the work for you when it comes to picking the best astrology links on the Web, so be sure to check out those bestowed with the Canopus Award of Excellence.

Astrologer Linda Reid, an accomplished astrology teacher and author, offers a complete online curriculum for all levels of astrology study, plus individual tutoring. To get your feet wet, Linda is offering a beginners' course at this site. A terrific way to get well grounded in astrology.

Visit an Astro-Mall

Surf to: America Online's Astronet at *http://www. astronet.com.* To cater to the thousands of astrology fans who belong to the America Online service, the Astronet area offers interactive fun for everyone. This site is also accessible to outside visitors at the above address. At this writing, there's a special area for teenage astrology fans, access to popular astrology magazines like *American Astrology* and *Planet Earth,* advice to the lovelorn, plus a grab bag of horoscopes, featured guests, a shopping area for books, reports, software, even jewelry.

Find an Astrologer Here

Metalog Directory of Astrology:
http://www.astrologer.com

Looking for an astrologer in your local area? Perhaps you're planning a vacation in Australia or France and would like to meet astrologers or combine your activities with an astrology conference there? Go no further than this well-maintained resource. Here is an extensive worldwide list of astrologers and astrology sites. There is also an agenda of astrology conferences and seminars all over the world.

The A.F.A. Website:
http://www.astrologers.com

This is the interesting website of the prestigious American Federation of Astrologers. The A.F.A. has a very similar address to the Metalog Directory and also has a directory of astrologers, restricted to those who meet their stringent requirements. Check out their correspondence course if you would like to study astrology in depth.

Tools Every Astrologer Needs Are Online:

Internet Atlas:
http://www.astro.ch/atlas/

Find the geographic longitude and latitude and the correct time zone for any city worldwide. You'll need this information to calculate a chart.

The Zodiacal Zephyr:
http://www.zodiacal.com

A great place to start out your tour of the Astrology Internet. It has a wide selection of articles and tools for the astrologer, such as a U.S. and World Atlas, celebrity birth data, information on conferences, software, and tapes. The links at this site will send you off in the right direction.

Astrology World:
http://www.astrology-world.com

Astrologer Deborah Houlding has gathered some of the finest European astrologers for this terrific website. A great list of freebies at this site. A must!

Web Fest:
http://hudson.idt.net/~motive/

The imaginative graphics on this beautiful site are a treat. There's compilation of educational material, as well as biographies of top astrologers who contribute to the festival mailing list. Here is the place to look for an astrologer or an astrology teacher, or for information about joining the top-notch mailing list.

Astrology Alive:
http://www.astrologyalive.com/

Barbara Schermer has one of the most creative approaches to astrology. She's an innovator in the field and was one of the first astrologers to go online, so there's always a cutting edge to this site. Great list of links.

National Council for Geocosmic Research (NCGR):
http://www.geocosmic.org/

A key stop on any astrological tour of the Net. Here's where you can find out about local chapters in your area, or get information on their testing and certification programs. You can order lecture tapes from their nationwide conferences or get complete lists of conference topics. Good links to resources.

Charts of the Famous

This site has birthdays and charts of famous people to download: *http://www.astropro.com*

You can get the sun and moon sign, plus a biography of the hottest new stars, here: *http://www.celebsite. com*

Best General Search Engine: Yahoo
http://www.yahoo.com

You get the maximum search for your time at Yahoo. This search engine enters your input into other popular search engines.

Matrix Space Interactive:
http://thenewage.com

Browse this New-Age marketplace for free interactive astrology reports, an online astrology encyclopedia, lots of celebrity charts, and information about Matrix's excellent Winstar Plus and other astrology programs. A fun place to spend time.

For Astrology Books

National Clearinghouse for Astrology Books:
http://www.astroamerica.com

A wide selection of books on all aspects of astrology, from basics to advanced, as well as many hard-to-find books.

These addresses also have a good selection of astrology books, some of which are unique to the site.

http://www.panplanet.com
http://thenewage.com
http://www.astrocom.com

Browse the huge astrology list of online bookstore Amazon.com at *http:www.amazon.com/*

Your Astrology Questions Answered

Astrology FAQ (Frequently Asked Questions):
http://www.magitech.com/pub/astrology/ info/faq.txt

Questions that are on everyone's mind. Especially useful information when you're countering astrology-bashers.

History and Mythology of Astrology:
http://www.elore.com

Be sure to visit the astrology section of this gorgeous site, dedicated to the history and mythology of many traditions. One of the most beautifully designed sites we've seen.

The Mountain Astrologer:
http//www.mountainastrologer.com/ index.html

A favorite magazine of astrology fans, *The Mountain Astrologer,* has an interesting website featuring the latest news from an astrological point of view, plus feature articles from the magazine.

CHAPTER 11

The Sydney Omarr Yellow Pages

Ever wondered where to find astrologers in your area, where to get a basic astrology program for your new computer, or where to take a class with a professional astrologer? Look no further. In this chapter we'll give you the information you need to locate the latest products and services available.

There are very well-organized groups of astrologers all over the country who are dedicated to promoting the image of astrology in the most positive way. The National Council for Geocosmic Research (NCGR) is one nationwide group that is dedicated to bringing astrologers together, promoting fellowship and high-quality education. They have an accredited course system, with a systemized study of all the facets of astrology. Whether you'd like to know more about such specialties as financial astrology or the techniques for timing events, or if you'd prefer a psychological or mythological approach, you'll find the leading experts at NCGR conferences.

Your computer can be a terrific tool for connecting with other astrology fans at all levels of expertise. Even if you are using a "dinosaur" from the 1980s, there are still calculation and interpretation programs available for DOS and MAC formats. They may not have all the bells and whistles or exciting graphics, but they'll get the job done!

If you are a newcomer to astrology, it is a good idea to

learn the glyphs (astrology's special shorthand language) before you purchase a computer program. Use the chapter in this book to help you learn the symbols easily, so you'll be able to read the charts without consulting a book. Several programs, such as Astrolabe's "Solar Fire" for Windows, have pop-up definitions. Just click your mouse on a glyph or an icon on the screen and a window with an instant definition appears.

Astrology software is available at all price levels, from a sophisticated free application like "Astrolog," which you can download from the Internet, to inexpensive programs for under $100, to the more expensive astrology programs such as "Winstar," "Solar Fire," or "Io" (for the Mac), used by serious students and professionals. These are available from specialized dealers and cost approximately $200–$350. Before you make an investment, it's a good idea to download a sample from the company's website or order a demo disk from the company. If you just want to have fun, investigate an inexpensive program such as Matrix Software's "Kaleidoscope," an interactive application with lots of fun graphics. If you're baffled by the variety of software available, most of the companies on our list will be happy to help you find the right application for you needs.

If you live in an out-of-the-way place or are unable to fit classes into your schedule, correspondence courses are available. There are also online courses being offered at astrology websites. Some courses will send you a series of tapes; others use workbooks or computer printouts.

The Yellow Pages:

Nationwide Astrology Organizations and Conferences:

Contact these organizations for information on conferences, workshops, local meetings, conference tapes, or referrals:

National Council for Geocosmic Research

Educational workshops, tapes, conferences, and a directory of professional astrologers are available. For a $35 annual membership fee, you get their excellent educational publications and newsletters plus the opportunity to meet other astrology buffs at local chapter events in cities nationwide. For further information, contact:

Beverly Annen
9307 Thornewood Drive
Baltimore, MD 21234
Phone: 410-882-2856

Or visit their web page: http://www.geocosmic.org

American Federation of Astrologers (A.F.A.)

One of the oldest astrological organizations in the U.S., established 1938, it offers conferences, conventions, and a correspondence course. It will refer you to an accredited A.F.A. astrologer.

P.O. Box 22040
Tempe, AZ 85382
Phone: 602-838-1751
FAX: 602-838-8293

A.F.A.N. (Association for Astrological Networking)

Did you know that astrologers are still being arrested for practicing in some states? AFAN provides support and legal information, working toward improving the public image of astrology. Here are the people who will go to bat for astrology when it is attacked in the media. Everyone who cares about astrology should join!

A.F.A.N.
8306 Wilshire Blvd.
Berkeley Hills, CA 90211

ARC Directory

(Listing of Astrologers Worldwide)
2920 E. Monte Vista
Tucson, AZ 85716
602-321-1114

Pegasus Tapes

(Lectures, Conference tapes)
P.O. Box 419
Santa Ysabel, CA 92070

International Society for Astrological Research

(Lectures, Workshops, Seminars)
P.O. Box 38613
Los Angeles, CA 90038

ISIS Institute

(Newsletter, Conferences, Astrology tapes, Catalog)
P.O. Box 21222
El Sobrante, CA 94820-1222
Phone: 800-924-4747 or 510-222-9436
FAX: 510-222-2202

Computer Software

Astrolabe

Check out the latest version of their powerful "Solar Fire Windows" software, a breeze to use. This company also markets a variety of programs for all levels of expertise, a wide selection of computer astrology readings, and MAC programs. It's a good resource for innovative software as well as applications for older computers.

Box 1750–R
Brewster, MA 02631
800-843-6682

Matrix Software

You'll find a wide variety of software in all price ranges, demo disks at student and advanced level, and lots of interesting readings. Check out "Kaleidoscope," an inexpensive program with beautiful graphics, and "Winstar Plus," their powerful professional software, if you're planning to study astrology seriously.

315 Marion Ave.
Big Rapids, MI 49307
800-PLANETS

Astro Communications Services

Find books, software for MAC and IBM compatibles, individual charts, and telephone readings. Find technical astrology materials here, such as "The American Ephemeris." A good resource for those who do not have computers—they will calculate charts for you.

Dept. AF693, PO Box 34487
San Diego, CA 92163-4487
800-888-9983

Air Software

This is powerful, creative astrology software. For beginners, check out the "Father Time" program, which finds your best days, or "Nostradamus," which answers all your questions. There's also the "Airhead" astrology game, a fun way to test your knowledge.

115 Caya Avenue
West Hartford, CT 06110
800-659-1247

Time Cycles Research

(Beautiful graphic IO Series programs for the MAC)

375 Willets Avenue
Waterford, CT 06385
FAX: 869-442-0625
E-mail: astrology@timecycles.com
Internet: http://www.timecycles.com

Astro-Cartography

(Charts for location changes)

Astro-Numeric Service Box 336-B
Ashland, OR 97520
800-MAPPING

Microcycles

Which software is right for you? The "world's largest astrological software dealer" can help you get up and running. Call for catalogs or demo diskettes:

PO Box 2175
Culver City, CA 90231
800-829-2537

Astrology Magazines

In addition to articles by top astrologers, most have listings of astrology conferences, events, and local happenings.

AMERICAN ASTROLOGY
475 Park Avenue South
New York, NY 10016

DELL HOROSCOPE
P.O. Box 53352
Boulder, CO 89321-3342

PLANET EARTH
The Great Bear
P.O. Box 5164
Eugene, OR 97405

MOUNTAIN ASTROLOGER
P.O. Box 11292
Berkeley, CA 94701

ASPECTS
Aquarius Workshops
P.O. Box 260556
Encino, CA 91426

Astrology Schools:

Though there are many correspondence courses available through private teachers and astrological organizations, up until now there has never been an accredited college of astrology. That is why the following address is so important.

The Kepler College of Astrological Arts and Sciences

By the time this book is published, Kepler College, the first institution of its kind to combine an accredited liberal arts education with extensive astrological studies, should be in operation. A degree-granting college that is also a center of astrology, has long been the dream of the astrological community and will be a giant step forward in providing credibility to the profession.
For more information:

The Kepler College of Astrological Arts and Sciences
P.O. Box 77511
Seattle, WA 98177-0511
Phone: 206-706-0658
or http://www.keplercollege.org

CHAPTER 12

Is Your Life at a Crossroads?

Consider a Personal Reading

Now that the millennium is here, you may wonder if, at this important crossroads, now is the time for you to get a personal reading to plot your future course or help clarify issues in your personal life. Here is some guidance to help you sort through the variety of readings available.

The first thing you'll discover is that there seem to be as many different kinds of readings as there are astrologers. Besides face-to-face readings with a professional astrologer, there are mini-readings at psychic fairs, pay-by-the minute phone readings that can either be tape recorded or a live exchange with an "astrologer," offerings of beautiful computer-generated readings and many pages of "personal" interpretation. If you have access to the Internet, a simple search under "Astrology" will produce a mind-boggling array of websites. Online chat rooms and mailing lists dedicated to astrology are other resources frequented by professional astrologers as well as interested amateurs.

To confuse the matter further, astrologers themselves have specialties. Some are skilled in the technique of horary astrology, which involves answering questions based on the time the question is asked. Some astrologers are psychologically oriented; others are more practical. Some use traditional methods; others use more exotic techniques from India or China.

Though you can learn much about astrology from

books such as this one, nothing compares to a one-on-one consultation with a professional who has analyzed thousands of charts and can pinpoint the potential in yours. With your astrologer, you can address specific immediate problems in your life that may be holding you back. For instance, if you are not getting along with your mate or coworker, you could leave the reading with some new insights and some constructive ways to handle the situation. If you are going through a crisis in your life, an astrologer who is also a trained counselor might help you examine your options . . . and there are many astrologers who now combine their skills with training in psychology.

Before your reading, a reputable astrologer will ask for the date, time (as accurately as possible), and place of birth of the subject of the reading. (A horoscope can be cast about anything that has a specific time and place.) Most astrologers will then enter this information into a computer, which will calculate your chart (perhaps several types of charts related to your situation) in seconds. From the resulting chart or charts, the astrologer will do an interpretation.

If you don't know your exact birth time, you can usually find it filed at the Bureau of Vital Statistics at the city hall or county seat of the state where you were born. If you still have no success in getting your time of birth, some astrologers can estimate an approximate birth time by using past events in your life to determine the chart.

How to Find a Good Astrologer

Your first priority should be to choose a qualified astrologer. Rather than relying on word of mouth or grandiose advertising claims, do this with the same care you would choose any trusted adviser such as a doctor, lawyer, or banker. Unfortunately, anyone can claim to be an astrologer—to date, there is no licensing of astrologers or established professional criteria. However, there are nationwide organizations of serious, committed astrologers that can help you in your search.

Good places to start your investigation are organizations such as the American Federation of Astrologers or the National Council for Geocosmic Research (NCGR), which offers a program of study and certification. If you live near a major city, there is sure to be an active NCGR chapter or astrology club in your area—many are listed in astrology magazines available at your local newsstand. In response to many requests for referrals, the NCGR has compiled a directory of professional astrologers, which includes a glossary of terms and an explanation of specialties within the astrological field. Contact the NCGR headquarters (see the resource list in this book) for information.

As a potentially lucrative freelance business, astrology has always attracted self-styled experts who may not have the knowledge or the counseling experience to give a helpful reading. These astrologers can range from the well-meaning amateur to the charlatan or street-corner gypsy who has for many years given astrology a bad name. Be very wary of astrologers who claim to have occult powers or who make pretentious claims of celebrated clients or miraculous achievements. You can often tell from the initial phone conversation if the astrologer is legitimate. He or she should ask for your birthday time and place and conduct the conversation in a professional manner. Any astrologer who gives a reading based only on your sun sign is highly suspect. Be especially wary of fly-by-night corner gypsies, who claim to be astrologers.

When you arrive at the reading, the astrologer should be prepared. The consultation should be conducted in a private, quiet place. The astrologer should be interested in your problems of the moment. A good reading involves feedback on your part, so if the reading is not relating to your concerns, you should let the astrologer know. Feel free to ask questions and get clarifications of technical terms. The reading should be an interaction between two people, rather than a solo performance. The more you actively participate, rather than expecting the astrologer to carry the reading or come forth with oracular predictions, the more meaningful your experience will be. An astrologer should help you validate your current experience and be frank about possible negative happenings, but suggest a positive course of action.

In their approach to a reading, some astrologers may be more literal, others more intuitive. Those who have had counseling training may take a more psychological approach. Though some astrologers may seem to have an almost psychic ability, extrasensory perception or any other parapsychological talent is not essential. A very accurate picture can be drawn from the data in your horoscope chart.

An astrologer may do several charts for each client, including one for the time of birth and a "progressed chart," showing the evolution from birth to the present time. According to your individual needs, there are many other possibilities, such as a chart for a different location, if you are contemplating a change of place. Relationships between any two people, things, or events can be interpreted with a chart that compares the two horoscopes. Another commonly used device is a composite chart, which uses the midpoint between planets in two individual charts to describe the relationship.

An astrologer will be particularly interested in transits—times when planets will pass over the planets or sensitive points in your chart, which can signal important events in your life.

Many astrologers offer tape-recorded readings, another option to consider. In this case, you'll be mailed a tape of a reading based on your birth chart. Though this reading is more personal than a computer printout and can give you valuable insights, it is not equivalent to a live dialogue with an astrologer, where you can discuss your specific interests and issues of the moment.

About Telephone Readings

Telephone readings come in two varieties. One is a dial-in taped reading, usually by a well-known astrologer.

The other is a live consultation with an "astrologer" on the other end of the line. The taped readings are general daily or weekly forecasts, applied to all members of your sign and charged by the minute. The quality depends on the astrologer. One caution: Be aware that these readings can run up quite a telephone bill, especially if you get into the habit of calling every day. Be sure that you are aware of the per-minute cost of each call beforehand. (It might be wise to keep a timer next to the phone, to limit your calls beforehand.)

Live telephone readings also vary with the expertise of the astrologer. The advantage of a live telephone reading is that your individual chart is used and you can ask about a specific problem. Usually the astrologer on the other end of the line will enter your birth data into a computer and use the chart it generates during the reading. However, before you invest in any reading, be sure that your astrologer is qualified and that you fully understand in advance how much you will be charged.

About Computer Readings

Most of the companies that offer computer programs (such as ACS, Matrix, ASTROLABE) also offer computer-generated horoscope interpretations. These can be quite comprehensive, offering a beautiful printout of the chart plus many pages of information. A big plus is that you'll receive an accurate copy of your chart, which can be used for future reference. The accompanying natal chart interpretation can be a good way to learn about your own chart at your convenience, since most readings interpret the details of the chart in a very understandable way. However, since there is no input from you, the interpretations will be general and may not address your immediate issues.

This is still a good option for a first reading, to get your feet wet, especially since these printouts are much lower in cost than live consultations. You might consider them as either a supplement or preparation for a live reading (study one before you have a live reading to get familiar with your chart and plan specific questions). They also make a terrific gift for someone interested in astrology. If you are considering this type of reading, look into one of the companies on our astrology resource list.

CHAPTER 13

Your Pisces Star Quality

All About Your Pisces Sun Sign

As a Pisces sun sign, you'll find that the qualities associated with this sign resonate through the many roles you play in life. And if there are other Pisces planets in your horoscope, or if your rising sign is Pisces, these conditions will intensify your Pisces-type personality. There'll be no mistaking you for another sun sign! For example, someone with a Pisces sun, Mars, and rising sign (ascendant) is likely to be much more obviously a "Pisces" type than someone with a Pisces sun combined with an outgoing Leo ascendant and an aggressive Mars in Aries. However, even if you have a different personality than the typical Pisces, you'll find that many of the traits and preferences described on the following pages will still apply to you.

The Pisces Man: Riding the Crest

The Pisces man has been characterized too often as a romantic adventurer with no roots in reality. In the last decade, however, Pisces men have come to the forefront with some of the biggest success stories. The proverbial boy from the mailroom who now owns the world's largest record company (David Geffen), the head of a global communications network (Rupert Murdoch), the arbiter of fashion tastes who decides what's IN and OUT (John Fairchild), and the head of a powerful entertainment conglomerate (Michael Eisner) are a few examples of the Pisces man who shows that he can be a shark as well as a charming goldfish, a surfer of life with an uncanny sense of when and how to catch the best wave.

The Pisces man often puzzles more predictable signs with your chameleon-like personality that seems to take on the colorations of each environment. You have an amazing ability to adapt to different situations and people, socializing with the jet set one day and hanging out at a working-class bar the next, reveling in a constantly changing cast of characters.

What makes you so adaptable is your sensitivity, which some Pisces go to great lengths to hide, with good reason. Your compassion also attracts many who take advantage of your good nature. And, since Pisces picks up moods from your surroundings, negative influences from these people can be disastrous. It is often a Pisces challenge to find a way to help others without being martyred yourself.

Once Pisces finds a place where your talents are appreciated, you can be extremely successful. Your intuitive ability to spot trends, your creative imagination, and your ability to second-guess the competition work in your favor. But before you settle down, you may go through a period of drifting and soul-searching until you determine who you are and where you are going. Many Pisces men fall under the influence of drugs and alcohol during this time, unless they have strong outside support. With positive, constructive influences, you'll use your varied experiences as grist for creative ideas or find work that gives you the variety you crave, like writer Tom Wolfe or film directors Spike Lee and Robert Altman.

In a Relationship

The positive Pisces man makes a loving partner who will keep the romance going long after the wedding. You are very susceptible to female charms, but you'll remain faithful if your wife gives you oceans of emotional support and steadily builds your self-esteem. Not the take-over type, you need constant stroking and reassurance. The woman who imposes her will on you or tries to boss you will find you slip through her fingers. If she can strike the right balance of support and stroking, however, you'll be an appreciative, sensual, and romantic lover for life!

The Pisces Woman: A Storybook Heroine

The Pisces woman is likely to have a life story worthy of a novel. She embodies a combination of glamour, talent, and sympathy that seems to attract dramatic scenarios. The most receptive, compassionate, empathetic sign of the zodiac, you often dive beneath the waters of the emotions. You're attracted to the underdog, and one of your paradoxes is that by helping the sick or needy, you miraculously gain prestige, power, and financial stability for yourself—if you don't become so involved in the troubles of others that you actually absorb them yourself. But many Pisces, like Elizabeth Taylor and Sally Jessy Raphael come out of the depths of difficult experiences to emerge victorious and stronger than ever.

Like your symbol, the fishes swimming in opposite directions while tied together, you're full of contradictions. You are really many women in one, and what fascinating characters you all are! Here is the ravishing beauty who swears like a dockworker, the socialite who runs off with her bodyguard, the sophisticated talk-show hostess with half a dozen children, the wholesome Miss America haunted by past scandal, the desperately impoverished teenager who became an ambassador. Never predictable, Pisces hides much strength and resourcefulness under her ultrafeminine exterior. Deceptively fragile and vulnerable, you only seem vague and dreamy. You're actually quite capable of fending for yourself, especially when you use your arsenal of creative talents.

Pisces's great challenge is to live up to your great compassion and sensitivity. Your sympathy encompasses everyone who is suffering, and you'll often champion causes that others reject as too controversial, such as Elizabeth Taylor's work on behalf of AIDS. But you must learn to discriminate in order to protect yourself against those who play upon your sympathies. By building up your own self-esteem, and by learning to discern the really needy from those who would merely drain your energy, you can truly help others and reward yourself with a feeling of accomplishment.

It is especially important for Pisces to find an outlet for your powerful feelings, preferably one that rewards your self-expression with financial security. Gloria Vanderbilt, once the poor little rich girl, made her own fortune after forty as a fashion designer. Rue McClanahan of *Golden Girls* and talk-show hostess Sally Jessy Raphael are other examples of Pisces who have had several profitable creative careers. Model and TV hostess Cindy Crawford is another Pisces who capitalized on her beauty and talent. Extremely compassionate, you can enter and absorb a role that makes you an excellent actress. Pisces women also do well in sports (Jackie Joyner-Kersee), where they can lose themselves in their activity.

Along with success stories are the inevitable tear-jerker tales of Pisces whose scandalous ups and downs, marriages, and bouts with alcohol and drugs are chronicled in the tabloids. The love lives of Patty Hearst, Elizabeth Taylor, Tammy Faye Bakker, Ivana Trump, and Dorothy Stratten became real-life soap operas. When you are drowning in your emotions, you can be easily threatened, jealous, possessive, a clinging vine. Or your feelings may get the better of you physically, creating illnesses. You become fulfilled when you can express your feeling in some artistic or creative way. This quickly puts you on the road to confidence, self-esteem, and financial independence.

In a Relationship

Even the most liberated and independent of this sign can easily perceive what her partner wants and switch into the appropriate role, often being both wife and mistress to the one you love. However, many men prefer not to marry their Pisces paramours, choosing them as a diversion from their confining domestic life. Because you are so willing to indulge a man's fantasies, you've been called the most dangerous "other woman" of the zodiac.

Though you may prefer to leave practical matters to your partner so you can focus on your creative talents, you have a surprisingly practical side, which is quite able to balance the budget. Negatively, you're not above using a bit of emotional manipulation, playing the martyr or victim to get your way. You need a mate who appreciates your many talents and helps you put them to constructive use.

The Pisces Family

The Pisces Parent

Having children brings out the loving, supportive side of Pisces, and can provide stability and a new sense of meaning and direction to your life. Children are often the anchor Pisces needs to stop drifting and set goals. Your intuitive sensitivity to young children's needs and developing feelings gives them gentle, nonjudgmental support, while your creativity makes learning and playtime special. Yours is the sign most capable of unconditional love, and you are particularly nurturing to a child who is needy or handicapped in some way. Typical of the caring nature of Pisces is the story of the famous actress who chose to adopt a crippled child and help it regain health. On the negative side, you should cultivate detachment and objectivity in order to deal with the emotional ups and downs of your child. A fulfilling marriage will assure that you will not overinvest emotionally in the child and will be willing to let go when the time comes for independence.

The Pisces Stepparent

As one of the most adaptable and compassionate signs, you can easily open your heart to stepchildren and sympathize with their feelings. You'll be especially supportive of your mate in the period of transition and willingly give up some of your own priorities to smooth over this delicate situation. Using your natural sense of theater and glamour, you can easily fascinate this young audience and channel their feelings into creative activities. But you may also have to assert your authority to gain their respect as well as their love. Since these children need your love and understanding, you will give it wholeheartedly.

The Pisces Grandparent

Pisces grandparents can share a magical world of fantasy with their grandchildren. When you enter their world, you become like a child again yourself. You're their special permissive playmate who never competes with parents for disciplinary rights. You're the accomplice who joins them in mischievous pranks. Through opening their minds to fantasy, you're their best teacher—the one who teaches them that it's okay to dream, for most creative ideas happen when you're playing. You'll live in their memories because you've touched their hearts and awakened their imagination.

CHAPTER 14

Show Off the Pisces in You

Pisces Self-Expression

Everyone's intrigued by their sun sign personality. But did you know that it also influences the styles that present you at your best, the colors and sounds that lift your mood, even the best places to vacation? Why not try putting more Pisces style in every area of your life and see if it doesn't make a happier difference!

Pisces at Home

Pisces likes to live out some of your fantasies in your environment, and what a safe place to live out the roles of your dreams. Many Pisces homes reflect a taste for the exotic, with artwork, crafts, and fabrics from faraway places. Ideally, you would like your home to overlook the ocean, but you can create your own water element inside with marine paintings, a shell collection, an aquarium, and walls painted in the many colors of the sea.

Pisces should pay special attention to comfort underfoot. Wonderful floor tiles, polished wood, and exotic carpets can make your home special. Dive into piles of beautiful pillows, walk barefoot on lush carpet, or lounge on floor pillows. Pisces often share their habitat with animal friends, so find some decorative baskets and scratch posts (and buy a powerful vacuum cleaner).

Talented Pisces should showcase their own artwork, ceramics, or photography at home. Photos of loved ones, romantic pools of light, and large mirrors reflect your live-in tastes and create the right atmosphere on a limited budget.

The Pisces Beat

Dreamy, emotional music by Chopin or Ravel stirs Pisces souls. Baroque music such as Handel's "Water Music" and Vivaldi's "Four Seasons" stimulate creative work. New Age meditative music and dance music, especially ballet themes, puts you in a relaxed mood. Pisces voices are James Taylor, Harry Belafonte, Johnny Cash, opera's Kiri Te Kanawa and Renata Scotto, and Nat (King) Cole.

Great Vacation Adventures for Pisces

Places with romance and fantasy appeal strongly to Pisces. And if they are near water, so much the better! Venice, Portugal, Alexandria, and Normandy fill the bill. Spiritual Pisces should seek out power spots such as Glastonbury, England, where King Arthur is buried; the ruins of Tulum, on the coast of Mexico; the mountains of Hawaii; and the sandy oceans of the Sahara desert. Or you might scuba dive in search of Atlantis off the coast of Bimini. In the United States, head for the crashing surf of Monterey, the Maine coast, or the coral reefs of the Virgin Islands. Romantic Vermont is an inland Pisces-ruled place.

Pisces with their minds on romance may forget their toothbrushes, so pack a case ahead of time with all the essentials. In fact, for an important trip, pack all your bags well in advance, when your concentration is best. The more advance planning the better, when you're traveling for business. To make your trip run smoothly, tap into the Virgo (your polar opposite) side of your nature; make countdown lists and check them off methodically; be sure you have double sets of directions, the proper insurance, and enough foreign money. Keep a special travel folder with all your papers organized. But not to worry: your charm is so enchanting that others are usually happy to help you during your travels (it's one way to meet new friends!).

Your Pisces Colors

All the colors of the sea—iridescent fish scales, coral, seafoam green, and the deep aquamarine of tropical waters.

Pisces Fashion Tips

Pisces likes a wardrobe that enables you to play many roles. You rarely limit yourself to one look. You'll switch with ease from crisp, efficient office clothes to romantic evening wear or casual sporty weekend outfits. But you are in your element when you wear glamorous clothes with a theatrical flair. After all, you are master of glamour and illusion. Like Sharon Stone, you can look like a mermaid in simple sequins, or wear a Gap T-shirt to a formal party with a few diamonds added for sparkle. Or take on another personality in tweeds. Keep your weight down so you can wear the dramatic styles you love best. Your makeup should play up your beautiful eyes to the max!

Pisces Fashion Leaders

For fashion inspiration, there are several Pisces designers who understand the looks that suit you best. For elegant, feminine fashion and fragrances, no one knows better than Hubert de Givenchy. For more colorful, young, avant-garde styles, there is Kenzo and Wendy Dagworthy.

Pisces Edibles

When in doubt, choose a place that specializes in seafood, especially if the restaurant has an ocean, lake, or river view. Exotic food has special appeal for adventurous Pisces. A romantic atmosphere, with candle-light and soft music, also wins big with Pisces. Stay away from places with loud noise and a frantic atmosphere.

CHAPTER 15

Unleash Your Pisces Potential—Find the Work You Love!

The key to Pisces success is to find a place where your sensitivity works for you rather than against you. That usually means a creative field, though Pisces can bring creativity to high finance, publishing, science, and medicine as well. You flourish in a supportive environment, where you are given the freedom to develop your ideas. Avoid rigid, structured companies, office politics, and overbearing employers who simply exploit your talents. Power games can sap your energy and divert your creativity. Instead, put your sensitive antennae to work psyching out the competition, divining the consumer mood, and understanding the hidden agendas of your coworkers. Choose associates and employers with positive mental attitudes who show appreciation for your efforts. You'll bloom in an open, unstructured situation, with plenty of encouragement. Pisces-influenced areas are the oil, perfume, footwear, and film industries. Alcohol and drugs are also Pisces-ruled, but work in those area will require self-discipline, since Pisces is very susceptible to alcohol and drug abuse. The caring and healing professions capitalize on your natural empathy with clients, offering many opportunities in psychotherapy, nursing, and home health care, especially. Glamour fields of fashion and beauty, as well as theater in any form, are always Pisces havens.

Pisces in Charge

The Pisces boss has uncanny intuition. You grasp the thoughts and trends in the air as if by magic. Extremely creative, you may prefer to work alone and do your real thinking in solitude, though you are very compassionate and caring of your subordinates and, oddly, they are protective of you in return, sometimes shielding you from office politics. Though they may be baffled by your unpredictable moods (sometimes your sweet temper can turn mean as a shark) and your vague sense of direction (be sure to put your order in writing), they adore you for your caring concern and standout talent.

Pisces Teamwork

Pisces does your best work when you are not tied down to a routine or made to punch a time clock. But even though you need creative freedom and require little supervision, you also need the security of a stable working environment. Because you are not one to step on toes to get ahead, or fight to keep your position, intense competition can upset your delicate sense of balance and distract you from the work you do best.

You'll turn out extraordinary work in a job where your talents are unique and appreciated. Because you can adapt to many situations easily and are extremely versatile, you may take time to discover your professional potential, floating from job to job, often going far adrift of your original direction. But perceptions gained from these diverse experiences only enhance your talent and professional value. You'll amaze others with your success and stamina when you finally find a job that fully engages your abilities.

To Get Ahead Fast

Look for a positive, supportive working environment with plenty of creative opportunity. Play up these attributes.

- Creativity
- Insight
- Tact
- Charm
- Empathy
- Intuition
- Talent
- Timing

Pisces Success Stories

Study these Pisces tycoons to learn how to capitalize on your sign's special talents.

David Geffen
Michael Eisner (Disney Studios)
Rupert Murdoch (press tycoon)
John Fairchild (*Women's Wear Daily* publisher)
Lawrence Tish and Harry Helmsley (real estate tycoons)
Alan Greenspan (Federal Reserve Chairman)
Gianni Agnelli (international billionaire)
Walter Annenberg
Robert M. Bass
Gloria Vanderbilt
Robert Mossbacher
Senator Daniel Patrick Moynihan

CHAPTER 16

Pisces Celebrities—From Hollywood to the Halls of Power

Here's a list of the current crop of celebrities born under your Pisces sun sign. Although it's fun to see who shares your birthday, this list can also be a useful tool to practice what you've learned so far about astrology. Use it to compare similarities and differences between the celebrities who embody Pisces traits and those who don't. Look up the other planets in the horoscope of your favorites to see how their influence might color the sun sign emphasis.

Prince Andrew (2/19/60)
Smokey Robinson (2/19/40)
Justine Bateman (2/19/66)
Sidney Poitier (2/20/25)
Kelsey Grammar (2/20/55)
Kurt Cobain (2/20/67)
Gloria Vanderbilt (2/20/24)
Cindy Crawford (2/20/66)
Ivana Trump (2/20/49)
Tyne Daly (2/21/46)
Rue McClanahan (2/21/34)
Mary-Chapin Carpenter (2/21/58)
Jill Eikenberry (2/21/47)
Drew Barrymore (2/22/75)
Kyle MacLachlan (2/22/59)
Julius Erving (2/22/50)

Peter Fonda (2/23/39)
Edward J. Olmos (2/24/47)
Paula Zahn (2/24/56)
George Harrison (2/25/43)
Tea Leoni (2/25/66)
Sally Jessy Raphael (2/25/43)
Michael Bolton (2/26/53)
Johnny Cash (2/26/32)
Elizabeth Taylor (2/27/32)
Mary Frann (2/27/43)
Joanne Woodward (2/27/30)
Mario Andretti (2/28/40)
Bernadette Peters (2/28/48)
Bugsy Siegal (2/28/06)
John Turturro (2/28/57)
Tommy Tune (2/28/39)
Dinah Shore (3/1/17)
Ron Howard (3/1/54)
Jon Bon Jovi (3/2/62)
Mikhail Gorbachev (3/2/31)
Desi Arnaz (3/2/17)
Jackie Joyner-Kersee (3/3/62)
Chastity Bono (3/4/69)
Niki Taylor (3/5/75)
Samantha Egger (3/5/39)
Tom Arnold (3/6/59)
Rob Reiner (3/6/47)
Stedman Graham (3/6/51)
Willard Scott (3/7/34)
Tammy Faye Bakker (3/7/42)
Michael Eisner (3/7/42)
Lynn Swann (3/7/52)
Daniel J. Travanti (3/7/40)
John Heard (3/7/46)
Cyd Charisse (3/8/23)
Lynn Redgrave (3/8/43)
Faith Daniels (3/9/57)
Kato Kaelin (3/9/59)
Raul Julia (3/9/40)
Chuck Norris (3/10/42)
Prince Edward (3/10/64)

Sharon Stone (3/10/58)
Shannon Miller (3/10/77)
Lawrence Welk (3/11/03)
James Taylor (3/12/48)
Liza Minelli (3/12/46)
Neil Sedaka (3/13/39)
Dana Delany (3/13/56)
Albert Einstein (3/14/1879)
Michael Caine (3/14/33)
Billy Crystal (3/14/47)
Prince Albert of Monaco (3/14/58)
Fabio (3/15/61)
Park Overall (3/15/57)
Jerry Lewis (3/16/26)
Kate Nelligan (3/16/51)
Kurt Russell (3/17/51)
Patrick Duffy (3/17/49)
Vanessa Williams (3/18/63)
Charley Pride (3/18/38)
Glenn Close (3/19/47)
Bruce Willis (3/19/55)
Ursula Andress (3/19/36)
William Hurt (3/20/50)
Jerry Reed (3/20/37)
Holly Hunter (3/20/58)
Spike Lee (3/20/57)
Mr. Rogers (3/20/28)
Theresa Russell (3/20/57)

CHAPTER 17

Astrological Outlook for Pisces in 2000

In the universal zodiac, Pisces rules the past, including prenatal influences, the manner of conception, and the impact of your ancestors, ethnic clans, and tribes. You will face the millennium with one foot in the future, the other in the past, because never do you want to lose sight of all that you learned through experience.

As a result, you will be fearless during this millennium. You'll recognize the new opportunities coming to you personally, as well as society as a whole. However, more carefully than others, you'll evaluate them in the light of history.

You will benefit from previous victories and defeats. You'll insist on honoring spiritual traditions and shy away from those who throw out the baby with the dirty bathwater.

Throughout the year, your twelfth house is packed. Aside from the sun, moon, and your personal planets (Mars, Venus, and Mercury), mighty Uranus, ruler of your twelfth house, and Neptune, your dominant orb, will be in your twelfth house, keeping you constantly aware of all that has gone before in your life. At times, these planets will be going forward, but between late May and late October, they will be hovering and giving you time to adjust and absorb.

You will be reviewing, changing your mind about some decisions made earlier. You will be strongly conscious of the fateful turns you took on destiny's long road.

Saturn, lord of your eleventh house of public interests, friendships, church and club membership and participation, will spend the millennium in Taurus and Gemini, giving stabilization and consolidation to everyday matters, family, home, ownership, and property.

Jupiter will confer good luck on the aforementioned interests.

Pluto provides foresight, awareness in your tenth house of career, professional, and authority interests.

Money flows your way over the spring. What you won becomes more valuable in May and June. The June–July interval is your season of love, of bonding more closely with your chosen one, of getting married.

Your learning processes due to the Uranus–Neptune transits are working overtime this year. You will be quicker than most to spot the occasional deception creeping into a society so constantly on the move that time itself is misunderstood and abused. Rely on your intuitive process to tell you when to make these Uranus-instigated changes and when to hold back.

CHAPTER 18

Eighteen Months of Day-by-Day Predictions—July 1999 to December 2000

All times are calculated for EST and EDT.

JULY 1999

Thursday, July 1 (Moon in Aquarius)   The moon joins Uranus and Neptune in your twelfth house, bringing reviews, investigations, and self-questioning about past decisions. Ultramarine and off-whites are your colors. Know when to drop old regrets and accusations. Do your best to collect what is due you. Hot combination numbers: 7 and 3.

Friday, July 2 (Moon in Aquarius)   You're turned off by those who talk liberty and practice license. Also, those who are preaching the doctrines of extreme changes cause you to fear their results. Throughout the month, Capricorn, Cancer, and Aquarius will be major influences. Hot combination numbers: 9 and 6.

Saturday, July 3 (Moon in Aquarius to Pisces 12:24 a.m.)   You're in your own element now and feel completely at home with the day's trends. Another Pisces is in the picture. Self-analysis will pay off; if you hold the initiative and demonstrate strong self-confidence, you will win big. Pea green and lime are your colors. Lucky lottery: 2, 11, 20, 29, 38, 47.

Sunday, July 4 (Moon in Pisces) Make social and travel decisions today. You are more closely in touch with the intangibles involved and others will feel that you know what you're recommending. Cancer and Scorpio will add spice to the day's happiness. Whites and blues go well together; your lucky number is 4.

Monday, July 5 (Moon in Pisces to Aries 7:21 a.m.) It's an excellent cycle for money making via special sales, promoting yourself and your product, and advertising. Aries takes a bow. At the track: Study the horses with the letters B, K, and T in their names or in the names of the jockeys. It's a good day for competing boldly. Your winning number is 8.

Tuesday, July 6 (Moon in Aries) Leo has a commanding position. Talks with your supervisors about salary requirements will produce good results. Today is also fine for hiring assistants and anybody who can help keep your home in better repair. Money flows freely and you feel that things can get even better. Hot daily doubles: 1 and 1, 1 and 4, 1 and 7.

Wednesday, July 7 (Moon in Aries to Taurus 11:22 a.m.) Sagittarius has a key role. Push financial opportunities for all they are worth. Discussions with your banker and broker can be profitable. Follow through on suggestions made to you. You are demonstrating more mars-ruled energy than earlier in the season. Lucky lottery: 3, 12, 21, 30, 39, 48.

Thursday, July 8 (Moon in Taurus) Taurus and Capricorn will influence your thinking. You do well to localize and concentrate, and to pounce on immediate and pressing duties. Minor details can be more important than the total job. This is a day when your learning processes are never idle. Sapphire is your color; your lucky number is 5.

Friday, July 9 (Moon in Taurus to Gemini 1:00 p.m.) Finish up any vital work that has been ne-

glected earlier in the week, so you can leave your job
for a relaxing weekend with a good conscience. Communications and short-distance travel are favored, but the
weather may interfere with beach and water fun. Kelly
green and gold go well together. Hot combination numbers: 7 and 2.

Saturday, July 10 (Moon in Gemini)   It's a favorable
day to share quality time with your family and other
loved ones. There will be plenty of good conversation
and much witty dialogue. Gemini will have a word for
everything. This evening calls for an exotic menu and
tropical drinks. Lemon is your color. Lucky lottery: 9,
18, 27, 36, 45, 6.

*Sunday, July 11 (Moon in Gemini to Cancer 1:27
p.m.)*   Libra and Aquarius can make this an unusual
day. You can be the center of the group's attention over
the morning and afternoon, but this evening is for you
and your beloved to escape from the world. It's not too
early to plan a memorable 15th and 24th. Your winning
colors are turquoise and primrose; your lucky number
is 2.

Monday, July 12 (Moon in Cancer)   Cancer and
Scorpio will have much to tell you. Love is the dominant
force now, and it's creative, imaginative, sympathetic,
and empathetic. Do favors, give compliments, and dine
away from home in an interesting place, featuring either
dancing or a cabaret. Your lucky number is 6.

*Tuesday, July 13 (Moon in Cancer to Leo 2:26
p.m.)*   The new moon illuminates your love needs,
desires, fantasies, and fears. There is sudden understanding in your close relationships. Give a party or a special
occasion that brings the generations together for good
food—perhaps a picnic. Bond more closely with your
beloved as Venus moves into your seventh house. Your
lucky number is 8.

Wednesday, July 14 (Moon in Leo)   A spurt of reserve energy will help you do some difficult chores. Fine aspects exist for catching up on odd jobs around the grounds of your home. Your employer may notice how well you are meeting all the demands made on you. Lavender and purple are exciting colors. Lucky lottery: 1, 10, 19, 28, 37, 46.

Thursday, July 15 (Moon in Leo to Virgo 5:39 p.m.)   Does your work stand out because others around you are not applying themselves? Don't take too many bows or there could be some backfiring. Rivalry on the job can be fierce when there is fear of downsizing. This evening requires better organization of time. Hot combination numbers: 3 and 9.

Friday, July 16 (Moon in Virgo)   Cooperation and compromise are required to get the best out of today's aspects, especially in marriage and coworker relationships. Virgo and Capricorn influence your thinking for the better. Stabilize your immediate environment. Mocha and cocoa are your colors; your lucky number is 5.

Saturday, July 17 (Moon in Virgo)   Talk youngsters into helping you around the house this morning. Your mate and you will achieve in tandem and, as a result, there is a good feeling of togetherness over this cycle. Problems and questionable situations can be talked away. Your winning colors are taupe and beige. Lucky lottery: 7, 16, 25, 34, 43, 3.

Sunday, July 18 (Moon in Virgo to Libra 12:19 a.m.) Study the financial pages of your newspaper and other economic periodicals to get a better handle on the way the economy is going. During the days ahead, you will want to differentiate between stocks that pay off and others that are too sluggish. Improve your financial position. Your lucky number is 9.

Monday, July 19 (Moon in Libra)   Libra and Gemini have good investment ideas. Insurance, tax shelters, refunds, applications for money due you, and all financial and investment interests are strongly supported by the aspects. This is a good day to push improvements and corrections. Cherry is your color: your lucky number is 4.

Tuesday, July 20 (Moon in Libra to Scorpio 10:30 a.m.)   You have a good handle on the economics of this cycle and will know which projects will make money and which should be abandoned. Today is fine for reviewing the way you and yours are handling time, including your free time. This evening is good for heart-to-heart talks. Hot combination numbers: 6 and 1.

Wednesday, July 21 (Moon in Scorpio)   Take a breather and change your scene for a day or two, as beach and water activities beckon. Scorpio and Cancer have front seats. Long-range thinking and planning is better than momentary uncertainty. Your appreciation of beauty is strong under prevailing aspects. Lucky lottery: 8, 17, 26, 35, 44, 2.

Thursday, July 22 (Moon in Scorpio to Sagittarius 10:48 p.m.)   Genuine relaxation includes keeping on the go, and this will become therapeutic. You move about at ease, enjoying the conversation, your mind and body fully cooperating. Sex is both physical and spiritual. It's wonderful getting away from the familiar. Hot daily doubles: 1 and 1, 1 and 4, 1 and 7, 4 and 7.

Friday, July 23 (Moon in Sagittarius)   If work has been slow, it can show new momentum under these sun–moon trends. Sagittarius and Leo are in commanding positions. Talks with your employer and supervisors will produce goodwill and a better feeling about work that has to be done before month's end. Hot combination numbers: 3 and 6.

Saturday, July 24 (Moon in Sagittarius)   Weekday responsibilities can spill over into the morning. If you think it wise, talk to your boss and coworkers on the phone. The great outdoors wants you to become a part of its exciting and adventurous panorama. Walks, chatting with local merchants and neighbors, are satisfying. Lucky lottery: 5, 14, 23, 32, 41, 50.

Sunday, July 25 (Moon in Sagittarius to Capricorn 11:08 a.m.)   You want to spend time with interesting people, good friends, members of your social groups, and perhaps a coworker with whom you are sympathetic. Camaraderie makes your day and gives you a sense of importance. Abandon the TV for Mother Nature's special places. Your color is Tawny; your fortunate number is 7.

Monday, July 26 (Moon in Capricorn)   You lean toward the conservative and can resent those who keep harping for extreme changes. You may feel that you have faced too many changes thus far in 1999, with Uranus storming about your twelfth house. Discussions can veer into arguments quite easily. Your color is light blue; your lucky number is 2.

Tuesday, July 27 (Moon in Capricorn to Aquarius 9:54 p.m.)   Capricorn will understand what you hope to do. Group activities sustain your morale and ego. Phone, write letters, and keep in closer touch with those who care. You may suddenly hear of a community or government stipend that you can collect for special work you do. Cerulean blue is your color: your lucky number is 4.

Wednesday, July 28 (Moon in Aquarius)   Lunar pressures stir up past mistakes and regrets. You are suspicious of what is taking place behind your back. There is a lot of backbiting going on now and those who enjoy being dependent are at war with the super-independent. Lucky lottery: 6, 15, 24, 33, 42, 51.

Thursday, July 29 (Moon in Aquarius)   Pressures activated by yesterday's lunar eclipse can make the past seem too much with you. There is a desire to get out

190

from under old anxieties as you wonder what is happening behind the scenes. Seek light and color, steering clear of chronic complainers. Hot combination numbers: 8 and 2.

Friday, July 30 (Moon in Aquarius to Pisces 5:27 a.m.) Teamwork needs more trust as Venus goes retrograde in your seventh house. You manage to get out from under other worries and come into the present. In your lunar-cycle high, you are more self-confident and self-reliant. Tell another Pisces all about it. Flame and orange are your best colors; your lucky number is 1.

Saturday, July 31 (Moon in Pisces) Arise early and get busy on a day that is ideal for catching up. You can pick and choose the odd jobs you want to do around the house, grounds, garage, and patio. Working outdoors gives you peace of mind. Gardening become a spiritual exercise. Lucky lottery: 3, 12, 21, 30, 39, 48.

AUGUST 1999

Sunday, August 1 (Moon in Pisces to Aries 12:47 p.m.) You enter the month fully confident that you can make things click in your own interest. Cancer and Scorpio are understanding and helpful. Hold the initiative as long as you can and keep on the move, establishing an environment of goodwill wherever you go. Your lucky number is 2.

Monday, August 2 (Moon in Aries) It's a promising money day, when wealth production trends are reassuring. Aries and Leo have key roles. Take the first step in an inquiry or investigation that could mean more money for you. You can be somewhat bold and daring in issuing an ultimatum. Your lucky number is 6.

Tuesday, August 3 (Moon in Aries to Taurus 5:09 p.m.) Talks with your banker and broker may be overdue. Know your economic worth and ways to increase your investment returns. A yard sale today can mean more ready cash. Also, advertising can be your means to a desirable gain. Your colors are mauve and beige. Hot combination numbers: 8 and 1.

Wednesday, August 4 (Moon in Taurus)　Narrow your sights and zero in on split-second opportunities. Local, everyday, usual, and familiar interests get strong lunar support. You are rather possessive of what you own now and this could be taken as miserliness by some of your critics. Lucky lottery: 1, 10, 19, 28, 37, 46.

Thursday, August 5 (Moon in Taurus to Gemini 7:57 p.m.)　Look around you and chores that are crying to be finished will attract your immediate attention. Relatives and neighbors may be strongly in evidence. Everyday details can be elusive at times, but not today. The hours pass more quickly than you would prefer. Hot combinations numbers: 3 and 9.

Friday, August 6 (Moon in Gemini)　Partnership matters pick up steam as Mercury resumes direct movement. Gemini preaches family values without encroaching on your personal freedoms. Real estate, ownership, and property matters get top billing. You'll want to share the upcoming weekend with youngsters. Canary is your color; your lucky number is 5.

Saturday, August 7 (Moon in Gemini to Cancer 9:53 p.m.)　Fine trends exist for greater activity, a family picnic, or a social club outing, and for escaping from polluted cities. Amusement parks will keep the kids excited and cheerful, and give you an opportunity to teach them manners. Lucky lottery: 7, 16, 25, 34 43, 3.

Sunday, August 8 (Moon in Cancer)　Cooperation with your mater will make the day proceed more smoothly. Discussions, at-home relaxation, sharing chores, and working around the lawn, veranda, and patio are preferred occupations. Togetherness reigns in your neighborhood. Purple is your color; your lucky number is 9.

Monday, August 9 (Moon in Cancer to Leo 11:56 p.m.) Your marital state, business partnerships, and teamwork are strongly evident trends. It's important that you get to career duties and responsibilities before the others on a day when obligations are on the front burner. You could be judged accordingly. Stick with the number 4.

Tuesday, August 10 (Moon in Leo) You could feel surrounded by Leo and Leo- ruled matters. You will not respond well to being pressured and overwhelmed with verbiage, or even overly "bossed." You require more breathing space than you get. At all tracks, keep your eyes on post position 6 in the first, fourth, and sixth races.

Wednesday, August 11 (Moon in Leo) A solar eclipse can pressure work and the expectations of others. You'll tire early if you dislike performing duties. Assignments can also be resented if there are sharp differences between the quick and brilliant workers on one hand and the slow-witted on the other. Keep the peace. Lucky lottery: 8, 17, 26, 35, 44, 2.

Thursday, August 12 (Moon in Leo to Virgo 3:22 a.m.) Your beloved has the key to your happiness. There are those at work with whom you can cooperate and others you would rather ignore under these aspects. Virgo and Taurus know the shortcuts and practical applications. Hot daily doubles: 1 and 1, 1 and 4, 1 and 7, 4 and 7. Spread your wings and take off.

Friday, August 13 (Moon in Virgo) Check things out with your beloved before making any family decision. You may feel that the lazy ones around your home need a talking to. There is some rebellion among the very young, who watch too much TV. Gemini and Sagittarius will have much to say this evening. Marigold yellows are in; your lucky number is 3.

Saturday, August 14 (Moon in Virgo to Libra 9:24 a.m.) This afternoon and evening favor financial decisions and the implementation of improvements and corrections. If you have extra time on your hands, settle some source of discord among the youngsters. You make a good King Solomon under these aspects. Lucky lottery: 5, 14, 23, 32, 41, 50.

Sunday, August 15 (Moon in Libra) Let Libra do the talking. Organize your time well, for there is much to do around your home. Prepare reports, reviews, and estimates. Documentaries on TV can add to your basic store of knowledge and help in decision making. Warm up to the work you will be doing tomorrow. Your lucky number is 7.

Monday, August 16 (Moon in Libra to Scorpio 6:40 p.m.) Today is fine for immersing yourself in projects that are pressuring your employer. It's one of those perfect days for the early birds. Record keeping, maintaining files, and facing shared tasks with a friendly approach are all indicated. Late evening finds you tired and yearning for a change of scene. Your lucky number is 2.

Tuesday, August 17 (Moon in Scorpio) Welcome Scorpio and Taurus. If you can't get away from the daily grind, then at least recycle an enjoyable trip in your imagination. Fine trends exist for beach and water activities and for sharing a trek with good companions, whose names include the letters C, L, and U. Your lucky number is 4.

Wednesday, August 18 (Moon in Scorpio) If you can change your scene, even for a few hours, the rest of the day will go better. Drive to and from work along a different route. Shop in a store that is unfamiliar to you. See people you haven't been in touch with this summer.

Your lucky colors are ivory and old rose. Lucky lottery: 6, 15, 24, 33, 42, 51.

Thursday, August 19 (Moon in Scorpio to Sagittarius 6:32 a.m.) Don't sit in one position too long. If possible, get into the great outdoors, enjoying August and its pleasant weather. You are conscious that the year is passing, yet there is much to be done. Sagittarius and Gemini come across. Hot combination numbers: 8 and 2.

Friday, August 20 (Moon in Sagittarius) Career demands can be burdensome, but once you accept more responsibility, everything goes more easy. Plan something social for the 23rd, and give others involved plenty of warning. Aries and Leo tend to get in the way, with their fiery expectations and bossing. Alabaster is your color; your lucky number is 1.

Saturday, August 21 (Moon in Sagittarius to Capricorn 6:59 p.m.) You may feel that your authority is being challenged, but be professional in the way you chastise or find fault. Nothing will be achieved by increasing the rebellion of a child or teenager. If you have difficulty sleeping, get into a good mystery novel or tape. Lucky lottery: 3, 12, 21, 30, 39, 48.

Sunday, August 22 (Moon in Capricorn) It's an excellent day to join an interesting group on a day when social expansion trends invite pleasure. Capricorn and Virgo play key roles. Your public life can make new and uncertain demands on your time. Church and club membership and participation are represented. Your fortunate number is 5.

Monday, August 23 (Moon in Capricorn) There can be some conflicts between your career and social interests. Also, your mate may be less interested in what you are doing socially, which can cause annoyance. This can be a memorable day for partying and for attending committee and planning meetings. Your lucky number is 9.

Tuesday, August 24 (Moon in Capricorn to Aquarius 5:49 a.m.) Virgo and Aquarius are in the day's scenario. You are interested in finishing some odd job, but there can be much interference and plenty of distractions. You may feel less free under these trends even though others can feel you are too independent. Your color is aquamarine. Hot combination numbers: 2 and 6.

Wednesday, August 25 (Moon in Aquarius) The wish to complete projects can be urgent, possibly because there is such confusion among assistants and in the boss's office. It's one of those days when people don't know what they want until they see what they don't want. Some channels are closed. Lucky lottery: 4, 13, 22, 31, 40, 49.

Thursday, August 26 (Moon in Aquarius to Pisces 1:50 p.m.) The full moon in your first house illuminates what you want to do and how you want to do it. Your personality and character are accented, and you can take the lead and control the situation. Another Pisces and an opposing Virgo are in the picture. Hot combination numbers: 6 and 1.

Friday, August 27 (Moon in Pisces) Step up to the plate, for it's your turn now. You can make an excellent showing now that you are in your lunar-cycle high. Others tend to get out of your way and to listen to your aspirations and intentions. You possess enormous sympathy for the losers. Your lucky number is 8.

Saturday, August 28 (Moon in Pisces to Aries 7:09 p.m.) It's another wonderful day, when you can hold the initiative and stay in the lead, sure of a generous following. Make your choices, then tell others all about them. Once others know that you intend to get things done, they won't get in your way. But the responsibility remains totally yours. Lucky lottery: 1, 10, 19, 28, 37, 46.

Sunday, August 29 (Moon in Aries) There are good trends for improving your speech as well as your personal appearance so that you can qualify for a promotion. There is no reason for younger Americans to make so many grammatical mistakes that their grandparents would have zealously avoided. Most stores have cosmetic counters with professionals to help you make the right choice. Your lucky number is 3.

Monday, August 30 (Moon in Aries to Taurus 10:41 p.m.)   Be cautious if an Aries or a Leo is trying to involve you in a get-rich-quick scheme. You dislike being pushed into a new interest by fire-sign people. Organizational interests tend to bore you. Pay attention to minor details as the month winds down. Your color is silver; your lucky number is 7.

Tuesday, August 31 (Moon in Taurus)   Taurus has the patience you may lack in local, immediate, and pressing matters. Your mind is aware that this summer is drawing to a slow close, and you are thinking of the joys that came to you at various times over the past three months. Spruce up your immediate working area. Hot combination numbers: 9 and 6.

SEPTEMBER 1999

Wednesday, September 1 (Moon in Taurus)   Teamwork is good. It's a fine day to spend away from home, perhaps at a budget resort, now that the season is ending. But be back by the 3rd, when your career demands will be stepped up. Immediate and pressing matters are being neglected all along the line. Amber is your color. Lucky lottery: 8, 17, 26, 35, 44, 2.

Thursday, September 2 (Moon in Taurus to Gemini 1:25 a.m.)   Gemini enters the picture with explanations, alibis, and impressive information. Domestic interests get strong backing from loved ones. You could hear that a favorite neighbor is about to move. The community's down-at-the-heels look is on the front burner. Hot combination numbers 1 and 7.

Friday, September 3 (Moon in Gemini) Push real estate, ownership, and property matters. There is a slowdown with five planets retrograding, so it may be difficult to get a handle on things that are constantly changing in intangible ways. People are isolating themselves with their TV sets. Wear taupe or tan; your best number is 3.

Saturday, September 4 (Moon in Gemini to Cancer 4:10 a.m.) At all tracks: post position number 5 in the fifth race looks promising. A Cancer and Capricorn can make your day seem more rewarding. Your children and other youngsters would love a picnic if you were to arrange it. The day is fine for having the last outdoor swim of the year. Electric blue is your color. Lucky lottery: 5, 14, 23, 32, 41, 50.

Sunday, September 5 (Moon in Cancer) Don't try to score points on your mate or other partner on a day when competition and rivalry are strongly indicated. Self-analysis and pride are not doing well as Venus retrogrades in your sixth house. Talk things over with a Scorpio, perhaps by phone. This evening brings peace of mind. Your number is 7.

Monday, September 6 (Moon in Cancer to Leo 7:29 a.m.) Don't neglect your physical or mental welfare. Watch any buildup of fatigue under these Venus–Moon trends. The work you do now may not be very rewarding in a personal sense, but it has to be done if you are to protect your job. Your winning colors are magenta and white; your lucky number is 2.

Tuesday, September 7 (Moon in Leo) You can catch up today. There are indications that if you take charge, the challenge pays off. In many ways, good work is therapeutic. Partnerships succeed because of the high-grade work done in unison. Information is flowing well. Emerald is your color. Hot combination numbers: 4 and 7.

Wednesday, September 8 (Moon in Leo to Virgo 11:57 a.m.) Scorpio and Taurus will impact a big part of this month. So will people, horses, and dogs with the letters D, M, V in their names. Doing joint projects and allowing sufficient reflection before making decisions will show good results. Information and research are favored. Lucky lottery: 6, 15, 24, 33, 42, 51.

Thursday, September 9 (Moon in Virgo)   The new moon, born in your seventh house, illuminates all partnerships, including marriage, and joint projects and agreements made at this time. Fine trends exist for brain-to-brain discussions. Improve relationships with your in-laws and with the friends of your mate. At all tracks: post position 8 in the eighth race is a winter.

Friday, September 10 (Moon in Virgo to Libra 6:16 p.m.)   There are some stirrings of revived interest in abandoned projects and in improving your personal appearance and hairstyle. A dignified and formal look, which can be majestic in your case, will play an important role in your advancement. Browns and blacks with white trimmings are fine; your lucky number is 1.

Saturday, September 11 (Moon in Libra)   Venus resumes direct movement in your sixth house of health and labor, and your overall physical well-being is snapping back. This is a fine day to implement changes that can make your life easier and more rewarding. Libra makes an important contribution. Lucky lottery: 3, 12, 21, 30, 39, 48.

Sunday, September 12 (Moon in Libra)   Figure out what you can do with accumulated funds, leisure time, and recycled energies. Keep taking your herbs and vitamins. There are recycled opportunities and more awareness of your personal advantages. Set your goals, evaluating your aims and methods. Your color is damask; your lucky number is 5.

Monday, September 13 (Moon in Libra to Scorpio 3:08 a.m.)   No quick decisions or shortcuts! Take the long-range view and go all the way with it. Travel is in the picture, and if you feel you need a change of scene, then today and tomorrow are ideal for it. Scorpio and

Cancer will impact your day. White and navy are your colors; your lucky number is 9.

Tuesday, September 14 (Moon in Scorpio)   The view is good and you enjoy contemplation and reflection. It's the season that strongly appeals to your sense of oneness with nature and with people who love small critters and all birds. Nothing is escaping your attention as you move about unfamiliar places. Fushsia is your color. Hot combination numbers: 2 and 6.

Wednesday, September 15 (Moon in Scorpio to Sagittarius 2:35 p.m.)   Your desire to stretch a trip out another day is compelling, but you may feel guilty about work that is waiting for you. Evening is for your grand return in an excellent and relaxed mood. You can warm up to the work you will be doing tomorrow. Lucky lottery: 4, 13, 22, 31, 40, 49.

Thursday, September 16 (Moon in Sagittarius)   A Sagittarius can give you good directions in your work. You admire the way an executive uses authority. The trends permit you to advance in your career goals and to invite the professionalism that you desire. At all tracks: post position 6 in the first, fourth, and sixth races will do well.

Friday, September 17 (Moon in Sagittarius to Capricorn 3:14 a.m.)   All business connected with savings and investments can be speeded up, and good financial decisions can be made. You put the afternoon to excellent use and win the admiration of supervisors. You excel in securing marvelous cooperation from underlings. Hot combination numbers: 8 and 2.

Saturday, September 18 (Moon in Capricorn)   Immerse yourself in the social opportunities available to you. Join a group on a trek through the woods, a city park, or at the base of a hill or mountain. Accept all invitations that come your way. Capricorn, Virgo, and Taurus are good companions. Reddish-browns delight you. Lucky lottery: 1, 10, 19, 28, 37, 46.

Sunday, September 19 (Moon in Capricorn)   The rural autumn sciences captivate you. Dining at a country inn, as well as some farm and roadside shopping, are in this picture. A drive through one village after another will prove inspirational. Items made of wood, glass, and plastic will appeal to you. Rust and russet are your colors; your lucky number is 3.

Monday, September 20 (Moon in Capricorn to Aquarius 2:38 p.m.)   The day can hold you to restrictions, but this evening offers more personal independence and the chance to complete household tasks. Any show of irresponsibility during the day can bring chastisement. Aquarius enters the picture. Auburn is your color; your lucky number is 7.

Tuesday, September 21 (Moon in Aquarius)   There are projects to be finished before the month closes and today is fine for getting a handle on them. Your intuitive processes work in all but money matters. You may have hung on to a stock or treasure too long. Some unruly kids are operating behind the scenes. Blueberry is your color; your lucky number is 9.

Wednesday, September 22 (Moon in Aquarius to Pisces 10:51 p.m.)   Past experiences, including failures and mistakes, can show up again. Try to laugh it all off on a day when others expect anger and hurt from you. There is some jealousy and a lot of vanity involved in the day's events. Gemini and Libra may be frowning. Lucky lottery: 2, 11, 20, 29, 38, 47.

Thursday, September 23 (Moon in Pisces)   Now in your lunar-cycle high, you can put things right. Take the lead, hold the initiative, and let others know that you mean business. Your surge of self-confidence and self-reliance pay handsome dividends. Another Pisces and a Cancer know the story. Hot combination numbers: 4 and 7.

Friday, September 24 (Moon in Pisces)　　Set the pace and the pattern for others to follow suit. Air your aspirations for today and the rest of the month. You encompass duties, responsibilities, and obligations better than others, and you do all this without useless chatter and fault finding. Trifecta special: 1–4–6; 4–6–1; 6–4–1.

Saturday, September 25 (Moon in Pisces to Aries 3:34 p.m.)　　The full moon illuminates your wealth production, ways of raising some cash, advantages of a fall sale, and the best way to advertise and sell what you no longer need. Aries and Leo know how to do all this, but you may not want to bring them into the matter. Your color is pinecone green. Lucky lottery: 8, 17, 26, 35, 44, 2.

Sunday, September 26 (Moon in Aries)　　A Sagittarius will have some good ideas about how you can find a new source of income. One of your near-professional skills could be put on a money-making basis. Although September is yet to end, you could have the feeling that the old year is dying. Keep children off the streets after dark. Your number is 1.

Monday, September 27 (Moon in Aries to Taurus 5:51 a.m.)　　You may find Taurus overly possessive under these aspects. You could feel that there are too many around who love wasting your time. The everyday routines go better than anything unfamiliar. Fine trends exist for ordering beautiful items by phone. Your winning colors are silver and vermillion; your lucky number is 5.

Tuesday, September 28 (Moon in Taurus)　　Your drive in career is strong, and your motivation is crystal clear. Focus on getting along with even the more difficult and jealous types. You could have the feeling that there are too many collections at your place of business and too many begging letters in the mail. Hot daily doubles: 3 and 5, 5 and 7, 3 and 7.

Wednesday, September 29 (Moon in Taurus to Gemini 7:21 a.m.)   Gemini is about your best conversational-ist today. There's a steadiness and consistency here that Aquarius will lack. Domestic and community interests can be well served without taking too much of your time. Property values in your community are rising. Russet is your color. Lucky lottery: 9, 18, 27, 36, 45, 3.

Thursday, September 30 (Moon in Gemini)   Close the month on a happy note in and near your own home. Your garden can draw your attention. The changing leaves will make you feel a little sad, for you know that the year is waning and you may feel that it has gone by too fast. Talk this over with Libra. Hot combination numbers: 2 and 6.

OCTOBER 1999

Friday, October 1 (Moon in Gemini to Cancer 9:31 a.m.)   This morning is for home chores; the afternoon is fine for planning and programming October's parties and entertainments. You become more original and cre-ative as you set your mind to social interests. You could please your children if you arranged a Halloween party for them. Your lucky number is 2.

Saturday, October 2 (Moon in Cancer)   A Cancer and another Pisces have key roles. You are loving and loved, and do well by spreading goodwill. It's a fine day to bond with a difficult child. You are in the mood to give of yourself, which can also endear you to mate and in-laws. Khaki is your color. Lucky lottery: 4, 13, 22, 31, 40, 49.

Sunday, October 3 (Moon in Cancer to Leo 1:13 p.m.)   It's an excellent day to invite people in for tea and cookies, especially church and club committees with whom you will be working more closely now that every-thing is in full swing after the summer hiatus. Don't be too quick to say no to an elected or appointed office. Apricot is your color; your lucky number is 6.

Monday, October 4 (Moon in Leo)   Leo has chores and would like your help, or at least your encouragement. Be on guard against viral ailments by not dining out in questionable places. It's also a day when children have to be watched for any signs of fatigue or stomach complaints. Pinecone is your color; your favorite number is 1.

Tuesday, October 5 (Moon in Leo to Virgo 6:40 p.m.)   The yen to travel becomes stronger as Mercury enters Scorpio. What is happening far away can impact your life. Long-range thinking and planning will do well, once you switch from present to future. Your colors are bright blue and orchid. At all tracks, notice the letters E, N, and W in the names of jockeys and horses. Your lucky number is 3.

Wednesday, October 6 (Moon in Virgo)   Reconciliation, compromise, and cooperation are the rules to put this day to highest use. Share, discussing plans with your mate and other partners. Sign legal agreements and make enduring decisions. Build bridges across the gender gap. Buff is your color. Lucky lottery: 5, 14, 23, 32, 41, 50.

Thursday, October 7 (Moon in Virgo)   Bond more closely with loving and helpful in-laws, and do something kind for a controversial friend of your spouse. The signs Gemini and Virgo can dominate the day's scenario. Shyness is of little use, on a day when you should question what you see and are told. Hot combination numbers: 7 and 3.

Friday, October 8 (Moon in Virgo to Libra 1:52 a.m.)   You can be the perfect spouse as Venus enters Virgo. There's love galore to serve you as you do kindnesses and show special consideration. Of course, it all comes back to you tenfold. Libra knows where you're headed, financially speaking. Your color is indigo; your lucky number is 9.

Saturday, October 9 (Moon in Libra)   The new moon illuminates proper ways of handling accumulations of money, time, and energy. Savings, investments, insurance, tax, and overall security matters are in focus. The challenge is to avoid repeating past mistakes. Aquarius and Gemini have advice for you. Lucky lottery: 2, 11, 20, 29, 38, 47.

Sunday, October 10 (Moon in Libra to Scorpio 10:01 a.m.)   You may feel that you should be in two places at the same time. Give detailed directions to your children and others you want to deputize to take your place. You will feel better outdoors than inside crowded rooms, or where arguments are taking place. Salmon and pink are your colors; your lucky number is 4.

Monday, October 11 (Moon in Scorpio)   Take an alternate route to work; dine in an unfamiliar place; shop where you haven't shopped before. The day calls for substitutes, objective thinking, and escape from boring routines, for you are tired of the usual. Gemini and Virgo understand. White and maroon are your colors; your lucky number is 8.

Tuesday, October 12 (Moon in Scorpio to Sagittarius 10:18 p.m.)   This can be a memorable day in travel as you move about with self-confidence, taking on City Hall, and airing your personal ambitions and convictions. Your sense of self-reliance wins much admiration. Phone and write strong letters. Ruby is your color. Hot combination numbers: 1 and 7.

Wednesday, October 13 (Moon in Sagittarius)   Welcome to a cycle when you can improve your career situation, throw your hat in the salary-increase ring, and attract favorable attention from your employer. Stand up and be counted, speaking up for yourself, and making sure that everybody knows you're running for the gold. Lucky lottery: 3, 12, 21, 30, 39, 48.

Thursday, October 14 (Moon in Sagittarius)   Sagittarius and Leo are in the picture as organizational matters need your attention. It's how things are perceived that counts now, not how they really are. You may see the audacious picking up the prizes and censure yourself for hiding some of your light under a bushel. Your lucky number is 5.

Friday, October 15 (Moon in Sagittarius to Capricorn 10:04 a.m.)   The good you did in the last few days can bring an ultimate payoff. The social side of your job shouldn't be neglected, for you may notice that supervisors are more lonely than underlings. Don't take part in the brutal criticism of an absentee. Your winning colors are russet and mauve. Daily doubles: 3 and 7, 3 and 5, 5 and 7.

Saturday, October 16 (Moon in Capricorn)   At all tracks: post position 3 in the sixth and ninth races looks good. Be part of the group and you'll be inviting more fun and laughter. Capricorn and Taurus have front seats on an ideal day for action. Dress comfortably but with consideration of the weather. Lucky lottery: 9, 18, 27, 36, 45, 3.

Sunday, October 17 (Moon in Capricorn to Aquarius 11:17 p.m.)   Mars enters Capricorn, which activates your eleventh house, a combination of the social and the practical. Issue and accept meaningful invitations. Show grace along with your usual candor. You can see beyond the obvious and you search for the spiritual meaning in your activities. Your lucky number is 2.

Monday, October 18 (Moon in Aquarius)   You can tire of boring, jaded, and obvious matters. A change of scene would do you good, so complete no-win tasks and go on to more challenging projects. A buildup of planetary power in your twelfth house can bring a recycling of past events. Melancholia sets in. Your lucky number is 6.

Tuesday, October 19 (Moon in Aquarius)   Aquarius and Gemini will take the credit. Winnow out no-win projects, making allowances for what is happening behind the scenes. Recycle and recontact. Your intuitive processes are sharp, and your insight is more perceptive than others may realize. People fall into traps easily. Hot combination numbers: 8 and 2.

Wednesday, October 20 (Moon in Aquarius to Pisces 8:33 a.m.)   You have the feeling that your winning time is coming, so be prepared to cash in on the dynamic aspects now forming in your horoscope. Kick the unimportant debris out of your path, blotting out all interference and distractions. Another Pisces and a Cancer are helpful. Lucky lottery: 1, 10, 19, 28, 37, 46.

Thursday, October 21 (Moon in Pisces)   Seize the initiative, take the lead, and let the world know you are out to win. It's a day for high achievement, as long as you push your self-confidence and self-reliance. Dress to the hilt and look the part of winner. Your most flattering colors are primrose and pinecone. Hot combination numbers: 3 and 6.

Friday, October 22 (Moon in Pisces to Aries 1:42 p.m.)   You're still in your lunar-cycle high, when you can possess this day. Immerse yourself in the competitions as you work rings around the others and narrow your sights and concentrate. Stick to the possible and let others chase the rainbows. The water signs (Cancer, Scorpio, and Pisces) are with you. Your lucky number is 5.

Saturday, October 23 (Moon in Aries)   Jupiter falls back into Aries, signifying money, a bonus, an award, or a reward. The moon illuminates where the treasures are waiting for you, money you should have received before. Some obstacles are removed from your path as Uranus resumes direct movement. Lucky lottery: 7, 16, 25, 34, 43, 3.

Sunday, October 24 (Moon in Aries to Taurus 3:25 p.m.) The month becomes more fascinating for you. Versatility, flexibility, and creativity all point your way to rewarding days. You handle your budgets well, spend wisely, and enjoy what you can afford. Give yourself a lift by phoning Gemini or Libra. Saffron and henna are your winning colors; your lucky number is 9.

Monday, October 25 (Moon in Taurus) All around you are opportunities for appreciating and approving. Nature is putting on a show for your benefit. Deal in totality, the end product, and completion of a cycle. Taurus wants to know all about it. Hazel, the quieter reds, and browns are your colors; your lucky number is 4.

Tuesday, October 26 (Moon in Taurus to Gemini 3:33 p.m.) Relatives and neighbors make good companions on a day that accents the local, wonderful communications, and enjoyable walks in your own neighborhood. The pumpkins are ready and the children seem to love Halloween. Decorate your lawn and get in a supply of treats. Your lucky number is 6.

Wednesday, October 27 (Moon in Gemini) The drama gets better and better. Make sure Gemini is on hand, providing sparkling dialogue that gives you a strong sense of participation. The more, the merrier is the rule under these aspects. You spread your personal nets over a wide territory. Lucky lottery: 8, 17, 26, 35, 44, 2.

Thursday, October 28 (Moon in Gemini to Cancer 4:09 p.m.) You can recycle good luck, calling back memories of love at its most dynamic. In the past, you can find all the hints, knacks, and suggestions for inviting ecstasy and victory. Neptune lifts veils that have been hanging over the past, and puzzles and mysteries are solved. Your fortunate number is 1.

Friday, October 29 (Moon in Cancer)   Party, entertain, and arrange a masquerade evening for your children and the neighborhood kids. Cancer and Capricorn
are active in this socializing. Jupiter and its good-luck
force are operating to your personal advantage in all
wealth production. Your winning colors are aquamarine
and emerald; your lucky number is 3.

*Saturday, October 30 (Moon in Cancer to Leo 6:47
p.m.)*   You will love what you are doing for yourself,
younger people, and your beloved. You are ultra-creative,
strongly original, and intensely imaginative today. Pass
on some good social ideas to neighbors who seem de-
pressed and withdrawn. Immerse yourself in the fun and
games. Lucky lottery: 5, 14, 23, 32, 41, 50.

*Sunday, October 31—Daylight Saving Time ends
(Moon in Leo)*   Emotions can get out of hand on this
fiery day. A sense of rivalry and competition can damage
relationships between relatives and in-laws. Mercury's
Sagittarius ingress is speeding up some projects that you
haven't been thinking enough about over this pleasant
weekend. Don't panic. Your lucky number is 7.

NOVEMBER 1999

*Monday, November 1 (Moon in Leo to Virgo 11:07
p.m.)*   Guard against fatigue as the month gets underway. Discussions with your mate and other partners will
relieve some tensions. It's not the day to try to go it
alone, but much better for sharing responsibilities and
dealing in joint endeavors. Your winning colors are
milky white and rust; your lucky number is 8.

Tuesday, November 2 (Moon in Virgo)   Virgo brings
a practical touch to the discussion. Harvest colors pre-
dominate and add a sense of new adventures. Take time
out before arriving at any extreme viewpoint. Organizational matters are muddled. Many of the leaves beneath
your feet are worth preserving. Your number is 1.

Wednesday, November 3 (Moon in Virgo) Agreements arrived at today will endure. Today is fine for signing legal documents, adding some fall fashion to your wardrobe, and checking with your spouse before making a big-item purchase. Taurus and Capricorn can impact your thinking. Azure and old rose are your colors. Lucky lottery: 3, 12, 21, 30, 39, 48.

Thursday, November 4 (Moon in Virgo to Libra 6:57 a.m.) Libra will evaluate and balance one argument against the other. Now you can make decisions you have been avoiding. Excellent trends exist for handling accumulations of money, time, and energy. In-laws have much to tell you. Improvements are underway. Hot combination numbers: 5 and 2.

Friday, November 5 (Moon in Libra) Your career and professional interests and actions slow down as Mercury goes erratic in your tenth house. There can be confusion about where authority begins and ends. Even so, the way to bring about corrections and improvements in money and time problems is wide open. Your lucky number is 7.

Saturday, November 6 (Moon in Libra to Scorpio 4:46 p.m.) If you feel a change is required, you won't have much trouble bringing it about, for Libra and Aquarius are there with you. Late evening favors communications and possibly recycling last year's holiday travel. Saffron is your color. Plan something exciting for the 11th. Lucky lottery: 9, 18, 27, 36, 45, 6.

Sunday, November 7 (Moon in Scorpio) Travel within a 300-mile radius of home will go well. You are at your best when you take a long-range view of things. Scorpio and another Pisces are on hand. Your intuition is good and your conscience is your best guide. Autumnal reds, golds, and browns are your colors; your lucky number is 2.

Monday, November 8 (Moon in Scorpio)   The new moon in your ninth house illuminates matters at a distance. The information is there for you to tap. Your point of view can influence the thinking of loved ones. Away from home, you feel as secure as when you are on familiar ground. Tan and mocha are your colors; your lucky number is 6.

Tuesday, November 9 (Moon in Scorpio to Sagittarius 4:15 a.m.)   You are challenged by your career and develop more ambition as the moon in your tenth house is favorably aspected by Venus. You manage to be both authoritative and professional, which is noticed by top executives. Emerald is your color; your lucky number is 8.

Wednesday, November 10 (Moon in Sagittarius) Sagittarius and Gemini figure prominently. Discussions about your assignments clue you in on the problems of top management. You want to be part of the larger picture and the marvelous intuitive powers emanating from Pluto in your tenth house give you unbeatable insight. Lucky lottery: 1, 10, 19, 28, 37, 46.

Thursday, November 11 (Moon in Sagittarius to Capricorn 5:00 p.m.)   This can be a memorable day, with a Libra and a Taurus in the promising scenario. Speak up, airing your convictions and offering conclusions and suggestions. You can become more valuable to your employer under these trends. Your ability to estimate the time required is sharp. Hot combination numbers: 3 and 6.

Friday, November 12 (Moon in Capricorn)   Capricorn has the knack of keeping you interested in any social exchange. Hot daily doubles: 2 and 5, 3 and 5, 5 and 2, 5 and 3. Post position 5 in the second, third, and fifth races should be considered. A kindred spirit wants to hear from you but is a little uncomfortable about requesting your presence. Your lucky number is 5.

Saturday, November 13 (Moon in Capricorn) It's fine for group meetings, social plans, and discovering that a payment is owed you. This could be connected with work done locating jobs for people on welfare, or for some other volunteer work you did. Taurus and Virgo figure prominently. Lucky lottery: 7, 16, 25, 34, 43, 3.

Sunday, November 14 (Moon in Capricorn to Aquarius 5:46 a.m.) The moon joins Uranus and Neptune in Aquarius, spotlighting electronic, intangible, and advanced communications. It's obvious that workers are going to have to learn a lot more about computers, websites, and the Internet if they hope to advance in their jobs. There's much evidence that our world is changing. Your lucky number is 9.

Monday, November 15 (Moon in Aquarius) Complete tasks so that new responsibilities can be assumed. Much of the work you have been doing this year seems to be no longer relevant. Electronic items are constantly being replaced by miraculous developments. Much is happening behind the scenes, which makes for confusion. Your lucky number is 4.

Tuesday, November 16 (Moon in Aquarius to Pisces 4:21 p.m.) The month becomes much more personal, and you identify opportunities that are well within your scope. Today and tomorrow favor self-analysis, self-confidence, and self-reliance. You grab difficult challenges and show your true mettle in triumphing. Olive is your color. Hot combination numbers: 6 and 1.

Wednesday, November 17 (Moon in Pisces) In your lunar-cycle high, you exceed the expectations of your employer. You are at home administering, investigating, and writing reports and evaluations. You estimate the time it will take to do certain jobs better than most. Another Pisces and a Libra admire your abilities. Lucky lottery: 8, 17, 26, 35, 44, 2.

Thursday, November 18 (Moon in Pisces to Aries 10:57 p.m.) Push your aims closer to your chosen goals. You are good at defining what your goals are and enjoy secret covenants with yourself about achieving them. You don't let yourself down once you have made a promise. Taurus and Scorpio are on your side. Your lucky number is 1.

Friday, November 19 (Moon in Aries) Aries has a marvelous financial tip for you. You are free to push your earning power and overall wealth production. You realize that the goodwill you are spreading on the job wins major favor with your supervisors. By contrast, many coworkers can't get along with their associates. Your lucky number is 3.

Saturday, November 20 (Moon in Aries to Taurus 1:26 a.m.) There are fine trends for discussing your career, your ultimate salary requirements, and perhaps a change of assignments that will challenge you sufficiently. There is special money earmarked for you in some quiet service to the military organizations stationed nearby. Lucky lottery: 5, 14, 23, 32, 41, 50.

Sunday, November 21 (Moon in Taurus) Control the changes taking place in your immediate locality and interests, keeping a steady handle on them. The more conservative you are in accepting questionable changes, the better. You are not one who can easily rewrite the past, despite all this hullabaloo in your twelfth house. Your numbers are 7 and 3.

Monday, November 22 (Moon in Taurus) Taurus helps you play your cards close to the chest, despite all the questions and opinions coming your way. It's a good learning and listening day, when you should evaluate your assets. Siblings and neighbors are involved in this scenario. Your colors are burgundy and turquoise; your lucky number is 2.

Tuesday, November 23 (Moon in Taurus to Gemini 1:14 a.m.)   Today's full moon illuminates domestic, property, and ownership interests. Family discussions can settle plans and programs for the rest of the month. Gemini and Sagittarius bring excitement to the scene. At all tracks: post position 4 in the third and seven races looks lively. Your color is pumpkin. Cooperation is good.

Wednesday, November 24 (Moon in Gemini)   Your family doesn't always agree, but compromises of time and work can be achieved. Young people seem uncertain about recommendations. This is not the day to ride roughshod over complaining kids, even when you are sure they are wrong. Lucky lottery: 6, 15, 24, 33, 42, 51.

Thursday, November 25 (Moon in Gemini to Cancer 12:29 a.m.)   Let love come first as the moon dominates your fifth house and Mercury resumes direct movement in Scorpio. Creativity, imagination, and living fantasies are all represented. It's a grandly social day, with people showing up and talking about their travel adventures. Melon yellows and greens are in; your number is 8.

Friday, November 26 (Moon in Cancer)   Today is perfect for socializing, partying, entertaining, and helping children with their homework. The world seems full of matriarchs and patriarchs, but generation gaps can be bridged. Cancer and Scorpio make a big splash. Flame is your color; try the number 1.

Saturday, November 27 (Moon in Cancer to Leo 1:19 a.m.)   Who feels like working? Neither you nor those about you. Let the month wind its way toward December graciously, without pressures. The day is fine for genuine relaxation and idle chatter. Leo may not approve, but you are a spiritual and eternal Pisces. Your winning color is apricot. Lucky lottery: 3, 12, 21, 30, 39, 48.

Sunday, November 28 (Moon in Leo)   Do things that make good sense to you, refusing to be rushed by the fire signs (Aries, Leo, and Sagittarius). You progress by contemplating the busy month ahead and making decisions about what's left of November. Some of your ideas carry big collar signs. Your number is 5.

Monday, November 29 (Moon in Leo to Virgo 5:11 a.m.) It's a perfect day for bonding more closely with your beloved. Joint investments can show plenty. There's good orchestration within the system so that things dovetail ideally. Trust Virgo to know how long an odd job should require. Chestnut and earth are your colors. Hot daily doubles: 3 and 6, 3 and 9, 6 and 9, 4 and 5.

Tuesday, November 30 (Moon in Virgo) For best results, work, in harmony with your partners. Today is fine for clearing away garden and lawn debris. Your sense of fashion and what loved ones will approve is fine. There are excellent hours for taking care of many minor details that will make the month ahead move more suitably. Try the number 2 for all it's worth.

DECEMBER 1999

Wednesday, December 1 (Moon in Virgo to Libra 12:29 p.m.) The day demands full disclosure and a solid partnership agreement. This evening is for arranging improvements and corrections within all changes. Fine trends exist for organizing teamwork, church and club committee programs, and for handling accumulated funds. Libra and Aquarius are on board. Lucky lottery: 2, 11, 20, 29, 38, 47.

Thursday, December 2 (Moon in Libra) Discussions with your broker can produce more promising results. Do you have adequate life and accident insurance? This is a good cycle to review all security interests and to implement new safety programs. At all tracks: post position 4 in the fourth race is worth considering. Hot combination numbers: 4 and 3.

Friday, December 3 (Moon in Libra to Scorpio 10:35 p.m.)   There are some bargains to be found in larger outlet stores. Budgeting can seem burdensome and, chances are, it won't work under prevailing aspects. Many problems can be encountered with credit cards. Youngsters can complain about financial shortages. Copper and bronze are your colors; your lucky number is 6.

Saturday, December 4 (Moon in Scorpio)   This is your last chance to get in a quick trip before the holidays. Take off if somebody is expecting you, or if you want to delight an aging parent. Information is flowing well, and news from a distance is full of sentiment and nostalgia. Lucky lottery: 8, 17, 26, 35, 44, 2.

Sunday, December 5 (Moon in Scorpio)   It's a fine day for shopping in stores that are distant from your home and good for forming holiday plans and getting in some needed supplies. Buy gift boxes and wrapping paper, and order some special items by mail or phone. You will feel good about beating the clock. Your number is 1.

Monday, December 6 (Moon in Scorpio to Sagittarius 12:27 p.m.)   Today favors planning, programming, committee work, locating Christmas decorations. Do some baking and roasting. It's a day to look beyond the present and get greeting cards addressed and into the mails. This evening reminds you that tomorrow will be busy. Your lucky number is 5.

Tuesday, December 7 (Moon in Sagittarius)   It's somewhat difficult dropping the weekend and getting back to the nuts and bolts of your job, and Sagittarius feels the same way. Your employer can be a bit critical where work has been neglected. The new moon illuminates the best ways to get on with the program. Foxy is your color. Hot combination numbers 7 and 3.

Wednesday, December 8 (Moon in Sagittarius to Capricorn 11:14 p.m.)   Make up for lost time by pouncing on your duties as soon as you arrive on the job. Take on more responsibilities as a means of keeping the good opinion of your coworkers. If possible, put in a little holiday effort on your lunch hour and immediately after work. Lucky lottery: 9, 18, 27, 36, 45, 6.

Thursday, December 9 (Moon in Capricorn) You are now into an intensely social period, with fatigue threatening when conflicts arise among career, home, and outside commitments. Though you know that time is rushing, you'll push ahead with committee, volunteer, and charity work today and tomorrow. Scarlet is your color. Hot combination numbers: 2 and 6.

Friday, December 10 (Moon in Capricorn) Capricorn and Taurus figure prominently. Goodwill and a sense of humor help you shift from one responsibility to another. Friends and coworkers prove more understanding than you expected. The group isn't complete and decisions have to be postponed. Your lucky number is 4.

Saturday, December 11 (Moon in Capricorn to Aquarius 11:59 a.m.) Your career and professional duties loom more and more, as you take care of household decorations, gift buying, and other holiday duties. You can feel you are shortchanging both as Mercury moves into Sagittarius. Your winning colors are reds and greens. Lucky lottery: 6, 15, 24, 33, 42, 51.

Sunday, December 12 (Moon in Aquarius) Plans are changed with the emphasis shifted from one obligation to another. Let willing youngsters take on some of your home responsibilities. Aquarius and Libra figure prominently. Phone calls could make you nervous as you give family and home first place. Wear pearl gray; try the number 8.

Monday, December 13 (Moon in Aquarius to Pisces 11:18 p.m.) Complete certain holiday projects. Give some thought to the week ahead and what supervisors will expect from you. As the day advances, you are more at home with shortcuts, alternatives, and substitutes. A spurt of energy gives you a better feeling about everything. Your lucky number is 3.

Tuesday, December 14 (Moon in Pisces)   Now in your lunar-cycle high, you can stretch time and dollar bills. The impossible no longer exists, if you let your self-confidence and self-reliance have full play. Cancer and Scorpio are your best teammates. A great deal of work gets done with good feelings all around. Hot combination numbers: 5 and 2.

Wednesday, December 15 (Moon in Pisces)   Another Pisces knows the score. Take the initiative and hold it firm throughout all competitions and rivalries. Highly personalized interests get top billing and you air your ambitions for the rest of December effectively. Blacks and whites are your colors. Lucky lottery: 7, 16, 25, 34, 43, 3.

Thursday, December 16 (Moon in Pisces to Aries 7:30 a.m.)   Once again, there is a need to consider costs, and fortunately, some good sales can be found. A certain boldness is evident as you conquer obstacles and give short shrift to the opposition. A little less worry about your credit-card buying would be wise. You can cut down on expenses next month. Your number is 9.

Friday, December 17 (Moon in Aries)   Know where the bargains are. Aries makes a good companion on these treks from store to store. The news arriving from a distance is good, full of cheer and sentimentality. You may find you have a little more money available than you realized earlier. Orchestrate your decisions with those of your mate. Your lucky number is 2.

Saturday, December 18 (Moon in Aries to Taurus 11:45 a.m.)   Plenty of reserve energies come into fuller play as you tackle last-minute household chores. Gifts are arriving and Santa looks more generous than you anticipated. Aries and Leo are magnanimous in their praise.

Some flaws in the character of a child may be revealed. Lucky lottery: 4, 13, 22, 31, 40, 49.

Sunday, December 19 (Moon in Taurus)   Taurus and Virgo present the practical solutions. You pull in at the seams, narrow your sights, concentrate, and get plenty of work done. There are still outside church and club responsibilities, but you take these in better stride than loved ones. Brown is your color; your lucky number is 6.

Monday, December 20 (Moon in Taurus to Gemini 12:39 p.m.)   Good news! Money earmarked for you can start arriving, as Jupiter moves into your second house. You are more cheerful, more confident, and everything extra that you have done seems worthwhile. Aries and Sagittarius have key roles. Your color is magenta; your lucky number is 1.

Tuesday, December 21 (Moon in Gemini)   The family tops your agenda. Good memories are being built up among children and teenagers. Phone a loved one long distance and you will feel much better about old times and all that they meant to you. Gemini and Libra make things right. Mocha is your color; your lucky number is 3.

Wednesday, December 22 (Moon in Gemini to Cancer 11:52 a.m.)   The sun moves into your eleventh house, accenting friendships, group activities, annual holiday parties, and your desire to have closest friends in one of these evenings. Your love life, creativity, originality, and any possible worries about your children are all illuminated by the full moon. Lucky lottery: 5, 14, 23, 32, 41, 50.

Thursday, December 23 (Moon in Cancer)   Smile to show others just how well disposed toward them you are. Cancer and Capricorn want to be with you Last-minute touches are your most creative and original of the month. Don't forget tips to delivery men and paper boys, and pay special attention to the elderly living alone. Your numbers are 7 and 3.

Friday, December 24 (Moon in Cancer to Leo 11:32 a.m.) Your deeper spiritual assets come into fuller play. There can be some minor changes in schedules imposed on you, but you take all in stride. Annoyances can't get through your strong coat of happiness and inner joy. Phone, read your mail, and isolate yourself for an hour to enjoy personal gratitude. Your lucky number is 9.

Saturday, December 25 (Moon in Leo) Of course, you are overly tired. You want to relax and let others take care of what has to be corrected. You've done more than anybody could have demanded of you. Leo and Aquarius tend to tire you even more as they try to impose changes in your schedule. Lucky lottery: 2, 11, 20, 29, 38, 47.

Sunday, December 26 (Moon in Leo to Virgo 1:34 p.m.) Make this a day of genuine rest, with no chasing of bargains at special sales and no formal entertainments. The children will pick up after themselves if encouraged. Yesterday's leftover food will do fine. This evening calls for some private quality time with your mate. Your lucky number is 4.

Monday, December 27 (Moon in Virgo) Your beloved knows what to say, and there can be closer bonding in marriage, with the feeling that you two have come through another, often difficult, year. Virgo and Taurus have the front seats. A movie, a TV program, or a good book are fine for getting to know your true feelings. Your fortunate number is 8.

Tuesday, December 28 (Moon in Virgo to Libra 7:14 p.m.) An earthy day gives you marvelous opportunities for sharing, cooperating, compromising, and keeping everything steady and stable. You can depend on the local scene to remain quiet, as Saturn hovers in Taurus in good relationship to the sun. Relatives and neighbors are on deck. Hot combination numbers: 1 and 4.

Wednesday, December 29 (Moon in Libra)   Last-minute dealings with your broker and tax agent before the year ends will go well. Avoid any sense of panic if things move slowly and lines are long. A Libra and a Gemini have key roles. It's not too early to consider wise resolutions for the coming year. Lucky lottery: 3, 12, 21, 30, 39, 48.

Thursday, December 30 (Moon in Libra)   Deal with accumulated money, IRA's, tax breaks, and last-minute switches in CD's and the like. Make sure you have the latest information on how to improve your financial position. Aquarius reminds you of all the extreme changes taking place in communications and transportation. Your lucky number is 5.

Friday, December 31 (Moon in Libra to Scorpio 4:36 a.m.)   If possible, change your scene for New Year's Eve. Go where peace and quiet reign, even if people are enjoying their escape. You warm up to the great outdoors. Socializing opportunities are stepped up as Mercury enters Capricorn. This evening will be different from what you expected. Your lucky number is 7.

Happy New Year!

JANUARY 2000

Saturday, January 1 (Moon in Scorpio)   Today's lunar phase emphasizes travel, long-distance phone calls, and contributions to distant overseas charities. Visit an older person you haven't seen in some time. The Pluto keynote puts your awareness in focus, especially where you are mulling over possible studies that will make you more valuable to your employer.

Sunday, January 2 (Moon in Scorpio to Sagittarius 4:33 p.m.)   Today's Venus keynote suggests relaxation with a coworker who loves the great outdoors. Weather permitting, a walk in a park and dining in a restaurant known for its gourmet foods will be enjoyable. Steer clear of increased accident-producing potential on crowded highways. Scorpio makes a fascinating companion.

Monday, January 3 (Moon in Sagittarius)   Avoid anything that smacks of self-centeredness. The Uranus and Neptune keynotes demand different ways of driving to and from work. Extract from past experiences situations that made you happy as the New Year gets underway. Focus on romance this evening. Your lucky number is 4.

Tuesday, January 4 (Moon in Sagittarius)   Today's Mars keynote promises plenty of energy in romance, courtship, spontaneous socializing, and giving advice to offspring. This lunar phase brings enlightenment in career and professional areas. Focus on technological changes that are winnowing out the less flexible. The Jupiter keynote adds the good-luck dimension in finance.

Wednesday, January 5 (Moon in Sagittarius to Capricorn 5:24 a.m.)   Lucky lottery: 3, 9, 15, 30, 39, 45. Friendships mean everything. Locally, a Capricorn has workable advice on immediate and pressing situations. Today's Saturn keynote warns against exposure to virustype ailments. Focus on things you can do, rather than on hopes and dreams.

Thursday, January 6 (Moon in Capricorn)   This lunar phase offers enlightenment in church and club assignments. Conscientious efforts aren't enough when dealing with a hard taskmaster. Twelfth Night celebrations can relieve much tension that has crept into close relationships.

Friday, January 7 (Moon in Capricorn to Aquarius 5:53 p.m.)   At the track. Post position special—number 7 p.p. in the fourth race. Pick six: 1, 7, 4, 4, 2, 8. Watch for these letters in the names of potential winning horses or jockeys: F, O, X. Hot daily doubles: 1 and 7, 1 and 4, 4 and 7. Sagittarius shows less daring, but wins big.

Saturday, January 8 (Moon in Aquarius)   Lucky lottery: 9, 27, 36, 45, 18, 40. The moon position highlights the views of Aquarius and people who don't mind being out of step. Your lover has no reason to complain when Mars is looming over Pisces. Youngsters may be relaxing too long in front of the TV. Watch your intake of sugar and salt.

Sunday, January 9 (Moon in Aquarius)   Read the financial and business magazines and try to keep up with technological and global economic trends that are filtered down into your life. You are exposed to many complaints from older loved ones and from workers who fear this era of massive and sudden changes.

Monday, January 10 (Moon in Aquarius to Pisces 4:59 a.m.)   Today's lunar phase favors lovemaking and expressing your personality and character in relationships with another Pisces and Virgo. Focus on what you can do to improve your personal appearance under this Venus in Pisces keynote. It's a day when you can ask personal questions of someone who looks to you for directions. Your lucky number is 6.

Tuesday, January 11 (Moon in Pisces)   Today's Venus–Jupiter keynote promises strong acceptance by people very different from yourself. Look for a chance to take change and show what you can do. New opportunities for increasing stability in day-to-day situations are there for you to grab. Focus on good memories this evening. Hot combination numbers: 8 and 2.

Wednesday, January 12 (Moon in Pisces to Aries 1:48 p.m.)   Lucky lottery: 1, 19, 28, 37, 46, 10. Consolidate local and immediate gains as Saturn resumes direct movement in your third house. The Mercury keynote brings sudden changes, unexpected criticism. It's a day when saying little rebounds to your advantage. Coordinate your evening plans with your mate and children.

Thursday, January 13 (Moon in Aries)   An excellent lunar phase to increase your income. Fine for talks with supervisors and your employer. You may note that the cost of groceries and household items is rising. Complaints come from older people on antiquated pensions and from youngsters trapped in low-paying jobs without incentive.

Friday, January 14 (Moon in Aries to Taurus 7:38 p.m.)   A good day for considering your personal financial worth, with the strong possibility that you will discover you have more money than you first realized. Discussions with an Aries and Sagittarius will be rewarded. Saturn empowers you to consolidate some recent business–financial gains. A new rereading of the past is recommended. Number 5 is lucky.

Saturday, January 15 (Moon in Taurus)   Lucky lottery: 16, 7, 25, 34, 43, 47. Local situations force themselves upon you. It may be difficult to escape complaints of your neighbors and siblings. You could begin to resent the possessiveness of a dear friend. The Saturday-evening blues can bring on tendency to deceive yourself. Taurus and Virgo are helpful.

Sunday, January 16 (Moon in Taurus to Gemini 10:25 p.m.)   An excellent day to relax at home with loved ones. A TV documentary can hold your attention. Gemini and Libra tend to build up your self-confidence. Nothing can make the week ahead go as well as when you warm up to your job on Sunday afternoon, planning your routines and schedules.

Monday, January 17 (Moon in Gemini)   Hot combination numbers: 4 and 7. Joint business, financial, and betting endeavors with a loved one can pay off. A community problem rears its ugly head. There's much talk about deterioration in your locality and the possibility of falling real estate prices. A love relationship is better than you anticipated.

Tuesday, January 18 (Moon in Gemini to Cancer 11:01 p.m.)   Minor conflicts between your career–job and home–family are in the picture. Overcome phony guilt feelings by accepting the dual responsibilities that you and millions of others have each day. Organizational matters tend to be a big bore. An Aquarius helps you understand major changes. Your lucky number is 6.

Wednesday, January 19 (Moon in Cancer)   Lucky lottery: 19, 8, 17, 26, 48, 35. Studies, basics, and communications are under a cloud. It may be difficult to get youngsters interested. The generation gap will be more prominent over the evening hours. The 20-something people pit themselves against the good advice you have for them. Clean your dresser drawers to get away from confrontations.

Thursday, January 20 (Moon in Cancer to Leo 10:59 p.m.)   An excellent day for making love, finding the romance of life that is close by. Courtships make amazing progress. Communications with your beloved were never better. The approaching lunar eclipse warns against dining in any greasy spoon and exposing yourself to virus-related ailments. Try numbers 1, 4, 7.

Friday, January 21 (Moon in Leo)   A total blackout in your sixth house can have you wearing the wrong clothes, experiencing fatigue and disinterest in your duties and responsibilities. You will find Leo domineering and Aquarius too extreme. It's important that you abide by your physician's recommendations under these adversities.

Saturday, January 22 (Moon in Leo)   There is increased accident potential in the wake of yesterday's
eclipse, so make sure children are not playing danger-
ously. The weather can also carry dimensions of risk and
violence. Publicity and advertising fail to produce. Guard
against soaking up the false tears of somebody dear to
you. Lucky lottery: 15, 5, 23, 33, 41, 48.

*Sunday, January 23 (Moon in Leo to Virgo 12:08
a.m.)*   This lunar phase brings enlightenment in your
marital state, other partnerships, the fine arts of sharing,
cooperating, and making joint decisions. Virgo and Cancer want to keep you on the right track. Try not to get
involved in the marital tangles of a friend, who tends to
tell you too much today.

Monday, January 24 (Moon in Virgo)   At the track.
Post position special—number 2 p.p. in the sixth race.
Pick six: 2, 1, 4, 7, 2, 2. Watch for these letters or initials
in the names of potential winning horses or jockeys: F,
O, X. Hot daily doubles: 1 and 4, 2 and 6, 4 and 6. Virgo
keeps your bets realistic.

*Tuesday, January 25 (Moon in Virgo to Libra 4:10
a.m.)*   Today's Venus keynote endears you to friends
and others interested in sharing church and club responsibilities. This lunar phase gives enlightenment in security matters, progressive changes, budgeting, savings, and
investments. A Libra helps you see the silver clouds. Hot
combination numbers: 4 and 3.

Wednesday, January 26 (Moon in Libra)   Lucky lottery: 6, 24, 33, 42, 15, 12. Fine trends for straightening
out a legal tangle, reaching a decision-making stage in
banking and insurance matters. Focus on improvements
and correction in all financial interests. Libra and Gemini will listen. The weather can be getting you down.

*Thursday, January 27 (Moon in Libra to Scorpio 12:02
p.m.)*   The Mercury keynote speeds up the process of
learning from past experiences. Be flexible in confer-

ences and where more adjustment to changes is required. A former neighbor or in-law can make a surprise appearance. The Neptune keynote can reveal past deception and present chicanery.

Friday, January 28 (Moon in Scorpio)   If you could get away from the grind this weekend, the rest of this season will go better. A Scorpio is your best companion on any travel caper you begin. A change of scene, unfamiliar faces prove to be good ego food under this current lunar phase in your horoscope. Hot combination numbers: 3 and 9.

Saturday, January 29 (Moon in Scorpio to Sagittarius 11:18 p.m.)   Lucky lottery: 14, 32, 41, 5, 17, 20. An excellent day for unusual foods in a name restaurant. Fine for a brain-to-brain conversation at mealtime, and heart-to-heart talks as the evening winds down. You can get a good lease on positive thinking by the way you spend today. Sort and sift; evaluate; investigate.

Sunday, January 30 (Moon in Sagittarius)   Discuss your career–job-assignment matters with Scorpio and Pisces. You can arrive at a better picture of what is at hand. There's a good chance of hearing about a sale or auction that fascinates you. Sightseeing will also be enjoyable. Old churches, humanitarian centers, nautical museums are a must on your schedule.

Monday, January 31 (Moon in Sagittarius)   Sagittarius and Aries are in today's scenario. Arrive on the job earlier than others. A chance discussion with someone in power can brighten your future. Professional and authority interests get a good airing. The spotlight is on your employers, supervisors, your friends at court. Your lucky number is 2.

FEBRUARY 2000

Tuesday, February 1 (Moon in Sagittarius to Capricorn 12:10 p.m.)   Career problems are rooted more in the global than the national economy. A Sagittarius sees the larger picture and can explain it well. The Mercury keynote later on in the day speeds up work and gives you more insight into business trends. The Mars keynote provides the clout and pluck you require. Hot combination numbers: 1 and 7.

Wednesday, February 2 (Moon in Capricorn) Lucky lottery: 3, 12, 21, 30, 39, 48. The Pluto keynote, moon in Capricorn, increases your awareness and transformation power in social expansion. Your reactions blend well with those of key executives. The Jupiter keynotes confers the dimension of enthusiasm to your decisions.

Thursday, February 3 (Moon in Capricorn) Under the current Uranus–Neptune keynote, you are empowered to extract new gains and profits from past involvements. It's a good day to review, evaluate, and let the present serve your future. Plans, programs, routines, and schedules are handled well. Your lucky number is 5.

Friday, February 4 (Moon in Capricorn to Aquarius 12:31 a.m.) You'll realize that you are not out from under the old year 1999 completely. Adjustments to new ideas are making the rounds in your locality are difficult. Last year's uncertainties are making inroads on both social and economic expectations. Clouds gather over past mistakes. Your number is 7.

Saturday, February 5 (Moon in Aquarius) Lucky lottery: 9, 18, 27, 36, 45, 19. Don't count too much on promised assistance. Some increases in the cost of living will not make sense. Those with whom you do business are capricious in their charges and attitudes toward customers. Generation gaps aren't tolerable. Get to bed early.

Sunday, February 6 (Moon in Aquarius to Pisces 11:02 a.m.) You are going to have to give yourself first consideration on a day like this. Younger loved ones zero in on your cogitating and plans. The Mercury keynote speeds up anxieties and hostilities. There are good trends in preparation and in focusing on the work you have to do in the week ahead.

Monday, February 7 (Moon in Pisces) Today's aspects are favorable for sprucing up your personal appearance and working on a more positive attitude. Left to your own devices, you can turn this day to good account. Try to avoid gossip, cliques, and constant butting in on your intentions. Hot combination numbers: 6 and 1.

Tuesday, February 8 (Moon in Pisces to Aries 7:18 p.m.) Another Pisces proves understanding and helpful. This lunar trend gives you enlightenment in what you should be doing to keep the boss happy. If you hold the initiative under this Mars keynote, you will reach desired goals more quickly. You solve mysteries well and see the lay of the business land. Your lucky number is 8.

Wednesday, February 9 (Moon in Aries) Lucky lottery: 1, 10, 19, 28, 37, 46. An excellent day for pushing your earning power, income, and overall wealth production. Take Aries and Sagittarius into your confidence. Your self-confidence is the most valuable dimension in your striving. Young knights drive hard bargains.

Thursday, February 10 (Moon in Aries) Claim what you are sure should be yours. This lunar phase gives you special knowledge of costs, charges, kickbacks, and squeeze. The Jupiter keynote wants you to have what you have earned and deserve. The cold world out there can be made somewhat friendlier by your approach. Hot combination numbers: 3 and 9.

Friday, February 11 (Moon in Aries to Taurus 1:21 a.m.) Focus on what has to be done, crowding out past and future considerations. Taurus and Virgo are in this scenario. Hit what is immediate, pressing, related to studies, business correspondence. Phone those who have something valuable to say. Your awareness in career matters is developing. Number 5 is lucky.

Saturday, February 12 (Moon in Taurus)   Lucky lottery: 7, 16, 25, 34, 43, 14. What you're looking for is right under your nose, so to speak. Siblings and neighbors are in today's scenario. You gain, if you are willing to take full responsibility. You are faster when you are on familiar ground.

Sunday, February 13 (Moon in Taurus to Gemini 5:23 a.m.)   A fine day for a Valentine party and the exchange of small loving expressions. Be sure to have at least one Gemini in the group. The day carries strong emphasis on family, home, community, old school chums, and others you have known for a long time. Short-distance and local travel will do fine.

Monday, February 14 (Moon in Gemini)   Good trends exist for patching up any disagreement you have had with a coworker. A smile does wonders. An offer to help does even more. Information flows freely. Wit and humor extricate you from any embarrassing situation. Your intelligence pays off. Your lucky number is 4.

Tuesday, February 15 (Moon in Gemini to Cancer 7:46 a.m.)   At the track. Post position special—number 6 p.p. in the ninth race. Pick six: 1, 6, 5, 1, 6, 6. Watch for these letters or initials in the names of potential winning horses or jockeys: G, P, Y. Hot daily doubles: 1 and 3, 3 and 6, 1 and 6. A Scorpio companion makes the outing even more fun.

Wednesday, February 16 (Moon in Cancer)   Lucky lottery: 8, 17, 26, 35, 44, 18. Lovemaking should top your agenda under this lunar phase. You see the romance that tends to surround you. A courtship will make definite progress under these configurations. The Mars keynote keeps money flowing in your direction.

***Thursday, February 17 (Moon in Cancer to Leo 9:12
a.m.)***   Socializing in a spontaneous way will make the
day more pleasant. Good trends for giving advice to
young people. Your creativity, originality, and imagination are working overtime and help you to stand out in
any group. Perk up a drab month by opening your home
to neighbors. Your lucky number is 1.

Friday, February 18 (Moon in Leo)   A majestic Leo
enters the picture with all manner of suggestions that
are meant to improve your appearance and overall physical well-being. You may find some of this a bit too intense. A more practical Virgo can relieve any possible
tension. The Venus keynote gives you an appreciation
of an older friend. Number 3 is lucky.

***Saturday, February 19 (Moon in Leo to Virgo 10:54
a.m.)***   Lucky lottery: 5, 14, 23, 32, 41, 25. The sun
makes its Pisces ingress, so this part of the year belongs
to you. The full moon gives special illumination to your
marital state, other partnerships, the fine art of sharing,
and cooperative efforts. You are enlightened about in-
law relationships.

Sunday, February 20 (Moon in Virgo)   Venus has
you seeing the past in a more gentle light. Jupiter brings
luck to your immediate and pressing decisions. There
are gains due to your pluck and clout in financial matters. Neptune lends allure and mystery to a past romantic involvement.

***Monday, February 21 (Moon in Virgo to Libra 2:21
p.m.)***   Discussions with your mate or business partner
extract the best from the day's trends. Knowing where
you are and where you are headed gives the day in-
depth meaning. Remember you are not alone when it
comes to a trouble-making in-law, very possibly a juve-
nile. Your number is 2.

Tuesday, February 22 (Moon in Libra)   Excellent
trends exist in savings, investments, budgeting, bargain

hunting, and insurance discussions. Libra and Aquarius are in the picture. It's a good day to begin making corrections, improvements, and major changes. Can another insurance policy or company serve you better? Your lucky number is 4.

Wednesday, February 23 (Moon in Libra to Scorpio 8:58 p.m.)   Lucky lottery: 6, 15, 24, 33, 42, 12. Personalized interests can slow down as Mercury goes retrograde in Pisces. This lunar phase has you rolling with the punches and quickly adjusting to changes. Your psychic impressions in your career and profession give you good directions.

Thursday, February 24 (Moon in Scorpio)   An excellent day for travel, taking care of what you have perking for yourself at a distance, and for viewing the larger picture. You organize projects well with the help of Scorpio. Be sure to keep in touch, phone and write important business letters. What you hear can be very helpful to you. Your lucky number is 8.

Friday, February 25 (Moon in Scorpio)   At home or away from home base, you are vitally interested in what is going on, in what you can do to improve your financial outlook and maintain your present happiness. You profit from the stability you are demonstrating in business and overall economic matters. Hot combination numbers: 1 and 4.

Saturday, February 26 (Moon in Scorpio to Sagittarius 7:10 a.m.)   Lucky lottery: 3, 12, 21, 30, 39, 48. Sightseeing, dining in seafood restaurants, being friendly to water sign (Cancer, Scorpio, and Pisces) people you meet casually are all favored. This freedom from usual surroundings will make the rest of the season go better. Exchange addresses; notice coincidences.

Sunday, February 27 (Moon in Sagittarius)   Sagittarius and Leo are in today's scenario. Phone a friendly coworker as soon as you arrive home. There are things you should know about that happened when you were away. Before retiring, prepare for the week ahead by getting your wardrobe just right and looking over pertinent notes.

Monday, February 28 (Moon in Sagittarius to Capricorn 7:45 p.m.)   Career routines and schedules top your agenda. Be totally professional in your attitude and approach for best results under these stellar conditions. Moon–Pluto trends give you amazing insight into new technological changes. Self-confidence is your best asset. Hot combination numbers: 9 and 3.

Tuesday, February 29 (Moon in Capricorn)   Are you collecting all that is owed you in the way of special stipends for humanitarian involvements? Friends, members of your church and social clubs are in this scenario. Capricorn is in charge of much that is going on. Your social expansion gets wide support from the lunar phase. Your lucky number is 2.

MARCH 2000

Wednesday, March 1 (Moon in Capricorn)   A fine day for social expansion, church and club activities. The Saturn and Jupiter keynotes favor local, immediate, and pressing interests. You can stabilize and consolidate communication and transportation, negotiating a possible reduction in the costs. Lucky lottery: 1, 10, 19, 28, 37, 46.

Thursday, March 2 (Moon in Capricorn to Aquarius 8:14 a.m.)   There are some conflicts between a retrograde Mercury in your sign as well as the sun. Things may not move as fast as you want them to progress. You may find yourself falling back upon reserves of energy from attempting too ambitious a program. People behave rather unexpectedly. Your number is 3.

Friday, March 3 (Moon in Aquarius)   Under this lunar phase, you reach deep inside your memory for the answers. Uranus brings changes that make society hustle to keep up with scientific gains. The Neptune keynote speaks of the allure of exotic ideas and the deception surrounding some advice. Hot combination numbers: 5 and 3.

Saturday, March 4 (Moon in Aquarius to Pisces 6:31 p.m.)   Lucky lottery: 9, 18, 27, 36, 45, 29. The Mars–Pluto keynote is promising for higher earning power, more profitable career assignments. It's a good day to put forth your arguments for a higher salary and more rewarding assignments. Seek career advice from a Sagittarius.

Sunday, March 5 (Moon in Pisces)   Lucky you! The new moon illuminates your decision-making power, the solution to puzzles, and your abilities to extract new gains from past involvements. Another Pisces will have doubled the pleasure and fun of the day. You oversee successfully. You investigate well.

Monday, March 6 (Moon in Pisces)   A promising day for a great leap forward in your life, in personalized interests, and in your career potential. The mercury keynote puts you ahead of the competition. Excellent trends exist in public relations and gains from advertising. Neptune favors the restoration of a former relationship. Your lucky number is 6.

Tuesday, March 7 (Moon in Pisces to Aries 1:55 a.m.)   The moon–Mars keynote intensifies the success potential in your higher earning power, income, and a new source of income. You have the drive and the self-confidence now to go after what you are sure you deserve. The value you put on yourself is the value an employer will put on you. Hot combination numbers: 8 and 2.

Wednesday, March 8 (Moon in Aries)   Lucky lottery:
1, 10, 19, 29, 28, 46. Hold the financial initiative throughout the day and the money will flow in your direction.
It's déjà vu in one sense, and the way success came years
ago will repeat today. Because you know the score, your
employer finds you more valuable.

***Thursday, March 9 (Moon in Aries to Taurus 7:02
a.m.)***   The Uranus keynote helps you to keep abreast
of the times. Via TV or your newspaper, you will receive
good clues about big changes later on in the month.
Special enlightenment under this planetary keynote gives
you the inside track in a better credit card situation.
Your lucky number is 3.

Friday, March 10 (Moon in Taurus)   There's a big
buildup of the moon, Saturn–Jupiter power in your third
house, improving communications, transportation, studies, and your learning processes. Siblings and neighbors
are involved in the day's drama. Local situations offer
many doors to a brighter future. Hot combination numbers: 5 and 2.

***Saturday, March 11 (Moon in Taurus to Gemini 10:46
a.m.)***   Lucky lottery: 7, 16, 17, 25, 34, 43. Your understanding of money was never better. Personal clout and
drive can change any sluggish financial trend. The
dreams of Gemini and the practicality of Virgo should
never be overlooked. Earthy and rooty vegetables are
right for you today.

Sunday, March 12 (Moon in Gemini)   Gemini makes
a dramatic entrance and has useful information for you
on home decoration, falling real estate prices in certain
areas, and possibly what some of your children are doing
behind your back. Gossip, rumormongering, imaginative
tales that never happened keep wit and humor flowing.

***Monday, March 13 (Moon in Gemini to Cancer 1:52
p.m.)***   Venus enters Pisces, giving you unbeatable
support for glamorizing your personal appearance. Look

into an updated hairstyle, a new line of miracle cosmetics, and shop for wardrobe accessories that will spruce up some of your garments. If you want to look beautiful, today's the day to learn how. Number 4 is lucky.

Tuesday, March 14 (Moon in Cancer)   At the track. Post position special—number 6 p.p. in the ninth race. Pick six: 6, 1, 3, 6, 5, 1. Watch for these letters or initials in the names of potential winning horses or jockeys: H, Q, Z. Hot daily doubles; 1 and 6, 4 and 6, 2 and 4. Creative juices are stirred. Your betting partner is a Cancer.

Wednesday, March 15 (Moon in Cancer to Leo 4:44 p.m.)   Lucky lottery: 8, 16, 17, 26, 35, 44. Love, romance, courtship, and a stronger commitment to your beloved are all part of this joyful scenario. There are fine trends for social expansion and for advising your children and other young people. The Mercury keynote is promising for increased speed in personal reaction time.

Thursday, March 16 (Moon in Leo)   An excellent day for your overall physical well-being, considering some new herbs, new medical alternatives, and generally taking a strong stand in health maintenance. The lunar trend warns against self-deception, however. Some advice may be coming from a person who believes he knows everything. Your lucky number is 1.

Friday, March 17 (Moon in Leo to Virgo 7:49 p.m.)   A Leo is very much in the day's drama, strongly elitist, overly self-confident, with an agenda very much his or her own. You find this Leo entertaining. You learn much about fashion from Leo. Pluto awareness and transformation power develop more slowly on a day like this. Hot combination numbers: 3 and 9.

Saturday, March 18 (Moon in Virgo)   Lucky lottery: 5, 14, 15, 23, 41, 32. The day favors a more practical and methodical approach to work and spending. Virgo is in the picture. You and your mate can work the bugs out of any negative situation—again, by being practical and logical. No threats or ultimatums, please.

Sunday, March 19 (Moon in Virgo to Libra 10:57 p.m.) No matter what you think, nobody understands you better than your mate, with long-term business partners, and live-in associate second on the list. Keep any maudlin, self-pitying pose from coming to the fore. It's a day for laughing instead of crying. There is humor in many disagreements.

Monday, March 20 (Moon in Libra) The full moon gives marvelous illumination of your seventh house of partnerships, sharing, cooperative efforts, from all of which you can extract power today. Brain-to-brain rather than heart-to-heart conversations will work miracles. Joint business and financial endeavors will succeed. Your lucky number is 2.

Tuesday, March 21 (Moon in Libra) Libra and Aquarius are in the day's scenario. There are excellent trends in security matters, savings, investments, bargain hunting, and budgeting. A fine day to make a new will. It's also good for disposing of items you overstocked and for spring cleaning in closets and storage areas. Your lucky number is 4.

Wednesday, March 22 (Moon in Libra to Scorpio 6:17 a.m.) Lucky lottery: 6, 12, 15, 24, 33, 42. An excellent day for travel, relaxation, sightseeing, making long-distance phone calls, and checking up on projects and investments at a distance. Scorpio and Taurus are helpful. People at or from a distance tend to be lucky for you under existing aspects.

Thursday, March 23 (Moon in Scorpio) Today's spring fever can give you the yen to change your scene, plan a foreign vacation. The emphasis is on islands, and actually taking off like a big bird. You excel in organizing, engineering, putting it all together. A Cancer and

237

another Pisces are in your corner. Hot combination numbers: 8 and 2.

Friday, March 24 (Moon in Scorpio to Sagittarius 3:43 p.m.) Take advantage of the unbeatable drive you have to familiarize yourself with what is happening behind the scenes. You are able to head off a scandal, to uncover chicanery, and to see what is being covered up. Corruption in high places is being revealed. Number 1 is lucky for you.

Saturday, March 25 (Moon in Sagittarius) Lucky lottery: 3, 12, 21, 30, 39, 48. Today's Mars keynote gives you excellent drive in local, communications, transportation, and in all dealings with siblings and neighbors. The lunar trend in your tenth house keeps workaday activities high on your agenda. There are fine trends for achieving in usual activities.

Sunday, March 26 (Moon in Sagittarius) Sagittarius has an important role to play. If a coworker offers an invitation, accept it graciously. There are things going on at work that you can discuss and gain new insight in the bargain. You will enjoy checking the advance of spring in parks and fields.

Monday, March 27 (Moon in Sagittarius to Capricorn 3:52 a.m.) Family, home, property, and ownership matters are high on your agenda as the moon moves in your fourth house. Things that may have been sluggish earlier in the month, can be speeded up masterfully today. Aries and Leo are very much in evidence. Hot combination numbers: 9 and 6.

Tuesday, March 28 (Moon in Capricorn) Capricorn and Cancer are in today's scenario. The urge to engage in expensive social expansion can be strong. The lure of luxuries is also tempting, but overspending will bring a strong sense of guilt under your Jupiter–Saturn keynote. After all, April 15 tax time is close by. Your number is 2.

Wednesday, March 29 (Moon in Capricorn to Aquarius 4:35 p.m.) Lucky lottery: 4, 13, 14, 22, 31, 40. There's good Mars-ruled instigation, origination, and unbeatable drive in your learning processes, effective communication, and profitable short-distance transportation and travel matters. Engage a successful business person in conversation.

Thursday, March 30 (Moon in Aquarius) A big lunar–Uranus–Neptune power buildup permits extracting new gains and profits from past successes. The answers to any baffling questions are rooted in former experiences. An Aquarius knows where the secrets are buried. You do well, because your psyche knows the answers. Your lucky number is 6.

Friday, March 31 (Moon in Aquarius) You are in charge of closing out this month, of evaluating accurately the progress made, and putting a lot of small pieces of the whole together. You feel confident, able to cope, to accept inevitable changes related to the technologies and methodologies of these times. Hot combination numbers: 8 and 2.

APRIL 2000

Saturday, April 1 (Moon in Aquarius to Pisces 3:13 a.m.) Lucky lottery: 7, 16, 17, 25, 34, 43. Today's Venus keynote is a big help in making your immediate surroundings more comfortable, attractive, and better organized. Many complaints are coming from the barely skilled, who fear downsizing and being winnowed out of the ever-changing time.

Sunday, April 2—Daylight Saving Time begins (Moon in Pisces) You can count on good lunar illumination of your personal interests, anxieties, and expectations. There is special enlightenment in ways to stabilize and consolidate your recent gains. You may want to consider leasing rather than buying a car, for example.

Monday, April 3 (Moon in Pisces to Aries 11:33 a.m.)   A financial surplus in some areas and shortage in others makes for much mulling over of expenses, tax requirements, and new budgeting arrangements. The money's there as the sun moves in your second house, but it may already have been allocated. The Mercury keynote tells you to postpone financial decisions.

Tuesday, April 4 (Moon in Aries)   Now there is special illumination of your earning power, income, the value of what you own, and the possibility of finding a new source of income. This lunar trend is a good time to estimate future as well as current expenses. Talk all this over with an Aries. Your lucky number is 6.

Wednesday, April 5 (Moon in Aries to Taurus 3:30 p.m.)   Lucky lottery: 8, 16, 17, 26, 35, 44. You have unbeatable drive, pluck, and clout when zeroing in on local, immediate, and rare opportunities. Taurus and another Pisces are in this scenario. You benefit from a new improvement in a long-held investment.

Thursday, April 6 (Moon in Taurus)   Today's lunar trends favor communications, transportation, learning processes, studies, and connections with neighbors and siblings. A fine day to open up new channels of communication in career, business, and financial matters. The Venus keynote provides appreciation of luxuries and antiques. Your lucky number is 1.

Friday, April 7 (Moon in Taurus to Gemini 3:59 p.m.)   Today's Jupiter keynote promises good luck and record gains through local politics and legislation. Because of some building plans, your property can become more valuable. Local events tend to play into your hands, whereas earlier changes may have been feared. Your lucky number is 3.

Saturday, April 8 (Moon in Gemini)   Lucky lottery: 5, 14, 15, 23, 32, 41. Family, home, property, ownership, and community developments top your agenda. There can be full disclosures under these configurations—nothing hazy or withheld. Nothing is covered up now. Because you now have the complete picture, you can take action.

Sunday, April 9 (Moon in Gemini to Cancer 8:16 p.m.)   Gemini and Libra are in today's scenario. Love is a strong force, which helps you understand what otherwise might have been an impossible situation. Aunts, uncles, and cousins have an important effect on the current conditions of your clan or tribe.

Monday, April 10 (Moon in Cancer)   Love is both spiritual and physical under this lunar trend. Strong as your commitment to a loved one may be, it can still be strengthened under existing aspects. A Scorpio and a Cancer both understand your ambitions. There's plenty of romance and adventure potential here. Your lucky number is 2.

Tuesday, April 11 (Moon in Cancer to Leo 9:16 p.m.)   A fine day to come to grips with any problem presented by your children. The generation gap can be bridged under current fifth house stimulation. The Venus keynote gives an appreciation of financial advisers. Spontaneous socializing should include unmarried students interested in meeting Mr. and Ms. Right. Number 4 is lucky for you.

Wednesday, April 12 (Moon in Leo)   Lucky lottery: 6, 15, 16, 24, 33, 42. Leo makes a dramatic entry and wins your admiration. The trends favor keeping abreast of new medical and scientific findings, which insure greater longevity and longer productive years. Consider adding to your spring wardrobe.

Thursday, April 13 (Moon in Leo)   A fine day for reading, studying health journals, and becoming familiar with herbal medicine. Increasingly, modern physicians are looking into healing power, which has escaped their attention for more than 100 years. Today is also favorable for hard work. Your lucky number is 8.

Friday, April 14 (Moon in Leo to Virgo 3:19 a.m.) Virgo and Capricorn are strongly represented in your horoscope today. Fine trends exist for bonding more closely with your mate and other partners. Cooperative efforts, joint projects, stimulating discussions will make this a vital day. A divorced couple seem anxious to get back together. Your lucky number is 1.

Saturday, April 15 (Moon in Virgo) Lucky lottery: 3, 12, 13, 21, 39, 48. Discuss betting with your partners and choose numbers that all agree upon. In-laws and ex-mates are in the picture. Quiet and calm discussions prevail, if you and your beloved want to make a joint decision about a purchase, trip, or party.

Sunday, April 16 (Moon in Virgo to Libra 8:36 a.m.) An in-law or former in-law may need your help. The aspects suggest you do what you can, your actions proving most pleasing to your former mate and children. Do what you can to help nephews, nieces, and cousins resolve a question about where they should be married, or religious issues.

Monday, April 17 (Moon in Libra) An excellent day to start making corrections, improvements, and changes. It's important to consider the legality of what someone is urging you to do. Despite many requests to change your insurance policy, stick with the company you have been dealing with for a long time. Your lucky number is 9.

Tuesday, April 18 (Moon in Libra to Scorpio 3:36 p.m.) The full moon forms in your eighth house, illuminating all security matters—alarm systems; locks on doors, windows, and vehicles; savings, investments, and so on. Avoid taking any questionable mortgage on your home, despite the solicitation mail that fills your box. Libra has good advice. Hot combination numbers: 2 and 6.

Wednesday, April 19 (Moon in Scorpio)   Lucky lottery: 4, 13, 14, 22, 31, 40. The moon in Scorpio illuminates travel plans, projects at a distance from your home. It also helps you decide on additional studies to meet the challenges of these changing times. Take a more conservative approach to finances.

Thursday, April 20 (Moon in Scorpio)   The sun–Saturn–Jupiter keynotes give unbeatable power for coping with studies, new office equipment, local problems, and any sudden changes in legislation governing your neighborhood and its taxing programs. If a sibling is certain that a piece of property now on the market will increase in value, then put up some money. Your number is 6.

Friday, April 21 (Moon in Scorpio to Sagittarius 12:59 a.m.)   Pay primary attention to your career on a day when you can register gains. Arrive on the job early, when there will be opportunities to discuss relevant matters with a supervisor. Steer clear of gossips and rumormongers who excel in getting all the stories wrong. Hot combination numbers: 8 and 2.

Saturday, April 22 (Moon in Sagittarius)   Lucky lottery: 1, 10, 19, 28, 37, 46. Your sense of control in home and community can be tested by both young people and senior citizens. The great outdoors beckons strongly, but a coworker or supervisor may pester you for opinions and decisions. Sagittarius and Leo have parts to play.

Sunday, April 23 (Moon in Sagittarius to Capricorn 12:48 p.m.)   This day of rest may not be very quiet. Many demands can be made upon your time and energy. Church and club committees may go begging for chairpersons. There's ego food here, but it would be wrong to take on more responsibilities than you can handle as spring advances.

Monday, April 24 (Moon in Capricorn)   Give your best shot to business and offer assistance to older loved ones, thereby making this a balanced day in line with the dominant aspects in your horoscope. This evening is for quiet socializing with long-term friends and coworkers. Capricorn and Virgo play vital roles. Your lucky number is 7.

Tuesday, April 25 (Moon in Capricorn)   The Mercury keynote and moon in Capricorn permit some financial dealings that couldn't get off the ground earlier in the month. A formerly indecisive partner can suddenly be ready for speedy actions. You may feel like celebrating this evening, now that a deal has been agreed upon. Your lucky number is 9.

Wednesday, April 26 (Moon in Capricorn to Aquarius 1:43 a.m.)   Lucky lottery: 2, 11, 20, 29, 38, 47. The moon joins Uranus and Neptune in your twelfth house, where there is illumination of changes in the works. You'll discover how to extract new gains from past studies and experiences. Old puzzling mysteries are solved when Neptune lifts the veil.

Thursday, April 27 (Moon in Aquarius)   New insight into changes imposed upon you earlier in the year can make this a red-letter day. The answers to many of the questions you are asking yourself are right there within you. Memory serves you greatly. You will love to reminisce with siblings and others you have known for a long time. Your lucky number is 4.

Friday, April 28 (Moon in Aquarius to Pisces 1:06 p.m.)   Gemini, Libra, and Aquarius help make this one of your truly intellectual days. Conversation is witty, informative, and just what you need. Discuss property, ownership, law, recent legal decisions, and what is happening behind the scenes. At work, computers or cooling systems may break down. Your lucky number is 6.

Saturday, April 29 (Moon in Pisces)   Lucky lottery: 8, 17, 18, 26, 35, 44. The lunar transit of your sign reveals what has been hidden, held back, denied you, and how you can make sure this doesn't happen again. As veils are lifted, the truth emerges from behind the coverup. Scandals are in the news.

Sunday, April 30 (Moon in Pisces to Aries 8:55 p.m.)   You can take the lead in spiritual matters, on a church committee, as a witness in a legal case. Your ability to walk that chalk line between right and wrong does you proud. No one dislikes deception more than you, but you also love privacy and often ignore what you suspect is going on.

MAY 2000

Monday, May 1 (Moon in Aries)   Push your earning power and financial matters under the current lunar transit. The Venus–Mercury keynotes keep local matters high on your agenda. Past experiences come to the fore again, under Uranus and Neptune trends. You could discover that your possessions are much more valuable than suspected. Your lucky number is 3.

Tuesday, May 2 (Moon in Aries)   There is great inequality, as the salaries of some go sky high, whereas others are downsized and unable to cope with the rising cost of living. There are some career uncertainties as Pluto retrogrades in your tenth house. The picture is there, but it is fuzzy and blurred. Hot combination numbers: 5 and 2.

Wednesday, May 3 (Moon in Aries to Taurus 12:54 a.m.)   Lucky lottery: 7, 16, 17, 25, 34, 43. Local situations and conditions may limit your actions today. Siblings and neighbors may interfere in a selfish way and expect you to solve their problems. Taurus and Virgo play key roles as you strive to chalk up gains.

Thursday, May 4 (Moon in Taurus)   The lunation happens in your third house, illuminating ways to overcome local setbacks, enrich your mind via a new course of studies, and improve your image in the eyes of those who are overly judgmental. The Mars keynote supports domestic, real estate, property, and ownership interests. Your lucky number is 9.

Friday, May 5 (Moon in Taurus to Gemini 2:24 a.m.)   The Saturn keynote stabilizes immediate and pressing matters. You can consolidate the recent advantages that have come your way. Opportunities to dispose of items you no longer require, including electrical and mechanical equipment, are promising. Advertising, phone calls, and letter writing serve you well. Your lucky number is 2.

Saturday, May 6 (Moon in Gemini)   Lucky lottery: 4, 13, 14, 22, 31, 40. The moon's position focuses on your creative ambitions. Is your camera giving you the professional pictures you want the world to evaluate? Your Neptune assets serve you well in creating and then solving mysteries.

Sunday, May 7 (Moon in Gemini to Cancer 3:14 a.m.)   The spotlight is on the reasons others love you so much. Your quiet, gentle, often mysterious ways seem both romantic and adventurous to all who like you. Your ruling planet, Neptune, gives you more allure than most. The glamorous look is easy for you to achieve.

Monday, May 8 (Moon in Cancer)   There are excellent trends for spontaneous socializing, for come-as-you-are parties and for letting the various generations get to know each other. Your children may be a little baffled at the extent of your knowledge of what they are thinking and doing. Your creativity makes you popular. Your lucky number is 1.

Tuesday, May 9 (Moon in Cancer to Leo 5:02 a.m.)   Leo and Sagittarius have key roles, as you evaluate mental and physical attributes. Your physician or clergyman can be in the picture. A current health doctrine may be that looking beautiful and fashionable reflects in your state of being. Hot combination numbers: 3 and 9.

Wednesday, May 10 (Moon in Leo)   Lucky lottery: 5, 14, 15, 23, 32, 41. Consult some of the health-maintenance books on the newstands. This is a time when you may seek health information on the Internet and wish to learn more about nutrition, diet, and many allied subjects that your physician never broached.

Thursday, May 11 (Moon in Leo to Virgo 8:42 a.m.)   There are fine aspects for adding new accessories to your wardrobe. You are at your best when you achieve the exotic, mysterious appearance, when you keep those attracted to you guessing. Your sense of privacy also is a great protection against unwanted attention. Your numbers are 7, 3, 5.

Friday, May 12 (Moon in Virgo)   The lunar spotlight is on your marital state, business partnerships, and what you can gain from joint projects and investments. The power to bond with your beloved is a powerful thread through these hours. The Mars keynote supports your authority in your home. It's a fine day for discussing house rules with teenagers. Your number is 9.

Saturday, May 13 (Moon in Virgo to Libra 2:28 p.m.)   Lucky lottery: 2, 11, 20, 29, 38, 47. Today's Neptune keynote tones down a gossip's ability to deceive and zero in on secrets you'd rather keep hidden. The methods of your beloved can stir your criticism. Married people must make allowances for the great differences between the genders.

Sunday, May 14 (Moon in Libra)   The Mercury keynote helps you feel comfortable in your own house and your own neighborhood. You articulate your needs well. You are carrying an aura of youth, no matter what your age, and will enjoy discussions with rebellious kids. Build bridges of understanding now.

Monday, May 15 (Moon in Libra to Scorpio 10:18 p.m.) A legal matter could take a turn for the better and may possibly be settled soon. Libra and Aquarius have key roles. You notice that there are some who don't want to discuss the source of their additional income. You won't pry and probe, but a relative will. Hot combination numbers: 8 and 2.

Tuesday, May 16 (Moon in Scorpio) A face-to-face meeting with your broker, insurance, and tax adviser can ultimately mean more money in the bank for you. Watch the cash registers at the checkouts on a day such as this. The yen to travel, to change your scene can be strong, but chances are you are unable to get away. Your lucky number is 1.

Wednesday, May 17 (Moon in Scorpio) Lucky lottery: 3, 12, 21, 30, 39, 48. You extend your thinking beyond the norm and take in more than others may realize. Long-distance phone calls will serve your purpose. People from foreign countries are lucky for you under Scorpio-ruled trends.

Thursday, May 18 (Moon in Scorpio to Sagittarius 8:10 a.m.) The full moon forms in your ninth house, which illuminates future travel plans. It's a fine day for planning your summer vacation. Islands such as Corsica, Malta, Jersey, Man, and Pitcairn appeal strongly to your desire for romance and history. Discuss these dreams with a Scorpio and another Pisces. Your lucky number is 5.

Friday, May 19 (Moon in Sagittarius) At the track. Post position special—number 7 p.p. in the first race. Pick six: 7, 2, 1, 4, 7, 6. Watch for these letters or initials in the names of potential winning horses or jockeys: A,

S, J. Hot daily doubles: 7 and 1, 7 and 4, 1 and 4. Sagittarius does well figuring the odds.

Saturday, May 20 (Moon in Sagittarius to Capricorn 8:02 p.m.)   Lucky lottery: 9, 18, 27, 36, 45, 49. Avoid thinking too much about your career, incompetent supervisors, and possible desire to find a new job. Let this be a fun day when you are an individual, not just an employee. Refuse to let business interfere with family and home duties.

Sunday, May 21 (Moon in Capricorn)   Gemini and Capricorn are in your day's scenario. Your Gemini friend often seems more like a relative, a soul mate who knows more about you than anybody else. There are things you can discuss with Gemini today that edge into your private life. With Capricorn, you can combine pleasure with business.

Monday, May 22 (Moon in Capricorn)   Invite a former coworker to an outdoor cafe to realize more fully that this is the glorious month of May. Recalling old times, problems shared and overcome, will give you extra self-confidence for the rest of this month. Your guest may have been a supervisor. Hot combination numbers: 6 and 1.

Tuesday, May 23 (Moon in Capricorn to Aquarius 9:01 a.m.)   An older, rather cranky friend, who fears retirement, may be issuing a cry from the heart for understanding. Your Piscean compassion can be strongly stirred. Children are not the only ones who require center-stage attention now and then. Your sense of fair play is its own reward. Your lucky number is 8.

Wednesday, May 24 (Moon in Aquarius)   Lucky lottery: 1, 10, 19, 28, 37, 46. Today's lunar transit lights up the past, secrets, confidential matters, and what is transpiring behind the scenes. Gemini and Aquarius would love to share your psychic impressions and learn how your Neptunian power can lift veils and uncover explanations.

Thursday, May 25 (Moon in Aquarius to Pisces 9:08 p.m.)   The sun and Mars keynotes accent the anxiety of students on the verge of examinations and vacation adventures. The parental "No" not only brings arguments, but some pretty racy language that can upset your quiet, gentle approach and attitude. Other parents are on your side. Hot combination numbers: 3 and 6.

Friday, May 26 (Moon in Pisces)   Venus moves into Gemini, which turns yesterday's monsters into today's charmers. Talks with children and their friends do much to restore your peace of mind. Summer plans are always more elaborate than they should be as May moves into its finale. Mars–Venus gender conflicts touch puppy love. Your lucky number: 5.

Saturday, May 27 (Moon in Pisces)   The moon in Pisces produces solutions to mysteries, negative findings, and information that has been concealed. Try to keep the impact of this from upsetting too many people, especially Taurus and Cancer. Everything comes out in the open. Your lucky lottery: 7, 16, 17, 25, 34, 43.

Sunday, May 28 (Moon in Pisces to Aries 6:08 a.m.) Study the financial pages of your Sunday newspaper. There are good pointers for future investments and a clue about where the global economy is headed. Neighbors complain about recent increases in the cost of living. The blame is carelessly allocated and there is nostalgia for the old, simpler days.

Monday, May 29 (Moon in Aries)   The moon in Aries produces knightly behavior in the presence of senior citizens. But underneath, there is resentment and aggression about financial worries and shortages. You learned long ago that it's futile to stand in the way of change and, what one hopes, is progress. Your lucky number is 4.

Tuesday, May 30 (Moon in Aries to Taurus 11:03 a.m.) There are financial opportunities if you pounce upon them as soon as they present their prologues. It's imperative that you rise early and punch that time clock before the competition. You excel at keeping others in the dark under these aspects and enjoy your gains even more. Your lucky number is 6.

Wednesday, May 31 (Moon in Taurus) Lucky lottery: 8, 16, 17, 26, 35, 44. The Taurus moon favors the practical, rather than what you may prefer to do. You may encounter much possessiveness or stubbornness on part of siblings and neighbors. Bank clerks will appear to be out of sorts. Keep your purchases to the minimum. Stick to your budget.

JUNE 2000

Thursday, June 1 (Moon in Taurus to Gemini 12:35 p.m.) A buildup of sun–Venus–Mars power in your fourth house puts domestic issues at the top of the day's agenda. Within your home, the generational differences must be bridged and in your calm, insightful ways you are chosen for this task. A show of your bullish temper erupts. Your lucky numbers are 1, 4, 7.

Friday, June 2 (Moon in Gemini) The lunation occurs in your fourth house, illuminating many ways to keep the peace between young and old. There is enlightenment about childrens' camps, novel ways to earn a little spending money, and how to steer your children away from the wrong companions. In your subtle ways, you can inspire youngsters.

Saturday, June 3 (Moon in Gemini to Cancer 12:31 p.m.) Lucky lottery: 2, 11, 20, 29, 38, 47. Today favors the flow of information about your community. Students tend to separate themselves from those with less education. It's time for an intelligent lecture on the cautious handling of any vehicle. Watch children with a tendency to disappear.

Sunday, June 4 (Moon in Cancer)   A fine day for love-making, bonding more closely with your beloved, and standing together in the face of youthful rebellions. The romance of the month comes to the fore, with strong emphasis on what you can do only in summer. Cancer and another Pisces make this a pleasant day for you.

Monday, June 5 (Moon in Cancer to Leo 12:47 p.m.)   Talks with children can produce the desired results. Always be ready for a gentle compromise or at least give the impression of reconsidering your initial attitude. The sublime dimension in your Pisces personality and character is a big advantage. Your lucky number is 8.

Tuesday, June 6 (Moon in Leo)   Leo will share a strong love of this month and appreciation of the flowers, harmony, and anticipation that engulfs people. Happiness is therapeutic under these aspects. You encounter some majestic attitudes and elegant fashions. Those local changes that came on strong earlier are sluggish now. Your lucky number is 1.

Wednesday, June 7 (Moon in Leo to Virgo 2:58 p.m.)   Lucky lottery: 3, 12, 21, 30, 39, 48. It's a day when casual dress still can win prizes. Comfort is in great demand. The fire signs (Aries, Leo, and Sagittarius) have vital roles to play as a placid afternoon gives way to an exciting evening of parties and pleasures.

Thursday, June 8 (Moon in Virgo)   Today favors partnership, talks with your mate and business associates. Joint projects will be more effective than a lone approach. Virgo and Taurus come center stage. The method chosen to accomplish is more important than you may have realized. Number 5 is right for you now.

Friday, June 9 (Moon in Virgo to Libra 8 p.m.)   It's a day for married couples to appear together in public, even when one prefers a solitary role. Light and dark harmonize; the day's trends support the night's trends. The inevitable becomes accepted and a stormy passage leads to future agreement and happiness. Your lucky number is 7.

Saturday, June 10 (Moon in Libra)   Lucky lottery: 9, 18, 19, 27, 36, 45. You enjoy the Midas touch in money matters, bargain-hunting, and wise budgeting. Savings and investments are favored as the moon transits your eighth house. Minor changes help, rather than upset, any applecarts. Your self-confidence invites gains.

Sunday, June 11 (Moon in Libra)   Intelligent discussions will accomplish much more than arguing. Libra knows how to look on the positive side and is a wonderful influence when disagreements arise. Doing the right thing nags at those who try to escape it. Yes, the poet said it: "What is so rare as a day in June?"

Monday, June 12 (Moon in Libra to Scorpio 3:56 a.m.)   It's time to change your scene, even if only for a few days. Scorpio is your best companion in testing the waters, relaxing in the sun, and organizing social expansion and unusual get-togethers. There is a strongly sensual trend in your makeup now. Choose number 6.

Tuesday, June 13 (Moon in Scorpio)   At the track. Post position special—number 8 p.p. in the second race. Pick six: 1, 8, 8, 3, 2, 4. Watch for these letters or initials in the names of potential winning horses or jockeys: B, K, T. Hot daily doubles 2 and 8, 8 and 1, 8 and 8. You spend a little more to win a little more.

Wednesday, June 14 (Moon in Scorpio to Sagittarius 2:19 p.m.)   Lucky lottery: 1, 10, 19, 28, 37, 46. Keep on the move. Enjoy the fresh offerings of a seafood restaurant that accents the food rather than the decor. Walks on the beach can make the sunset heavenly. For someone who isn't boistrous, you can enjoy the happy noise of youngsters.

Thursday, June 15 (Moon in Sagittarius) Career demands take precedence. Be on the job earlier than most, rested, ready to take on your weight in wildcats. Sagittarius makes a splendid companion under prevailing aspects. Today favors conferences, seminars, increased production, and fast-moving production lines. Your lucky number is 3.

Friday, June 16 (Moon in Sagittarius) Take the problem for a pleasant stroll away from the job. The answers show up almost immediately, once you are freed of the working environment. You can win the approval of a difficult supervisor by the way you present your recommendations. Hot combination numbers: 5 and 2.

Saturday, June 17 (Moon in Sagittarius to Capricorn 2:27 a.m.) Lucky lottery: 7, 16, 17, 25, 34, 43. Capricorn and Virgo will influence your thinking. It can be a grand day for socializing with those with whom you do business, if you set the pattern and pace at the outset. An older person can throw a monkey wrench in an otherwise peaceful evening.

Sunday, June 18 (Moon in Capricorn) An outing, picnic in a park, but not sun bathing will make this a wonderful Sunday. It's an earthy day, when your appreciation of the approach of summer is first-rate. Taurus and Virgo make good companions who certainly will relieve you of a lot of the hard work.

Monday, June 19 (Moon in Capricorn to Aquarius 3:26 p.m.) Friendships, a positive approach to work, and the ability to cope with a lot of idle chatter will make this a good day. The Venus keynote gives allure to everyday activities. Mars accents spontaneous lovemaking. The beast will not be denied his beauty. Fire signs ignite with water signs.

Tuesday, June 20 (Moon in Aquarius) You stir the smoldering embers of a past love. The least expected stranger can reappear. The past encroaches on the present. Aquarius and Gemini understand the situation and can be helpful. Sort and sift right from wrong, with both regrets and an accompanying feeling of escape. Your lucky number is 6.

Wednesday, June 21 (Moon in Aquarius)   Lucky lottery: 8, 17, 18, 26, 35, 44. Close out no-win situations, doomed projects, and past uncertainties. Prepare; gather your wits together; your time is coming. This is the eve of your lunar rebirth. Finish, complete, and get ready for your golden tomorrow.

Thursday, June 22 (Moon in Aquarius to Pisces 3:52 a.m.)   The moon in Pisces gives you a sense of rebirth. You are very much at home, as your psychic awareness encompasses the entire day and night. There is splendid illumination of your personal interests, where you want to head from here and how to go about getting there. Your lucky number is 1.

Friday, June 23 (Moon in Pisces)   The perfect time to solve mysteries, learn what is happening behind the scenes, extract new gains from old successes, remember what others seem to have forgotten. Another Pisces and a Cancer make good companions under prevailing aspects. Your lucky number is 3.

Saturday, June 24 (Moon in Pisces to Aries 1:56 p.m.)   You are in your season of romance with the sun, Venus, Mercury, and Mars permitting power plays. The love ball certainly is in your court; if single make the most of these trends. You possess an aura of adventure. Courtship triumphs. Lucky lottery: 5, 14, 23, 32, 41, 15.

Sunday, June 25 (Moon in Aries)   Financial discussions with a relative or neighbor will go well as the moon moves in your second house. There can be some bold decisions made now for the week ahead. The urge to seize the initiative and prove what self-confidence can achieve for you is strong.

Monday, June 26 (Moon in Aries to Taurus 8:20 p.m.)   There is enormous inequality in the matter of salaries and this truth is a favorite topic for Pisces. People who understand the computer, but who can't speak proper English, and are ignorant of U.S. geography are making a fortune. TV study programs may be the answer in both cases.

Tuesday, June 27 (Moon in Taurus) There is plenty of lunar, Saturn, and Neptune power in your third house, which makes short-distance travel and communications beneficial. A better understanding of the day's significance can be drawn from a discussion with Taurus and Virgo. It's an earthy day. Stick with the facts and avoid fancies. Your lucky number is 4.

Wednesday, June 28 (Moon in Taurus to Gemini 11:01 p.m.) Lucky lottery: 6, 15, 24, 33, 42, 21. Studies, learning processes, broadening your scope, and probing areas where you recognize your limitations are all favored under prevailing aspects. It's a perfect night to take the initiative in lovemaking.

Thursday, June 29 (Moon in Gemini) The moon makes a dynamic entry into your fourth house, giving you special insight and in-depth conclusions about domestic, community, property, and ownership interests. You know where to get the information loved ones need to make wise choices. There's nothing wrong in asking questions of independent youngsters. Your lucky number is 8.

Friday, June 30 (Moon in Gemini to Cancer 11:11 p.m.) The moon–Jupiter advance in Gemini implies upcoming good fortune through property sales, joint projects with your mate and children. Sagittarius wants speedier action and explanations, but may rely on your more spiritual advice. Family situations are stabilized. June should prove to be a fine prologue for July.

JULY 2000

Saturday, July 1 (Moon in Cancer) Do not take a loved one for granted during the eclipse pattern in your fifth house. No innuendos, thoughtless retorts that put the partner of your enduring romance in a bad mood, to say nothing about the guilt it brings you later on. This solar eclipse pressures ships and boats. Lucky lottery: 1, 10, 19, 28, 37, 46.

Sunday, July 2 (Moon in Cancer to Leo 10:39 p.m.)   Caution is required on and near the water in the wake of yesterday's eclipse. Puppy-love affairs fizzle out; the rejected one needs your understanding. Absenteeism and tardiness can work against poorly planned socializing. The Jupiter keynote is promising for today's cash flow.

Monday, July 3 (Moon in Leo)   Leo gives a sense of majesty and elegance to your day. Some health complaints come from senior citizens. Youngsters may also show a lack of energy. Some may be attempting too much in the way of play, games, and striving to keep up with the crowd. Your special numbers: 7, 3, 5.

Tuesday, July 4 (Moon in Leo to Virgo 11:20 p.m.)   Stick with the fire signs (Leo, Sagittarius, Aries) when it comes to celebrating Independence Day. You are privately more independent than most, but do not make a federal case of this. Find an unobstructed view from which you and your children can watch a display of fireworks. Your lucky number is 9.

Wednesday, July 5 (Moon in Virgo)   Lucky lottery: 2, 11, 20, 29, 38, 47. Today favors marriage, other partnerships, closer bonding with your beloved, and standing together to keep the entire world at bay. Joint projects are ideal. Sharing responsibilities and rewards is recommended. Virgo provides a practical, logical point of view.

Thursday, July 6 (Moon in Virgo)   It's a good day for conferences, joint decisions, full disclosures. The boardroom is the place for facts and realities, not for theories and unrealistic dreams. It would be easy to upset a senior official under these aspects. There is a cosmic bridge for the genders to walk.

Friday, July 7 (Moon in Virgo to Libra 2:48 a.m.) A good day for talks with your banker and broker. Pay close attention to burglar alarm systems, locks on windows and doors, structural deficiencies in your garage. Make sure youngsters are not tampering with your vehicle through natural childish curiosity. Avoid parking in unfamiliar and dark places. Your lucky number is 6.

Saturday, July 8 (Moon in Libra) Lucky lottery: 8, 17, 18, 26, 35, 44. Libra and Cancer figure prominently in your day's experiences. Security matters are still accented. Savings, investments, insurance, inheritance, budgeting, and bargain hunting get superior grades. Schedules are changed this evening.

Sunday, July 9 (Moon in Libra to Scorpio 9:49 a.m.) Start improvements such as a cleanup and inspection of your garage, basement, or attic. Identify any source of a potential accident in these areas, as well as your lawn and backyard. Are utility wires about to become entangled with tall trees? Is the driveway deteriorating?

Monday, July 10 (Moon in Scorpio) A fine day to begin your summer vacation, buy a recreation vehicle, head for the seashore with family togetherness prominent. The Mars keynote in your horoscope is a guarantee that loving exchanges are your responsibility. In your own mysterious ways, always sublime, always subtle, you hold the key to family joys.

Tuesday, July 11 (Moon in Scorpio to Sagittarius 8:06 p.m.) Enjoy sightseeing, visiting places of historic interest, meeting friendly strangers whose youngsters are attracted to yours. The feeling that the holidays are the best days of the year is strong and very much shared with older and younger loved ones. You take special pleasure in a Scorpio's opinion. Your lucky number is 7.

Wednesday, July 12 (Moon in Sagittarius) The great outdoors is your castle. At home or on the road, you'll want to spend time in the sun. Ball games, boat rides, delicious foods are all part of this positive scenario. Cement new friendships. A secret dream of more independence is realized. Lucky lottery: 9, 18, 19, 27, 36, 45.

Thursday, July 13 (Moon in Sagittarius) Travel offers a kind of higher education for parents and children. Mother returns with new recipes and she is not shy about going into the kitchen of a restaurant to see just what they did to make a dish so delectable. Father encounters someone who's been doing his type of work for years. Your lucky number is 2.

Friday, July 14 (Moon in Sagittarius to Capricorn 8:28 a.m.) Fine trends for collecting along the way: attractive pebbles, sand and lake shells, a menu Junior shouldn't have walked off with, hotel soap and miniatures of shampoo. Your Venus keynote views some odds and ends as beautiful. Saturn practicality loves to gather symbols of happy memories. Your lucky number is 4.

Saturday, July 15 (Moon in Capricorn) Lucky lottery: 6, 15, 16, 24, 33, 42. Capricorn and Taurus impact your day significantly. Spend time with friends you have known for a long time. Your togetherness is based on both joyful and sad experiences. Because your children are developing so much this summer, you may find them almost unrecognizable.

Sunday, July 16 (Moon in Capricorn to Aquarius 9:27 p.m.) A total lunar eclipse in your eleventh house brings pressures through delays, postponements, and cancellations. A financial stipend can suddenly cease. An older loved one may fight assisted-living or nursing home transfer. Friendly neighbors may learn that new job requires a big move.

Monday, July 17 (Moon in Aquarius) Nautical disasters and a buildup of other accident potential arrive in the wake of yesterday's eclipse. A coverup is exposed. Some gains come from falling back on the old way of performing a difficult task. Caution pays off. An Aquarius and another Pisces understand your feelings. Hot combination numbers: 3 and 9.

Tuesday, July 18 (Moon in Aquarius) Your long-ago-learned "know-how" serves you well during the absence of an executive when unfamiliar responsibilities fall on you. You excel in reaching into the past; your sign rules all past events, including prenatal experiences. You are made strongly aware of this today. Hot combination numbers: 5 and 2.

Wednesday, July 19 (Moon in Aquarius to Pisces 9:45 a.m.) Lucky lottery: 7, 16, 25, 34, 43, 27. There is considerable reliance on memories and the way things were done in the past. The Uranus–Neptune regression in your twelfth house leaves many anticipated renovations of former methods undecided. Changing technologies will pick up steam again in October.

Thursday, July 20 (Moon in Pisces) The lunar power spotlights your personality and character assets and accents your method of getting things done in painless ways. You'll continue to oppose violent methods and the imposition of changes before the general public is ready for them. Push highly personalized wishes today. Hot combination numbers: 9 and 6.

Friday, July 21 (Moon in Pisces to Aries 8:10 p.m.) The day belongs to you; the way is clear to improve your savings plan, annuities, investments, and budgeting. A Leo helps you see the bigger picture in all this. Those in your immediate environment feel you know the score and perceive beyond what is obvious. Your lucky number is 2.

Saturday, July 22 (Moon in Aries) Lunar power gives you special enlightenment in wealth production. You are strongly aware of costs, charges, expenses, and value under prevailing aspects. A boldness characterizes the way you pursue bargains and engage in back-and-forth humorous offers. Lucky lottery: 4, 13, 22, 31, 40, 14.

Sunday, July 23 (Moon in Aries)　The sun enters Leo, accenting your developing new health, nutrition, and herbal interests. Growing your own berries and grapes is more than a dream. Discussions based on ways of offsetting questionable imported fruits and vegetables are popular. Aries encourages your views.

Monday, July 24 (Moon in Aries to Taurus 3:45 a.m.)　The buildup of moon–Uranus power in your third house favors increased understanding of local changes, recommended studies. You open improved channels of communication and may decide to lease, rather than buy, your next car. Taurus and Virgo have key roles. Your lucky number is 1.

Tuesday, July 25 (Moon in Taurus)　Siblings, neighbors, former school friends show up today. Phone, write letters, and reestablish old contacts. You are strongly aware of what is splendid and also of what is wrong in your locality. For relaxation this evening, try the best-selling memoirs of a celebrity. Your lucky number is 3.

Wednesday, July 26 (Moon in Taurus to Gemini 8:03 a.m.)　Lucky lottery: 5, 14, 15, 23, 32, 41. People you see every day may begin to get on your nerves. The failure of elementary schools causes great concern, and you are beginning to wonder if throwing more money at them will actually help. Some children assert: "It's not our fault; it's the teachers!"

Thursday, July 27 (Moon in Gemini)　Gemini brings a breath of fresh air and provides interesting gossip. The answers you seek are readily available under today's stellar currents. Family situations are better understood during this lunar phase. Leo and Libra prefer more serious topics. Hot combination numbers: 7 and 1.

Friday, July 28 (Moon in Gemini to Cancer 9:31 a.m.)
Family and home top your agenda. As the month winds
down, there can be some disagreement with children
over a possible late August trip to an expensive resort.
The general opinion is that resort prices will be lowered
right after Labor Day. The managerial generation feels
senior loved ones could use a visit. Your lucky number
is 9.

Saturday, July 29 (Moon in Cancer)   Lucky lottery:
2, 11, 20, 29, 38, 47. Children get the upper hand—it's
known as parental indulgence! Fine trends exist for
spontaneous socializing, discussions with your mate and
children, and for making love with the one who understands you best and worries about your happiness.

Sunday, July 30 (Moon in Cancer to Leo 9:24 a.m.)
A Scorpio and a Cancer figure prominently in the day's
events. You are creative, original, and imaginative under
prevailing aspects. Your deep love is stirred for your
family. Senior citizens let you know how unhappy life's
scenario turns out when faced with giving up their homes
and moving to a retirement community.

Monday, July 31 (Moon in Leo)   The partially
eclipsed lunation occurs in your sixth house and warns
against inviting fatigue. Avoid questionable food. Be
sure imported fruit has been washed several times. Steer
clear of the coughers and sneezers. Even if you're on
the road and famished, bypass the greasy spoons.

AUGUST 2000

***Tuesday, August 1 (Moon in Leo to Virgo 9:28
a.m.)***   The sun–Venus–Mars keynotes accent your
sixth house of overall physical health maintenance. The
power of taking care of yourself is strong, and your
abundance of energy is a big advantage in planning
proper diet and exercise. You join in the praise of your
herbal remedies. Hot combination numbers: 7 and 3.

Wednesday, August 2 (Moon in Virgo)   Lucky lottery: 9, 18, 19, 27, 36, 45. Today's Jupiter keynote is promising for good fortune in family, home, and ownership matters. Fine trends exist for real estate transactions. The service you give to your community is noticed by many and rebounds to your ultimate popularity.

Thursday, August 3 (Moon in Virgo to Libra 11:32 a.m.)   The Saturn keynote in your third house produces stability in studies, learning, communications, and transportation matters. You consolidate all the progressive moods you have made in adjusting to changes and building between older and younger loved ones. Your lucky number is 2.

Friday, August 4 (Moon in Libra)   The lunar transit of your eighth house protects your security. There's evenness in savings, investments, insurance, and budgeting. Your money is covered with the legality of Libra. Talks with your banker, broker, and a successful friend increase your self-assurance and sense of security. Your lucky number is 4.

Saturday, August 5 (Moon in Libra to Scorpio 5:05 p.m.)   Lucky lottery: 6, 15, 24, 33, 42, 16. A perfect day to correct anything wrong on the lawn or in the backyard. Shrubbery and trees need this annual inspection. It's fine for making definite changes in routines and schedules that have become jaded and boring. Aquarius and Gemini approve.

Sunday, August 6 (Moon in Scorpio)   A fine day for travel, enjoying beach activities, boating excursions, and being part of the big playful scenario. Scorpio encourages you to relax by day and make love by night. Dancing and dining in a lovely setting are in the picture. Your surroundings give your morale a big boost.

Monday, August 7 (Moon in Scorpio)   Venus in your horoscope favors your marital state, close bonding with your beloved, and total enjoyment in being together.

Mercury is promising for a strengthened physique from walking and other beneficial exercise. You enjoy enormous energy and drive under prevailing aspects. Your Lucky number is 3.

Tuesday, August 8 (Moon in Scorpio to Sagittarius 2:31 a.m.) Career requirements, professional and authority matters take first place on today's agenda. Your employer expects you to do more than your usual share of work, possibly because others are away on vacation. Sagittarius and Leo figure prominently. Don't loiter or let others waste your time. Your lucky number is 5.

Wednesday, August 9 (Moon in Sagittarius) Work piles up and you may have to stay late. Some assistance isn't up to snuff, but avoid making too much of this. You want to confirm your employer's belief that you are good at pinch-hitting and also at getting along with coworkers. Lucky lottery: 7, 16, 17, 25, 34, 43.

Thursday, August 10 (Moon in Sagittarius to Capricorn 2:45 p.m.) You may be able to relax over the late afternoon when some competent assistants return from vacation. Capricorn and Taurus have key roles. There are social events being planned by your coworkers. Your beloved has something special in mind for the two of you this evening. Dress up; enjoy people. Your lucky number is 9.

Friday, August 11 (Moon in Capricorn) The social side of your job is in this picture. Management likes to see all levels of the company picnic together. It's a chance to show off your children and to acknowledge that you are having a good time. The Saturn keynote protects family attitudes. In fact, your children will impress the executives. Your lucky number is 2.

Saturday, August 12 (Moon in Capricorn) Lucky lottery: 4, 13, 14, 22, 31, 40. Take advantage of the day by doing a little sightseeing within a 300-mile radius of home. Hills and mountains are in your mind, even if not nearby, for it's an earthy day. Taurus, Virgo, and Capricorn are perfect companions.

Sunday, August 13 (Moon in Capricorn to Aquarius 3:44 a.m.)   You are free of past concerns and are living completely in the present. An ultra-liberal Aquarius may be responsible for this flight to independence. You yearn to experience new feelings, arrive at new conclusions, meet people different from yourself. The food you choose may be exotic and foreign.

Monday, August 14 (Moon in Aquarius)   The past may be too much with your beloved, which calls you back to your old self. There are fine trends now for coming to grips with an old mystery. The urge to move furniture about, to add more light and color to the dark corners of your home was never more urgent. Hot combination numbers: 1 and 7.

Tuesday, August 15 (Moon in Aquarius to Pisces 3:42 p.m.)   The full moon spotlights past experiences, confidential matters, and starts you wondering about classmates of long ago. Courses of study you once thought difficult now seem simple. All the knowledge you have acquired in life gives you a feeling of truly belonging. Your lucky number is 3.

Wednesday, August 16 (Moon in Pisces)   The moon in Pisces reveals, uncovers, discovers, and makes clear what has been hidden from view and what has baffled. Neptune is lifting veils. Decision making is easier. The complicated becomes simplified. There is almost complete understanding of your own motivation. Lucky lottery: 5, 14, 15, 23, 32, 41.

Thursday, August 17 (Moon in Pisces)   Yesterday's trends in your personal life continue. You feel confident about taking steps into the future. A fine day to ask much of yourself, for presenting difficult questions and then insisting on logical answers. Another Pisces and a Cancer have vital roles. Your lucky number is 7.

Friday, August 18 (Moon in Pisces to Aries 1:45 a.m.) Now you can pick up the payoffs for all the good work you have been doing, for having placed yourself in the know, so to speak. A certain boldness is recommended, as you go after a salary increase, an improved assignment, and a better parking spot for your vehicle. Hot combination numbers: 9 and 6.

Saturday, August 19 (Moon in Aries) Bargain hunting, comparative shopping, and wise budgeting mean more money in the bank. Aries and Sagittarius will impact your day. Shopping is all the more adventurous when you tackle the job early in the morning, accompanied by your beloved. Lucky lottery: 2, 11, 20, 29, 38, 47.

Sunday, August 20 (Moon in Aries to Taurus 9:32 a.m.) Stay in your own community, participating in a religious service and having breakfast in a local chain restaurant. Siblings and neighbors love to see you around. Encourage youngsters to entertain their friends. Taurus and Virgo are in this picture. Fine trends exist for studies and communications. Your lucky number is 4.

Monday, August 21 (Moon in Taurus) Short-distance travel, combining business with pleasure is favored. Everyday routines are less boring when carried out pronto. Criticism rises, as you notice some ill-kept lawns. A monstrous cat is ready to pounce on a beautiful bird, detracting from your peace of mind. Your lucky number is 8.

Tuesday, August 22 (Moon in Taurus to Gemini 2:56 p.m.) The Mercury keynote coaxes a partner out of the magnolias, so to speak. Postponed conferences and decisions can be put together at last. The rest of the day takes on a hurried trend and much work gets done. Your marital state gets a good shot in the arm and the evening is shared with your beloved. Your lucky number is 1.

Wednesday, August 23 (Moon in Gemini) Lucky lottery: 3, 13, 21, 30, 39, 48. Today's Venus keynote gives more sensuality in the search for ecstasy with your beloved. The assets of your mate's personality and character are revealed again in all their glory. Tonight is a special time for expressing your glorious love.

Thursday, August 24 (Moon in Gemini to Cancer 6 p.m.)   Domestic, property values and taxes, and family togetherness are accented. The air signs (Gemini, Libra, and Aquarius) are active in your experiences. It's an intellectual day, with much talk about your children's educational plans. The high cost of operating family vehicles is an oppressive thought. Your lucky number is 5.

Friday, August 25 (Moon in Cancer)   Listen to what Scorpio and Cancer have to say. You are loving and loved, busy, anxious to keep members of your clan happy. Shopping for students' clothing can be tiresome, especially when a critical youngster is with you. Hot combination numbers: 7 and 3.

Saturday, August 26 (Moon in Cancer to Leo 7:17 p.m.)   The moon's transit of your fifth house increases your popularity with in-laws and business partners, especially the latter's family. It's a fine evening for spontaneous socializing; be sure idle youngsters are recruited to help you. Be casual. Lucky lottery: 9, 18, 27, 36, 45, 19.

Sunday, August 27 (Moon in Leo)   A Leo captivates you with splendid self-centeredness and egotism. Leo knows all the expensive stores where you should be shopping, as well as the best plastic surgeons and the special pills and herbs that will put you on top of the world. Don't be too quick to let your water sign put Leo's fire out.

Monday, August 28 (Moon in Leo to Virgo 7:56 p.m.)   You can't beat Leo's advice when it comes to looking elegant, proper dieting, and joining the right exercise group. Another Pisces may accuse you of taking it too easy when hot tubs and daily swimming are the "in" thing. Your excuse might be that you are more spiritual than physical. Your lucky number is 6.

Tuesday, August 29 (Moon in Virgo)   It's a day when you and your beloved can bond more strongly and face the entire world as an unbeatable team. The amazing protection found in a right, loving partnership threads through your awareness. You reach out. You provide joy and happiness. Hot combination numbers: 8 and 2.

Wednesday, August 30 (Moon in Virgo to Libra 9:34 p.m.)   Yesterday's lunation power is still with you in your seventh house of sharing, cooperative efforts, and joint projects. Heart-to-heart discussions are better than intellectual talks. Or as the poet said: "The heart has its reasons." Your lucky lottery: 1, 10, 19, 28, 37, 46.

Thursday, August 31 (Moon in Libra)   You would love to stop the clock and hold on to this month as it is about to pass into history. There is something about the post–Labor Day period that means extra responsibilities for Pisces. Your children may have this feeling also. Hot combination numbers: 3 and 6.

SEPTEMBER 2000

Friday, September 1 (Moon in Libra)   Saturn and Jupiter keynotes guarantee domestic stability, as well as good luck in your interfamily relationships. A lot of this is due to the free flow of information and the basic intention of understanding a different generation. Your lucky number is 2.

Saturday, September 2 (Moon in Libra to Scorpio 1:56 a.m.)   Strong efforts are made to hold on to summer. Family beach activities at a resort preparing to close down are favored. Minor travel to have a good time and a last shot at sunbathing and a boating excursion are favored. And how your children will love it! Lucky lottery: 4, 13, 22, 31, 40, 49.

Sunday, September 3 (Moon in Scorpio)　　Keep busy, clinging to summer pastimes, spending quality time with your mate and children. End-of-summer parties are in full swing. It's a day when you realize that, beyond normal patriotism, you really find much to admire in your fellow Americans, many of whom really know how to live, love, and enjoy life.

Monday, September 4 (Moon in Scorpio to Sagittarius 10:10 a.m.)　　All good things must end, but even a return trip is enjoyable under today's ninth house trends. Scorpio and Cancer are sympathetic and also helpful. Children are reaching for new ideas and you are glad to see them anticipating a school year. Your lucky number is 1.

Tuesday, September 5 (Moon in Sagittarius)　　You may feel that your boss is asking too much of you during rumors of downsizing and the specter of new, more complicated electronic and digital equipment. The fearful complaints from coworkers stir your sympathy. Sagittarius will answer your questions. Hot combination numbers: 3 and 9.

Wednesday, September 6 (Moon in Sagittarius to Capricorn 10:10 a.m.)　　Lucky lottery: 5, 14, 15, 23, 32, 41. Pluto-engendered awareness gives you strong support in your career. You present a strongly professional presence, which finds favor with those in power. You excel in encouraging coworkers to settle down.

Thursday, September 7 (Moon in Capricorn)　　Capricorn and Virgo figure prominently. Friendships, social-expansion, and a strong sense of togetherness with coworkers make this a pleasant day. You are getting along well with senior citizens, who fear retirement and its possible loneliness. A new source of minor income presents itself. Your lucky number is 7.

Friday, September 8 (Moon in Capricorn)   The Mercury keynote in your horoscope speeds up security matters. Repairs on an alarm system, locks on windows and doors can be taken care of today. Small print announcements are annoying, and all the more so when they come from banks and brokerage houses. Hot combination numbers: 9 and 6.

Saturday, September 9 (Moon in Capricorn to Aquarius 10:46 a.m.)   Lucky lottery: 2, 11, 20, 29, 38, 47. The Mars keynote provides an abundance of energy and gains from sprucing up your personal appearance. Pay some attention to beautifying your premises with special attention to shrubbery and annuals. You're making your neighbors happy.

Sunday, September 10 (Moon in Aquarius)   Don't be baffled. Do it the way you did it long ago and chances are you will succeed. From past experiences, you can find good clues for the present. Your sign has jurisdiction over the past, including prenatal experiences and what your ancestors put together for you. You're important!

Monday, September 11 (Moon in Aquarius to Pisces 10:35 p.m.)   Aquarius and Libra are in your corner. You do well by extracting faith and courage from childhood experiences and from the wisdom of parents and grandparents. Perspective and scope are favored. Fine trends exist for taking up the cudgels in defense of senior citizens. Your lucky number is 8.

Tuesday, September 12 (Moon in Pisces)   It's your turn to show your mettle as the moon transits Pisces. You'll have the right answers at your fingertips. Beauty and harmony are serving you. You locate things that are lost better than most. You please others by your obvious concern. Hot combination numbers: 1 and 7.

Wednesday, September 13 (Moon in Pisces)   Lucky lottery: 3, 12, 21, 30, 39, 48. All is revealed, proclaimed, pontificated under this full moon in your sign. Watch your newspaper as crimes are solved, and witnesses speak out. In your personal life, you know more than ever what you need.

Thursday, September 14 (Moon in Pisces to Aries 8:01 a.m.)   You are empowered to make correct decisions, right turns, and to open the proper doors into a brighter future. Take full advantage of your intuition about your career, ambitions, and about how changes can play into your hands. Hot combination numbers: 5 and 2.

Friday, September 15 (Moon in Aries)   At the track. Post position special—number 7 p.p. in the fourth race. Pick six: 1, 2, 4, 7, 9, 1. Watch for these letters or initials in the names of potential winning horses or jockeys: E, N, W. Hot daily doubles: 1 and 7, 7 and 7, 4 and 7. Invite a Sagittarius to accompany you.

Saturday, September 16 (Moon in Aries to Taurus 3:06 p.m.)   The money is flowing in, as the moon transits your second house. Aries and Leo are in the day's scenario. The more you progress into this electronic and digitalic world, the more money you put in your bank. You experience sympathy for those who are being left behind. Lucky lottery: 9, 18, 19, 27, 36, 45.

Sunday, September 17 (Moon in Taurus)   Local, everyday, usual routines, studies, communications, and transportation matters are boring. Attend religious services in a large downtown church, where you are likely to meet people you rarely encounter. Spread your wings, cast your nets over the entire world.

Monday, September 18 (Moon in Taurus to Gemini 8:23 p.m.)   Today's Mars keynote urges you to take the lead in marital improvements, working for a closer bonding with your mate. The Saturn keynote demands consolidation of family efforts rather than each going off unprepared. Virgo and Capricorn stick to more conservative approaches.

Tuesday, September 19 (Moon in Gemini) Good trends exist in real estate costs, transactions, and rewards. There can be some dissatisfaction with community-based taxation. Gemini and Libra are cheerful and positive. They can coax you out of the doldrums. It's a good day to confront issues, but in a gentle way. Hot combination numbers: 8 and 2.

Wednesday, September 20 (Moon in Gemini to Cancer 12:16 p.m.) Lucky lottery: 1, 10, 19, 28, 37, 46. An interfamily conference on problems all must consider will be effective. Look at all sides of the issue when evaluating a senior citizen's future living arrangements or a child's violent temper. It's a day to offset a bigger problem.

Thursday, September 21 (Moon in Cancer) A big love day, full of romance, enjoyable courtship, and important decisions. Know where your kids are and what they are doing. Spontaneous socializing can clear the atmosphere of recriminations. Your creativity and originality are stirred. Hot combination numbers: 3 and 6.

Friday, September 22 (Moon in Cancer) There's an adventurous trend to the day. Autumnal splendor invites your inspection. A fine day to trace the advance of Indian summer in stream and park. Collect leaves of splendid hue for pressing in books. Help children to understand what is going on in Nature. Your lucky number is 5.

Saturday, September 23 (Moon in Cancer to Leo 3:01 a.m.) Lucky lottery: 7, 16, 25, 34, 43, 52. The sun enters Libra while the moon transits Leo, favoring gender equality, parental evaluation of children's potential, your sense of security and interest in health maintenance. Keep abreast of what is happening in the thinking of an agitated senior.

Sunday, September 24 (Moon in Leo) The season calls for new approaches to your family's overall physical well-being. Watch children's food preferences and a tendency to postpone schoolwork on weekends. Your horoscope shows a strong resolve to hold on to all of summer's pleasures, even as storm windows and doors are installed.

Monday, September 25 (Moon in Leo to Virgo 5:03 a.m.) Venus-in-Scorpio was once called the hushed-up aspect, because it implied sensuality galore in the search for sexual ecstasy. This Venus keynote in your horoscope can be discussed with your beloved and produce the desired results. The moon illuminates your marriage vows. Your lucky number is 4.

Tuesday, September 26 (Moon in Virgo) Your marital state and other partnerships get strong lunar stimulation. It's a good day to share ideas, evaluate the attitudes of those in power, consider taking a stronger stand on the part of disgruntled workers. Virgo and Taurus have key roles. Hot combination numbers: 6 and 1.

Wednesday, September 27 (Moon in Virgo to Libra 7:23 a.m.) The lunation occurs in your eighth house, which calls attention to savings, budgeting, comparative shopping, investments, and insurance matters. This is a fine day to make changes in security and allied money matters. Libra and Aquarius have key roles. Lucky lottery: 8, 16, 17, 26, 35, 44.

Thursday, September 28 (Moon in Libra) You sparkle; you're brilliant; you want to tell Gemini all about it. Your innate creativity, active imagination, and dualism want those cosmic fish that symbolize your sign to swim in the same direction for a change. Another Pisces speaks up bravely. Your lucky numbers are 1, 4, and 7.

Friday, September 29 (Moon in Libra to Scorpio 11:31 a.m.) The Mercury keynote in your horoscope speeds up actions on the job and aims for a production record. You cover a great deal of territory, without leaving the building very often. Scorpio and another Pisces know the score and work brilliantly together. Your lucky number is 3.

Saturday, September 30 (Moon in Scorpio)   Good trends exist for getting away from the familiar, usual, and traveling within a 300-mile radius. Sightseeing is a big part of this grand day, when Nature is making such a strong statement. Phone long-distance, write letters to contacts far away. Lucky lottery: 5, 14, 15, 23, 32, 41.

OCTOBER 2000

Sunday, October 1 (Moon in Scorpio to Sagittarius 6:51 p.m.)   The month gets off to a good start, with much momentum. You can set your own pattern and pace. Libra, Scorpio, and Aquarius strongly impact your day. Money is coming up as the month advances and you can invite an even cash flow today. It's important to aim for more stability in your lifestyle.

Monday, October 2 (Moon in Sagittarius)   Sagittarius shows up, full of suggestions for upward mobility in both economic and social departments. In your career, you are helped along by your own hard-working psychic impressions. Pluto gives you the transformation power to change a career dream into a reality. Your lucky number is 9.

Tuesday, October 3 (Moon in Sagittarius)   Discussions with supervisors can show you the way out of a quandary. Coworkers are not in agreement, inasmuch as some are getting richer and the rest are standing still economically. You achieve and win big if you are professional, fair, and exercise your authority wisely.

Wednesday, October 4 (Moon in Sagittarius to Capricorn 5:44 a.m.)   Lucky lottery: 4, 13, 22, 31, 40, 49. Capricorn and Virgo figure prominently. It's an excellent day for friendships, social expansion, and for church and club membership and participation. Phone that friend you haven't heard from since summer. Don't neglect those who have retired.

Thursday, October 5 (Moon in Capricorn)   There are good combinations of business with pleasure. It's fine for dealings with senior citizens, unfriendly executives, but give cliques and rumormongers a wide berth. Look into the possibility of a stipend for some extra work you are doing, especially anything that helps people who are just off welfare. Your lucky number is 6.

Friday, October 6 (Moon in Capricorn to Aquarius 6:34 p.m.)   Work can be pleasant, but it will prove to be of no avail if done with constant chatter and interruptions. Try to isolate yourself when you are tackling a big important job. Self-discipline is a big help to you. Taurus and Gemini are also helpful. Hot combination numbers: 8 and 1.

Saturday, October 7 (Moon in Aquarius)   Lucky lottery: 1, 10, 19, 28, 37, 46. Aquarius and Gemini have vital roles to play. The retrograde Saturn and Jupiter keynotes seek patience and perseverance in family and home interests. Good trends for reevaluating past experiences and seeing some of them in gentler lights.

Sunday, October 8 (Moon in Aquarius)   Preparation, prologues to definite decisive actions, and estimate giving are in this picture. You sense busier times are coming and want to be ready for them. The gulf between liberal and conservative coworkers is growing, and it's hard to find any common ground.

Monday, October 9 (Moon in Aquarius to Pisces 6:37 a.m.)   Bing-bang, suddenly that busy day is before you! Organize without any fanfare for the best results. No help is better under these aspects than that of half-hearted malcontents. The moon in your sign gives you good directions. You find what you need in the way of perseverance. Your lucky number is 7.

Tuesday, October 10 (Moon in Pisces)   Another Pisces helps you double the work output as well as the fun. You have the answers, thanks to your strong knowledge of methods and quality control. Your employer is also aware of your great value to production schedules. You can rush when it is necessary. Your lucky number is 9.

Wednesday, October 11 (Moon in Pisces to Aries 3:52 p.m.)   Lucky lottery: 2, 11, 20, 29, 38, 47. You gain from your suspicion of what is being hidden, covered up, festering behind the scenes. You instinctively know how to lift these veils, thanks to your Neptune keynote. You solve puzzles well and work your way out of any maze.

Thursday, October 12 (Moon in Aries)   Now the money is rolling in. Wealth production is rising. This lunar trend favors your earning power and points to where additional capital can be found. There can be sudden awareness that your possessions are more valuable than you realized. Aries and Leo are in the picture. Your lucky number is 4.

Friday, October 13 (Moon in Aries to Taurus 10:06 p.m.)   The full moon spotlights additional income sources. People in military uniforms are lucky for you. You admire those who storm and pioneer in these ever-changing times. Profits and gains are more than you anticipated. An in-law has a good money-making idea. Hot combination numbers: 6 and 1.

Saturday, October 14 (Moon in Taurus)   Lucky lottery: 8, 17, 18, 26, 35, 44. Concentration pays off. Special skills are indicated but they may require up-to-date tools and materials. You are creative and original in ways that can be transformed into cash. Taurus and Virgo love your handiwork crafts.

Sunday, October 15 (Moon in Taurus)   The Saturn keynote wavers between family cooperation and studies, before conferring stability on one of them. Don't count any gains before the report is in. Studies win out as the day advances. Learning processes fascinate you, as more practical knowledge is absorbed.

Monday, October 16 (Moon in Taurus to Gemini 2:19 a.m.)   Listen to Gemini. Interfamily sharing and cooperation pay off. Good trends in household repair work, garage and basement cleanup programs, removing evidence of oil spills from the driveway and floor of the garage. The help you hire today will do good work. Your lucky number is 5.

Tuesday, October 17 (Moon in Gemini)   The newly direct Neptune in Aquarius adds glamour to your old wardrobe items. Your well-known allure and mysterious glances will work to your overall advantage. Children pick up interesting behavior patterns from your example, even when you are not aware of this. Hot combination numbers 7 and 4.

Wednesday, October 18 (Moon in Gemini to Cancer 5:38 a.m.)   Lucky lottery: 9, 18, 19, 27, 36, 45. It's a fine day for giving and receiving love, favors, and compliments. Romance is in the air, threading its way through the work that has to be done and the necessary and unnecessary chatter. Courtship makes progress and a future bride and groom are more confident.

Thursday, October 19 (Moon in Cancer)   Today's Venus keynote wins you popularity in the executive offices. There is much enjoyment of special courses related to new work you are assigned. It's not a good day to begin any long-distance travel, however, with traffic problems and confusing schedules distracting. Your lucky number is 2.

Friday, October 20 (Moon in Cancer to Leo 8:43 a.m.)   October's traditional bright blue weather catches the artist's eye in you and other creative and imaginative types. Nature expresses romance in its paintings today. You take an additional moment out now and then to just look and listen. The force of love proves again that it is the strongest. Go with number 4.

Saturday, October 21 (Moon in Leo)   Lucky lottery: 6, 15, 24, 33, 42, 51. Leo and Sagittarius figure prominently. Get some vigorous exercise today. Walking is one of your best methods of keeping fit. It's also fine for camping out with the kids, strolling through parks, going for a hayride.

Sunday, October 22 (Moon in Leo to Virgo 11:54 a.m.) Keep on the go, dressing appropriately, and making certain that your children are working their baby fat off in the right type of exercise and games. Sports can offer much to the entire family. A football, softball, tennis racquet, set of golf clubs are in this happy picture.

Monday, October 23 (Moon in Virgo)   The sun enters Scorpio, giving you wander lust and assuring you happiness from good physical exercise. Jogging before breakfast is a big help to a well-ordered day. Try to talk your mate into joining you on a day when your marital state gets strong lunar support. Your lucky number is 3.

Tuesday, October 24 (Moon in Virgo to Libra 3:31 p.m.)   Partners, including your beloved, are inclined to expect more than usual from you now. Little chinks in gender equality can be spotted—if you look for them. The better way is to tolerate differences. Dress up this evening. Hot combination numbers: 5 and 2.

Wednesday, October 25 (Moon in Libra)   Libra and Leo play vital roles. Talks with your broker can pay off in profits and freedom from anxiety. Good bargains are to be found along rural roads. Harvest festivals will do well under prevailing aspects. Find the appropriate time to ask the embarrassing questions. Lucky lottery: 7, 16, 17, 25, 34, 43.

Thursday, October 26 (Moon in Libra to Scorpio 8:25 p.m.)   Some good bargains can be found in the larger outlet stores. Shop for woolen items, things that create space in the crowded areas of your kitchen. A dear friend wants your company on a short trip. And how you would love to get away! There's more money in your escrow account than you anticipated. Your lucky number is 9.

Friday, October 27 (Moon in Scorpio)　　The lunation happens in your ninth house, and that short trip moves into focus. Get away today, and have an enjoyable weekend. Loved ones will help you keep to your travel plan by taking on some of your weekend chores. Scorpio and another Pisces are making their contributions. Your lucky number is 2.

Saturday, October 28 (Moon in Scorpio)　　Fine for travel, taking care of business, doing some interesting shopping and sightseeing. You make acquaintance with hunters and younger ghosts and goblins at the inn where you are lodged. The place itself is not taking any backseat to the people. You'll want to return. Lucky lottery: 4, 13, 22, 31, 40, 14.

Sunday, October 29—Daylight Savings Time ends (Moon in Scorpio to Sagittarius 2:42 a.m.)　　Travel, grand returns, shopping along the way are all favored. But career demands can enter the picture as soon as you are home. There have been phone calls you could have done without. Someone is jealous that you have been away. No TV dozing tonight. Go to bed!

Monday, October 30 (Moon in Sagittarius)　　Sagittarius and Aries are glad to see you. Another Pisces feels slighted. You are left with the feeling that you are a necessary fixture at your place of employment. Business meetings go well and generally the higher-ups are in agreement. A perfect evening at home. Your lucky number is 1.

Tuesday, October 31 (Moon in Sagittarius to Capricorn 1:03 p.m.)　　It's a busy trick-or-treat night. Have plenty of wrapped candies in the front foyer. Give your own kids a 9:00 P.M. curfew. You will notice that Halloween is becoming more popular and costly than ever. Many youngsters rent costumes for just one night. Hot combination numbers: 3 and 6.

NOVEMBER 2000

Wednesday, November 1 (Moon in Capricorn) Lucky lottery: 2, 11, 20, 29, 38, 47. The Mercury keynote in your horoscope turns travel sluggish, with traffic problems in the air and on the ground. This lunar trend stimulates your public appearances, church and club participation, committee meetings. In humanitarian work, you are aware of the special problems of the old and newly born.

Thursday, November 2 (Moon in Capricorn) The Venus keynote is promising for the enjoyment of career assignments and the friendliness of those with whom you work. Mars gives you drive in marriage and other partnerships. Fine for arranging office parties, a harvest festival. Your employer loves to see people working well together. Your lucky number is 4.

Friday, November 3 (Moon in Capricorn to Aquarius 1:41 a.m.) The moon stimulates your packed twelfth house, where sudden changes are temporarily delayed. A good luck dimension provided by Jupiter gives you needed rest, more time to adjust to and absorb the changes experienced earlier in local matters, studies, and a sense of being unduly pressured by associates. Your lucky number is 6.

Saturday, November 4 (Moon in Aquarius) Lucky lottery: 8, 16, 17, 26, 35, 44. Mars enters Libra, giving you unbeatable drive and good motivation in security matters: alarm systems, car club, locks on doors and windows, savings, budgeting, investments, and insurance. You have a better understanding of a legal entanglement.

Sunday, November 5 (Moon in Aquarius to Pisces 2:15 p.m.) The Pluto keynote increases the strength of your psychic impressions. You can act upon your intuition in a matter related to your job, relationships with coworkers, supervisors, and the top boss. When to speak up and when to hold your peace are in focus now and prepares you for the week ahead.

Monday, November 6 (Moon in Pisces) The lunar trend in Pisces gives your personal interests a helpful boost. Anticipate upcoming career and assignment changes. When you ask questions, be sure you receive definite answers. Conflicts arise when the Piscean cosmic fish attempt to swim in two directions. Your lucky number is 5.

Tuesday, November 7 (Moon in Pisces) Although travel was held up earlier, Mercury now starts those engines and motors running. Chances are, you won't be able to get away unless you can talk your boss into a business–pleasure combination within the 200-mile radius. The answers you require are found via meditation. Hot combination numbers: 7 and 3.

Wednesday, November 8 (Moon in Pisces to Aries 12:03 a.m.) Lucky lottery: 9, 18, 19, 27, 36, 45. Go for the big money today. The lunar trend tells you where it is and how you can get it. A discussion about your salary, your chance of taking on additional and more vital assignments may be the answer. Doors are opening for you.

Thursday, November 9 (Moon in Aries) Today favors wealth production, your earning power, and the discovery of a new source of income. You learn that what you own is more valuable than you formerly realized. Aries and Leo are in the day's scenario. It's fine for bargain hunting in the company of a child. Your lucky number is 2.

Friday, November 10 (Moon in Aries to Taurus 6:13 a.m.) Today favors studies, communications, and transportation matters. Siblings and neighbors are in this picture. A Taurus and Virgo advise the practical approach. You are likely to be more possessive than usual. A grumbling relative may accuse you of being miserly. Your lucky number is 4.

Saturday, November 11 (Moon in Taurus) Lucky lottery: 6, 15, 24, 33, 42, 51. Time to catch up on preparation for winter chores. Ask your friendly local hardware store for some answers. It's a good day to spend quality time with children, give them the feeling they are appreciated and loved.

Sunday, November 12 (Moon in Taurus to Gemini 9:29 a.m.) After worship services, spend some time with fellow parishioners. Good talk takes place over coffee and includes local property tax problems and sliding values. There is a shared annoyance over the way one neighbor is letting his property deteriorate. You get a good picture of what is going on today.

Monday, November 13 ˙ (Moon in Gemini) The Venus keynote in your horoscope is promising for the enjoyment of friends, committee work, church and club social assignments, and your public life. Capricorn and Taurus have key roles. Set a good example if you are intent on encouraging others and offering advice. Your lucky number is 3.

Tuesday, November 14 (Moon in Gemini to Cancer 11:22 a.m.) Gemini and Aquarius figure prominently. Good trends exist in all domestic chores, in family togetherness. Give quality time to daughters, who tend to be resistant to advice. An inspection of your property gives you good feelings about your role as a conscientious citizen. Hot combination numbers: 5 and 2.

Wednesday, November 15 (Moon in Cancer) Lucky lottery: 7, 16, 25, 34, 43, 52. It's perfect for making love, engaging in a marvelous prologue that completely involves your mate in this quest for ecstasy and wholesome health. Romance, courtship, creativity, originality, and successful hosting of a party are favored.

Thursday, November 16 (Moon in Cancer to Leo 1:20 p.m.) The Uranus–Neptune keynotes continue to foster changes in the way you view past events. You do well to extract new gains from accomplishments performed years ago. Your résumé can be improved. Urge those loved ones who are resisting the many changes taking place in society to be more flexible. Your lucky number is 9.

Friday, November 17 (Moon in Leo) Leo and Aries have key roles. Fine trends exist for a physical examination, a talk with your physician and dentist, and for awareness of the strong link between thinking healthy and being healthy. Don't be so quick, however, to dismiss the complaints of an older person. Hot combination numbers: 2 and 6.

Saturday, November 18 (Moon in Leo to Virgo 4:17 p.m.) Lucky lottery: 4, 13, 22, 31, 40, 49. Exercise recommended by your physician is favored. A walk in the woods, contemplation of the advance of autumn, jogging with your children are all good. This evening calls for a family dinner, with traditional recipes.

Sunday, November 19 (Moon in Virgo) Fine lunar trends exist for knowing what your beloved expects of you. Sharing, cooperative efforts, and joint projects, are in this picture, along with a Virgo and Cancer. Discussions should be heart-to-heart as well as brain-to-brain. Think back to early courting days.

Monday, November 20 (Moon in Virgo to Libra 8:36 p.m.) Today favors your marital state, in-law talks, and closer bonding with partners and coworkers. The changing times could be placing a strain on relationships. Sort and sift, carefully evaluate, and choose the proper approach before offering meaningful advice. Remember, some prefer to solve their own problems. Your lucky number is 1.

Tuesday, November 21 (Moon in Libra) Fine for budgeting, talks with your broker, evaluating tax and annuity programs. The cost of living is rising, although the government will deny this. The chasm between the economic mouthpieces and the average daily shopper is growing. Some shoddy merchandising practices are uncovered. Your lucky number is 3.

Wednesday, November 22 (Moon in Libra) Lucky lottery: 5, 14, 23, 32, 41, 50. The sun enters Sagittarius, accenting your career, relationships with those in power and also with malingering coworkers. In trying to keep the peace, you may have to walk a tightrope from time to time today. The unskilled complainers may get too much of your compassion.

Thursday, November 23 (Moon in Libra to Scorpio 2:34 a.m.) How you would like to get away from it all! The lunar transit of Scorpio puts escape tactics in focus. Closing your ears to complaints from coworkers is impossible. What you have going for yourself at a distance boosts morale. Scorpio and Cancer figure prominently. Your lucky number is 7.

Friday, November 24 (Moon in Scorpio) If planning a short trip, it would be wise to make tracks as soon as the workday ends. Just being on the road can restore your peace of mind. Taurus makes a good companion. Your mate will prove understanding, if you leave your family behind. Before the weekend is over, you will sense a rebirth. Hot combination numbers: 9 and 6.

Saturday, November 25 (Moon in Scorpio to Sagittarius 10:34 a.m.) Lucky lottery: 2, 11, 20, 29, 38, 47. An excellent day for moving about, dining in unusual settings, enjoying conversations with strangers, examining and buying a few local products. Sightseeing takes in some autumnal splendor. A brief respite from the grind will long be remembered. The lunation illuminates your responsibilities.

Sunday, November 26 (Moon in Sagittarius)   As you turn attention toward your home, career problems are unable to get the hold they had earlier. Look to your own marvelous intuition for the answers to handle vicious cliques at work and to refrain from appearing partisan.

Monday, November 27 (Moon in Sagittarius to Capricorn 8:58 p.m.)   Concentrate on the work you must do alone and block out those who would interrupt with gossip and rumors. You might speak a little sharply, saying you don't have time to talk or to listen. Sagittarius and Leo are in the picture. Your awareness tells you which superior will ultimately listen to your complaints.

Tuesday, November 28 (Moon in Capricorn)   Capricorn and Virgo are in the day's scenario. The accent falls on your public image, membership and participation, committee work, friendships based on mutual interests, and the possibility of deserving a small stipend for some of the humanitarian work you are doing. Hot combination numbers: 1 and 4.

Wednesday, November 29 (Moon in Capricorn) Lucky lottery: 3, 12, 21, 30, 39, 48. You will enjoy meetings, conferences, investigating committees, analysis reports connected with groups in which you hold membership. Some of these people with whom you find yourself in total agreement can become close friends. Take those social steps.

Thursday, November 30 (Moon in Capricorn to Aquarius 9:27 a.m.)   Changes present themselves somewhat unexpectedly under Uranus–Neptune aspects. Progress never was as fast-moving as it is today, especially in the new sciences governing organization and employment matters. Today's method or style is next week's anachronism. Your lucky number is 5.

Friday, December 1 (Moon in Aquarius)   Career demands, new assignments, the fear of more changes in your office routines and equipment are all in this picture. Some confusion exists in the front offices, where partners seem to disagree over the value of purchasing new equipment. The problem is that changes are consistently coming day after day. Your lucky number is 5.

Saturday, December 2 (Moon in Aquarius to Pisces 10:24 p.m.)   Lucky lottery: 7, 16, 25, 34, 43, 52. Past mistakes are showing up. Where there was unthinking acceptance of change, the bill is now coming in. Aquarius and Gemini are in the day's script. Someone you haven't seen in a long time could reappear in your life today. Memories take over.

Sunday, December 3 (Moon in Pisces)   It's your day, with personal interests illuminated by the moon. You can make your own decisions without opposition and have little difficulty winning others over to your point of view. Another Pisces and a Cancer have vital roles. Begin the holiday month by dining out.

Monday, December 4 (Moon in Pisces)   The Mercury keynote in your horoscope speeds up work that has to be done. You can wring decisions out of a reluctant supervisor without half trying. You have the knack of encouraging the malingerers to put forth greater efforts. By the end of the day, you feel on top of the world. Your lucky number is 4.

Tuesday, December 5 (Moon in Pisces to Aries 9:19 a.m.)   Another good day to get a lot of work done. Sagittarius and Gemini are helpful. By being on the job before most coworkers, you will be able to have a conversation with a supervisor who appreciates your knowledge. If handing out assignments, however, be prepared for a lot of palaver. Your lucky number is 6.

Wednesday, December 6 (Moon in Aries) Lucky lottery: 8, 17, 26, 35, 44, 48. The money is rolling in and you can increase your take by working longer hours or more diligently and meriting a quality-salary increase. Aries and Leo figure prominently in the day's events. Invest in something beautiful or in government bonds.

Thursday, December 7 (Moon in Aries to Taurus 4:28 p.m.) Increase your production and give joy to the heart of those in charge. If a malingering complainer doesn't understand the work, offer to stay on this evening and teach him; you may be surprised at how fast he starts producing. Newer additional assignments you want are coming to you. Your lucky number is 1.

Friday, December 8 (Moon in Taurus) The Venus keynote gives you more appreciation of the past and of those you loved long ago. You may find yourself thinking about grandparents, great-aunts and -uncles who have passed on. Something you learned on an early job also resurfaces and gives you a sense of self-approval. Hot combination numbers: 3 and 9.

Saturday, December 9 (Moon in Taurus to Gemini 7:52 p.m.) Lucky lottery: 5, 14, 23, 32, 41, 50. The Mars keynote in your horoscope gives drive and good motivation to bargain hunting and seeking new sources of capital. Working evenings in a store during the Christmas rush may work out well, giving you a discount on presents you intend to buy.

Sunday, December 10 (Moon in Gemini) A Gemini exudes enthusiasm, stirring your creativity in home decoration. Gemini and a Libran friend will know where to locate materials that add light and color to some areas of your household. And listen: the art of handicrafting more beautiful holiday decorations than you can purchase commercially is well within your scope.

Monday, December 11 (Moon in Gemini to Cancer 8:50 p.m.) The full moon illuminates your family, home, property, ownership, community, interior and exterior decoration, and communication with relatives. You are bubbling with enthusiasm and joy, and are in a fine mood for the holiday season, Immerse yourself in the church and charitable work others expect of you. Your lucky number is 2.

Tuesday, December 12 (Moon in Cancer) Express your spiritual and physical love. Try to get some quality time alone with your soul mate. There are many things to discuss about gifts you wish to give parents and relatives. Also, despite the busy hours, there must be time for lovemaking on a day that is perfect for it. Hot combination numbers: 4 and 7.

Wednesday, December 13 (Moon in Cancer to Leo 9:10 p.m.) Scorpio and a Cancer play key roles. You sense gratitude, as well as affection, emanating from loved ones. Many children are more careful about their behavior at this time of year. There is a respite from bickering and the demands of youngsters. Lucky lottery: 6, 15, 24, 33, 42, 51.

Thursday, December 14 (Moon in Leo) A good cycle for shopping with an Aquarian, who seems enthusiastic about purchasing expensive items. You can do this person a favor by steering Aquarius into other, more moderate stores, where realistic and affordable items can be obtained which still fit the bill. You can also shop for and find the ideal presents for children on your holiday gift list. Your lucky number today is 8.

Friday, December 15 (Moon in Leo to Virgo 10:31 p.m.) Leo and Libra have key roles. A touch of fatigue may catch up with you by quitting time. Get some genuine rest tonight, so that you can give the season your best shots tomorrow. Don't fall asleep in front of the TV and make sure small children are not doing likewise. Your fortunate number today is 1.

Saturday, December 16 (Moon in Virgo) Lucky lottery: 3, 12, 21, 30, 39, 48. The perfect day to bond with your mate and also to shop together. There's good talk over the cafeteria lunch. It's time to recognize your limitations before taking on any more charitable or humanitarian work. Your mail carrier and newspaper deliverer may prefer checks as holiday gifts.

Sunday, December 17 (Moon in Virgo) A fine day for talks with your beloved, clergyperson, and parishioners who may expect more hours from you this month than you have to spare. Always let those who depend on you know what your time constraints are. Minor entertaining of neighbors and coworkers in your own home is on the agenda.

Monday, December 18 (Moon in Virgo to Libra 2:02 a.m.) Libra takes strong stands on what is right and what is inappropriate. It's a good day for bargain hunting, shopping for friends and coworkers, and planning any entertainment you would like to schedule for preholiday dates. Any shortages in your spending capital will become obvious during today's planetary aspects. Your lucky number is 9.

Tuesday, December 19 (Moon in Libra) Savings, investments, budgeting, bargain hunting, and overall security matters are emphasized. It's the time of the year when many break-ins happen, when hurried shoppers forget their car keys, and the desperate misbehave for a little cash. Keep all this in mind as you wander about. Your lucky number is 2.

Wednesday, December 20 (Moon in Libra to Scorpio 8:13 a.m.) Lucky lottery: 4, 13, 22, 31, 40, 49. Follow yesterday's warning. Be sure clerks give back your credit card. Don't leave your checkbook on any counter while chatting or looking elsewhere at merchandise. In family relationships, there is a lot of mutual understanding.

Thursday, December 21 (Moon in Scorpio)　　A little roadside shopping and finding special holiday items at a distance from home will go well today. Also, if minor travel is required to deliver gifts to older relatives and to visit other shut-ins, this is your best day for taking to the road. Scorpio understands. Hot combination numbers: 6 and 1.

Friday, December 22 (Moon in Scorpio to Sagittarius 4:58 p.m.)　　The sun enters Capricorn and this becomes the proper evening for a major party in your own home. Youngsters will prove helpful. Mix coworkers with close friends and neighbors. Don't forget a recent acquaintance you want to know better. Casual dress can still show elegance. Your lucky number is 8.

Saturday, December 23 (Moon in Sagittarius) The Mercury keynote gives a party arranged for children and their friends plenty of gusto. Phone friends who have been under the weather; squeeze another humanitarian chore into your busy schedule. Some criticism can come your way from an older relative who wants more attention. Lucky lottery: 1, 10, 19, 28, 37, 46.

Sunday, December 24 (Moon in Sagittarius)　　Some unexpected problems arise that can throw a monkey wrench into your Christmas plans. Do what you can to shift things around to suit those with time problems. Try to calm your natural annoyance with those who wait until the last minute to advise of a change in plans.

Monday, December 25 (Moon in Sagittarius to Capricorn 3:55 a.m.)　　More complications arise as the lunation in your eleventh house is partially eclipsed this evening. The cook has good reason to complain, and second suppers may be required for latecomers. You are particularly annoyed when there is interference with the old traditions. Even so, you remember that this is a spiritual holiday and this demands forgiveness.

Tuesday, December 26 (Moon in Capricorn)　　Favorable for visiting, minor entertaining, answering correspondence, phoning people at a distance. Capricorn and

Taurus have key roles. Older loved ones need more attention at this time of the year. Youngsters surprise you by being understanding of your time problems. Hot combination numbers: 9 and 6.

Wednesday, December 27 (Moon in Capricorn to Aquarius 4:27 p.m.) Lucky lottery: 2, 11, 20, 29, 38, 47. Self-discipline makes you a good role model for younger coworkers. Be prepared to do some pinch-hitting for those on vacation. The decisions you are called upon to make are well within your scope. Use authority carefully.

Thursday, December 28 (Moon in Aquarius) Gemini and Libra will impact your day. It's fine for figuring out ways to help neighbors adjust to many changes in the local tax situation. Other changes tend to neutralize past concepts. The entire way of farming without eroding topsoil is changing. Hot combination numbers: 4 and 7.

Friday, December 29 (Moon in Aquarius) Aquarius demonstrates the ultra-liberal approach to prevailing problems. The Uranus–Neptune keynote has you seeing the past in more gentle lights than most people who are complaining today. There is natural concern about the costs of changes that are being imposed upon business and self-employed people. Your lucky number is 6.

Saturday, December 30 (Moon in Aquarius to Pisces 5:29 p.m.) Lucky lottery: 8, 17, 26, 35, 44, 18. It's your turn to have the last laugh on a know-it-all executive. Things are not as they appeared to be some time ago. There is good luck coming to you from the moon in Pisces in all of your personal interests. You find things others lose.

Sunday, December 31 (Moon in Pisces) It's up to you to decide how you and yours will spend this joyful evening. You will have little difficulty persuading relatives and friends to go along with your ideas to create peace, harmony, a chance for people to let their hair down safely.

Happy New Year!

ABOUT THE AUTHOR

Born on August 5, 1926, in Philadelphia, Omarr was the only person ever given full-time duty in the U.S. Army as an astrologer. He also is regarded as the most erudite astrologer of our time and the best known, through his syndicated column (300 newspapers) and his radio and television programs (he is Merv Griffin's "resident astrologer"). Omarr has been called the most "knowledgeable astrologer since Evangeline Adams." His forecasts of Nixon's downfall, the end of World War II in mid-August of 1945, the assassination of John F. Kennedy, Roosevelt's election to the fourth term and his death in office . . . these and many others are on the record and quoted enough to be considered "legendary."

ABOUT THIS SERIES
This is one of a series of twelve
Day-to-Day Astrological Guides
for the signs of 2000
by Sydney Omarr

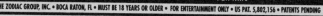